Being
Posthuman

ALSO AVAILABLE FROM BLOOMSBURY

Žižek on Race, Zahi Zalloua
Continental Philosophy and the Palestinian Question, Zahi Zalloua
Philosophical Posthumanism, Francesca Ferrando
Posthuman Glossary, edited by Rosi Braidotti and Maria Hlavajova

Being Posthuman

Ontologies of the Future

Zahi Zalloua

BLOOMSBURY ACADEMIC
LONDON · NEW YORK · OXFORD · NEW DELHI · SYDNEY

BLOOMSBURY ACADEMIC
Bloomsbury Publishing Plc
50 Bedford Square, London, WC1B 3DP, UK
1385 Broadway, New York, NY 10018, USA

BLOOMSBURY, BLOOMSBURY ACADEMIC and the Diana logo are trademarks of
Bloomsbury Publishing Plc

First published in Great Britain 2021

Cover design by Charlotte Daniels
Cover image © Brainmaster / Getty Images

Library of Congress Cataloging-in-Publication Data
Names: Zalloua, Zahi Anbra, 1971- author.
Title: Being posthuman : ontologies of the future / Zahi Zalloua.
Description: London, UK ; New York, NY, USA : Bloomsbury Academic, 2021. |
Includes bibliographical references and index. | Summary: "In Being
Posthuman, Zahi Zalloua interrogates the notion that "post-" does not
necessarily mean 'after' or that what comes after is more advanced than
what has gone before. He pursues this line of inquiry across four
distinct, yet interrelated, figures: cyborgs, animals, objects, and
racialized and excluded 'others'. These figures disrupt the narrative of
the 'human' and its singularity and by reading them together, Zalloua
determines that it is only when posthumanist discourse is combined with
psychoanalysis that subjectivity can be properly examined"– Provided by publisher.
Identifiers: LCCN 2020034751 (print) | LCCN 2020034752 (ebook) | ISBN
9781350151086 (hb) | ISBN 9781350151093 (pb) | ISBN 9781350151109 (edf) |
ISBN 9781350151116 (ebook)
Subjects: LCSH: Humanism. | Philosophical anthropology.
Classification: LCC B821 .Z35 2021 (print) | LCC B821 (ebook) | DDC 144–dc23
LC record available at https://lccn.loc.gov/2020034751
LC ebook record available at https://lccn.loc.gov/2020034752

ISBN: HB: 978-1-3501-5108-6
PB: 978-1-3501-5109-3
ePDF: 978-1-3501-5111-6
eBook: 978-1-3501-5110-9

Typeset by Deanta Global Publishing Services, Chennai, India
Printed and bound in Great Britain

To find out more about our authors and books visit www.bloomsbury.com and
sign up for our newsletters.

For the undercommons

Contents

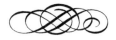

Acknowledgments

The question of the posthuman has long haunted and fascinated me. I must confess a greater affinity with theorists of anti-humanism than with devotees of humanism. I find it more and more difficult to frame my commitment to teaching in humanist terms—not the least because I frequently teach authors who are at war with the idea/l of the human. In recent years, I've become increasingly concerned with the ways the human persists in our critique and teachings. We, who teach in the humanities, are *a priori* considered humanists. Fortunately, I'm able to draw on Edward Said's musings on humanism as a form of endless critique to comply with my interpellation as a humanist teacher and scholar. But here still, in the back of my mind, I keep asking, even of Said, is the human as such beyond or immune from critique?

In my classes in Race and Ethnic Studies at Whitman College, we read and learn about the ways racism often manifests itself through the dehumanization or animalization of certain minorities. It would seem, then, that anti-racism is about the important labor of rehumanizing—of returning the human—to the racialized others, and thus correcting the murderous conflation between human and animal. In one class, for example, I remember showing my students a photograph of a Ferguson protester holding a sign that says, "We are human too." The message is clear: those who can claim to be

human—who can convince privileged others of their humanity—
receive protection and recognition, and those who can't . . . well . . .
you know the story.

Being Posthuman wants to tell another story, where critique
follows the errant or queer path of the posthuman and where, for
instance, the objection to racialization or animal cruelty does not go
immediately to a critique of dehumanization or a defense of animal
rights. To be sure, resisting the lure of security is not an easy task or
ask. It requires as much unlearning as learning. At home, I've learned
a great deal about/from my furry creatures across the years. If people
think that ethics is exclusively a human affair, they've never really
encountered cats. My brother Mounir has been an endless source
of encouragement, and I'm grateful to him, and to his own furry
companions, for the joy and energy they bring to life.

At Whitman, I couldn't be more thankful to my students, especially
the participants in "Afro-Pessimism and Its Critics" and "Race,
Class, Violence" as well as in the very rewarding independent study
on "Psychoanalysis" (well, it was mostly on Žižek!). I found myself
constantly returning to my manuscript after our class discussions
and meetings. My work has also benefited from exchanges with
my colleagues at Whitman. I wish to thank, in particular, Shampa
Biswas, Matt Bost, Chetna Chopra, Tarik Elseewi, Bruce Magnusson,
Gaurav Majumdar, Lydia McDermott, Suzanne Morrissey, Alvaro
Santana-Acuña, and Lisa Uddin. Jordon Crawford provided crucial
research assistance in the early stages of the project. Two events at
Whitman also left their imprint on this book. In the fall of 2019, I
participated in a Gender Studies Research Roundtable on the theme
"Futures of Color," organized and chaired by Nicole Simek. That
semester my colleague and friend Gaurav Majumdar invited me to
dialogue with Benjamin Boysen at his talk on the "Material Turn" in
the humanities. Both of these events created a space for invaluable

intellectual conversations and allowed me to test out my ideas from Chapters 3 and 4 of my book.

For the many fruitful encounters and exchanges outside of Whitman, I want to thank Jake Blevins, Benjamin Boysen, Chris Breu, Clint Burnham, Jeffrey Di Leo, Jennifer Kwon Dobbs, Peter Hitchcock, Ilan Kapoor, Sophia McClennen, Paul Allen Miller, Christian Moraru, John Mowitt, Brian O'Keeffe, R. Radhakrishnan, Russell Sbriglia, Robert Tally, and Harold Veeser. Particular thanks go to Jake Blevins and Benjamin Boysen for generously reading earlier versions of the manuscript. I would like to thank Lisa Goodrum and Lucy Russell from Bloomsbury for their enthusiastic support of this project. Lastly, without Nicole Simek's incalculable love and unwavering commitment, this work would have faltered long ago.

Portions of Chapter 3 appeared elsewhere in a revised form, "On Not Selling Out the Subject," *symplokē* 27, no. 1–2 (2019): 291–300, and "Forget Latour," in *What's Wrong with Anti-Theory?* ed. Jeffrey R. Di Leo (New York: Bloomsbury, 2019), 236–49. I also want to thank the various presses for granting me permission to reproduce my epigraphs. This project was supported in part by a Louis B. Perry Summer Research Grant.

Introduction
The Improper of the
Human

*I have seen no more evident monstrosity and miracle in the world
than myself. We become habituated to anything strange by use and
time; but the more I frequent myself and know myself, the more my
deformity astonishes me, and the less I understand myself.*

MICHEL DE MONTAIGNE[1]

Yet to define the human not through any nota characteristica, *but
rather through his self-knowledge, means that man is the being
which recognizes itself as such, that* man is the animal that must
recognize itself as human to be human.

GIORGIO AGAMBEN[2]

The term "posthumanism" suggests uneasiness with the
representation of human subjectivity, doubts about the nature of
the human self and its givenness. From Donna Haraway's cyborg to
the hit AMC show *The Walking Dead*, a posthumanist attitude has
marked the Western cultural imaginary, attesting to a desire for a
conception of the human—and for a humanism—that is otherwise
than anthropocentric. More than a name for a condition or a kind
of new Zeitgeist, posthumanism is increasingly being mobilized as
a "generative tool," to borrow Rosi Braidotti's words, as a creative
response to the biogenetic age dubbed the "Anthropocene," an

unprecedented global state in which human activity has become the determining factor influencing the climate and the environment.[3] But how did we become posthuman? Or conversely, and more skeptically, are "we" posthuman? And what does it mean to be posthuman? Is there a proper of the posthuman? Do today's musings ironically repeat the earlier, classic humanist question, "What is the proper of man?"? Are posthumanists in the business of yielding positive knowledge of the posthuman? Or more iconoclastically still, is posthumanism a proper, if paradoxical, embrace of the improper? Inquiries into posthumanism's origins, goals, and fantasies quickly lead to a host of questions: If posthumanism ostensibly represents a turn *away* from the human and humanism, what is it a turn *toward*? What is its relation to the competing or alternative terms/turns of "anti-humanism," "transhumanism," and the "nonhuman"?[4] More fundamentally: What is humanism after all? What is the nature of its privileged unit, the *being* of the human?

The Persistence of the Human and Its Others

Humanism, in its most abstract or general sense, refers to a set of beliefs that place the human subject at the center of reflection and concern. Humanism has unquestionably supplied Western discourse with a resilient model of subjectivity. Vincent Descombes attests to humanism's strong mark on the philosophy of the subject, which affirms

> that the only conceivable suppositum of a "properly human" action is the being that identifies itself, not with the empirical person that it also is, but with the autonomous subject. Not the individual, taken up as he is in the tissue of the world, but a being

capable of positing itself as *ideally* (or ultimately) different from everything that history has made, from everything that society has conditioned, from everything that institutions have fixed, from all the futures that past events have already marked or cleared the way for. But it is also the being that decided to conduct itself in such a way that it can think of itself, at the end of an infinite effort, as the author of all its worldly determinations (emphasis in original).[5]

Humanism nurtures a philosophy of the subject, endowing the subject with agency and purpose.

In Western antiquity, we can trace this humanist sensibility in Protagoras's famous claim that "man is the measure of all things." Man displaces the gods as the center of discourse. In the Renaissance, humanism takes the form of an interest in identifying what distinguishes humans from other beings, a concern with the condition and singularity of "man" ("man" here stands ideologically for all human beings, occluding the fact that it represented, and still continues to represent, unmarked white, European, heterosexual, able-bodied men). Take, for example, fifteenth-century Italian thinker Pico Della Mirandolla, for whom man's ontological specificity is tied to his malleability, to his "chameleon"-like nature: "It is given to him [man] to have that which he chooses and to be that which he wills."[6] Giorgo Agamben places Pico's text at the center of what he names "the anthropological machine of humanism"[7]—which creates the human in relation to and against the animal—calling attention to its "ironic apparatus that verifies the absence of a nature proper to *Homo*, holding him suspended between a celestial and a terrestrial nature, between animal and human—and, thus, his being always less and more than himself."[8] The human is not given; it is a "mobile border," an "intimate caesura,"[9] without an essence or distinguishing feature. Becoming human requires a cognitive intervention, an act of self-recognition:

"*man is the animal that must recognize itself as human to be human* (emphasis in original)."[10] With the absence of a fixed model, a "proper place," "specific rank," or even a unique "face" (his choice ranges from beast to angel), the human is constituted by his "inhumanity,"[11] and must constantly separate himself from the animal; it is his constitutive outside. To claim his humanity, the humanist subject must work to exclude his own strangeness or animality. "The humanist discovery of man is the discovery that he lacks himself, the discovery of his irremediable lack of *dignitas*,"[12] astutely comments Agamben.

Complementing—if not smoothing over—this image of a self-forming subject is Dutch humanist Desiderius Erasmus's dictum, "Homines non nascuntur, sed finguntur" ("Men are not born, they are fashioned"). As did Pico, Erasmus foregrounded the creative activity of self-fashioning, committed to the humanist belief that the human subject is not given and unchangeable, but is something to form, to cultivate, or to create. Erasmus's open-ended definition of the subject becomes, as Thomas Greene puts it, "the motto of the Humanist revolution."[13] With such portraits of the Renaissance self, Pico and Erasmus helped to inaugurate the humanist myth of the self-made man, a man endowed with the capacity of cultivating himself and elevating himself to divine heights, particularly through the study of "good letters" (ancient literature, philosophy, rhetoric, philology, etc.). Only through the study of "good letters," which became synonymous with the study of humanity (*studia humanitatis*), could human beings ever achieve their full humanity, and be who they truly are.[14]

Not all subscribed to this humanist myth. Michel de Montaigne adopted a far more skeptical stance vis-à-vis this Erasmian ideal, objecting to this elevation of the human. The potential for greatness—à la Pico, the human can aspire to the divine—transforming the mere human into an angelic form, often results in its opposite: "That is madness: instead of changing into angels, they change into beasts;

instead of raising themselves, they lower themselves" (856). While this could easily be read in humanist terms—becoming animal is undesirable, beneath the subject's humanity—Montaigne's point, I believe, is different. A "spiritualized" form of self-care—a type of care that denies human embodiment, that denies our matter and our animality—does violence to the "human" self, which Montaigne conceives as *both* mind and body. Rather than devalorizing what in fact we share with nonhuman animals, denigrating what is perceived as improper to man, Montaigne complicates the exceptionalism of man. He points to our uncanny proximity to animals, troubling the ontological border separating humans from animals: "There is more difference between a given man and a given man than between a given animal and a given man" (342). For Montaigne, animals do not lack speech, reason, and intelligence; their difference from us is a question of degree, not kind. The humanist performance of civilization is thus at best overstated (since our difference from animals is not that ontologically significant), and at worst devastatingly violent, taking a more sinister turn in the "encounter" between Europe and the New World. More than any thinker of his times, Montaigne critically interrogated the humanism of his period by bringing to attention the ways philosophy's investment into the propriety of man is inseparable from Europe's colonial enterprise. The question "What are the essential and distinguishing features of European man?" is, then, part and parcel of a Western imperial project.

Lacking any humanity in the eyes of the European colonizers, the indigenous peoples of the New World—deemed "Cannibals"—were silenced and excluded from the civilized world of men, without any hope of humanistic protection.[15] In "Of Cannibals," Montaigne questions the superiority of his fellow Christian Europeans, their (self-appointed) privileged place in the Chain of Beings (*scala naturae*), ranked below God and angels but above all else, at the summit of humanity, higher than Jews and Muslims, and far higher than "Africans, Asians, and native Americans"—those whose humanity itself was disputed and who were "lower or nonexistent on the Chain."[16] Montaigne declines to police the anthropological border; he destabilizes the logic that hierarchizes and ontologizes the order of beings, this logic that would wall off Europeans (the standard of humanity) from Cannibals, locating the latter on the other side of civilization.

As we shall see, Montaigne locates the "true" Cannibals—those rightly charged with savagery, with inflicting excessive cruelty on others—not out there in the New World, as reported by travelers like Jean de Léry and André Thevet, but in the midst of French life, in the midst of a France divided by a horrific civil war. Montaigne's defense of the Cannibals, however, is not without qualification. He holds that they are guilty of barbarism in the *negative sense of the term*, describing his disdain toward "the barbarous horror of such acts" (155), and referring to their warfare as a *"human disease"* (156). In "Of Moderation," the essay just preceding "Of Cannibals," Montaigne expresses a more damning critique, recording his strong distaste for the "horrible cruelty" (149) practiced by the indigenous population of the New World, who "burn the victims alive, and take them out of the brazier half roasted to tear their heart and entrails out. Others, even women, are flayed alive, and with their bloody skins they dress and disguise others" (149). Sameness and difference between the native Americans and the Europeans are by no means mutually exclusive. What they both share is an inhuman impulse for excessive cruelty. Europeans all too easily identify it in the indigenous other, while simultaneously disavowing it at home.

In a move that must have astonished, if not scandalized, his humanist readers, Montaigne "animalizes" his contemporaries. He counters their Eurocentric blindness by accusing his countrymen of cannibalism of an even worse kind:

> I think there is more barbarity in *eating a man alive* than in eating him dead; and in tearing by tortures and the rack a body still full of feeling, in roasting a man bit by bit, in having them bitten and mangled by dogs and swine . . . than *roasting and eating him* after he is dead. (155, emphasis added)

Although Montaigne diffuses somewhat his charge, since we realize by the end of the sentence that his fellow Frenchmen don't actually eat the flesh of others but give it to dogs and pigs, he remains unwavering in his indictment of the practices of torture. The force of his claim that there is *more* barbarity in torturing and burning living human beings—"on the pretext of piety and religion" (155)—than in the cannibalism of the indigenous population who eat them *after* they are dead, after their ritual murder, is unaltered. Montaigne repeats this insight in "Of Cruelty": "Savages do not shock me as much by roasting and eating the bodies of the dead as those who torment them and persecute them living" (314). Despite the moral turpitude of the anthropophagic act (an act said to be improper to humanity), it seems clear that Montaigne considers the "natural" barbarity of the Cannibals more excusable, or at least less intolerable, than the "civilized" barbarity of the Europeans. The term "Cannibal" therefore no longer refers solely or primarily to those primitives who eat human flesh but also—or especially—to Montaigne's civilized countrymen who inflict the most horrific forms of torture.

Montaigne's critical discourse on the New World restages philosophy's timeless question of *what is proper to man?*—revealing that it only masquerades as a universal question, that it is in fact Eurocentric, aimed at solidifying European man's sense of superiority, legitimizing his status as the arbiter of human values.[17] The Cannibal legitimizes Europe's imperialist human-animal divide, its exclusive claim to civilization and humanity, and its idea/ideal of the subject immune from all the ills and barbarity Europeans witness in the New World. The indigenous other is "used to mark the constitutive outside of humanity proper,"[18] made to stand for a kind of "missing link"[19] between humans and animals. Against his countrymen, Montaigne short-circuits the premodern anthropological machine, what enables the European colonizer to see the Cannibal as an animal with human characteristics ("the non-man . . . produced by the humanization of an animal"[20]) by giving his contemporaries a most anti-humanist answer to the question what is *proper* to the human: it is the penchant for inhuman, excessive cruelty. We might say, following Slavoj Žižek, that (the excess of) cruelty is "absolutely immanent, the very core of subjectivity itself."[21] It is part of our ontological makeup from the Old World to the New World. Whereas Agamben draws on Pico for an account of the nonhuman as an immanence of the human, Žižek credits Immanuel Kant's distinction between the negative and infinite judgments for opening radically new ways of conceptualizing the human. There are, for instance, two ways to negate the statement "he is human." We can say, "he is not human" and "he is inhuman." But Žižek insists that the two are not the same:

> "He is not human" means simply that he is external to humanity, animal or divine, while "he is inhuman" means something thoroughly different, namely that he is neither human nor not human, but marked by a terrifying excess which, although negating what we understand as "humanity," is inherent to being human.[22]

If in the pre-Kantian world, "the core of subjectivity" was reason, always tempering "the excesses of animal lusts and divine madness," with Kant and German idealism that core is always already traversed by excess, so that "madness" is not a slipping of mastery but "signals the unconstrained explosion of the very core of a human being."[23] The humanist desire for perfection (from the Latin *perfectio*, meaning completion) dreams of evacuating all excesses from the subject, disavowing that "there is an inhuman core in all of us, or, that we are 'not-all human.'"[24]

But to be clear, this is not to naturalize or justify cruelty. Quite the contrary, the avowal of cruelty enjoins us to confront cruelty, to fight it, and to resist gentrifying the *in*human, as is typical in humanist discourse and its rhetoric of *perfectio hominis*, a discourse that regards civilization (i.e., reason and eloquence) as the intrinsic property of the (European/colonial) human. Demonizing the non-European for exhibiting cruelty (a supposed sign of the other's animality, or uncivilized culture) while ignoring both colonialist savagery and cruelty's crushing presence at home can only augment and fuel its destructiveness. Montaigne voices his unconditional objection to cruelty with his self-reflexive and ironic comment: "Among other vices, I *cruelly* hate *cruelty*, both by nature and by judgment, as the extreme of all vices" (313, emphasis added). Montaigne criticizes "cruelty" (it is unconditionally deemed the greatest vice) while signaling or, better yet, gesturing to its insurmountability with the paradoxical adverb "cruelly." "Cruelly" names here Montaigne's affective commitment to "putting cruelty *first*"[25] in his ethical orientation. This ineradicable vice, deemed improper to the human, this unshakable otherness, is reminiscent of the monstrosity that Montaigne "discovers" within: "the more I frequent myself and know myself, the more my deformity astonishes me, and the less I understand myself" (787, emphasis added). Self-study *gives* Montaigne a precarious and monstrous presence: "I have seen no more evident monstrosity and miracle in the world than myself" (787). Montaigne's humanity becomes unknowable and unrecognizable. He avows the "inhuman core" of his humanity; the destitution of the self follows a Montaigne who ceases *to be* human (in its phantasmatic form) and becomes more animal (more human). The improper is monstrous; the posthuman/inhuman of the human is monstrous.

From the perspective of the European subject, what is feared or unknown invariably takes the form of a monster; turning the indigenous other into a monster goes hand in hand with asserting the humanity of the European subject. But the improper also troubles definitions. It must be at once kept at bay and related back to what is proper. In the case of the human(ist), the improper serves a purely negative function. It is the nonhuman that tells European humanists what is not intrinsic, natural, or essential to the human. To put it slightly differently, before determining what the being of the human *is*, what the human is *not* must be first articulated. At this key politico-hermeneutic moment, the European man needs his maligned others: the inferior animal and the menacing non-European/the nonwhite/the non- or subhuman—with the latter, as witnessed in Montaigne's "Of Cannibals," undergoing a process of dehumanization, considered an animal in human form.

Cartesian Humanism and the Impropriety of Matter

If the Renaissance made man's powers of eloquence and the study of letters essential to humanism, and if Montaigne proved to be an irritant to his humanist tradition, refusing to validate its narcissistic self-image and nascent colonial logic, René Descartes and the Enlightenment foregrounded man's reason and agency. In the *Meditations* (1641), Descartes embarked on a search for epistemological certainty, maintaining that beliefs must be infallible if they are to serve as a reliable source of human knowledge. His radical method led him to hypothesize the existence of an evil deceiver, causing him to question all knowledge of the external world—including knowledge of his own existence. In the face of unbearable skepticism, Descartes discovered an indubitable and self-evident truth, namely that he exists, since he cannot doubt and not exist simultaneously—hence was born the Cartesian subject, the *cogito*, an autonomous and rational subject that was to serve as the metaphysical bedrock of many humanisms to follow. With the inauguration of the *cogito* come also Descartes's "corrections" of Montaigne: the affirmation of epistemic certainty (the Cartesian response to Montaigne's skeptical motto, "What do I know?") and the ontological petrification of animals as soulless automata.

In *The Passions of the Soul*, Descartes offers his *cogito* more protection from the pitfalls of self-knowledge, which, in turn, furthers the chances of successfully becoming "masters and possessors of nature."[26] Before mastering the world, the *cogito* must get its house in order and master itself. Descartes takes stock of philosophy's epistemic shortcomings, blaming its failure to attain a "better state" on an unhealthy excess of wonder: "Astonishment [*étonnement*] is an excess of wonder [*admiration*] which can never be anything but bad."[27] Astonishment is effectively banned, deemed improper to philosophical inquiry. Working against a pathologized mode of thinking, a healthy or proper philosophy must yield a cognitive payoff or extraction: the successful translation of the new into a well-digested, mastered familiar. If Descartes announces modernity's epistemic enlightenment, Montaigne refuses to see astonishment as something to be categorically dismissed, something from which the subject needs to be immunized. Montaigne's invitation to revel in the improper, his hospitality to alterity—be it human or animal—will provide posthumanists with an invaluable, earlier counter-model to Cartesian humanism.

At the same time, Cartesian humanism produced its own materialist responses. Ever since Descartes identified the human body as a machine (a characteristic we share with animals), philosophers have been eager to counteract the Cartesian bias in favor of the mind by giving a more prominent role to the body, and, by extension, to the animal. Eighteenth-century philosopher Julien Offray de La Mettrie's *Man Is a Machine* (1747) is a case in point. Against Cartesian dualism, which serves to privilege man (as mind) and disprivilege the nonhuman (as body), La Mettrie constantly reminds his readers of the primacy of the body, metonymically represented by the stomach: "What power a meal has! It rekindles joy in a sad heart, and joy flows into the souls of guests who sing glad songs in which the French excel. Only the melancholic is overcome, and the scholar is no longer good for anything."[28] To remedy the mind of a sad person, the powers of a good meal cannot be underestimated. Eating, however, is hardly the proper of the human. It is what humans share with animals and other living creatures—and this is precisely La Mettrie's point.

In the hands of La Mettrie, the improper body, and matter itself, gives the lie to Cartesian humanism, underscoring the entanglement of mind and body. With Victor Frankenstein, the protagonist of Mary Shelley's 1818 novel *Frankenstein*, this matter becomes the canvas to test out man's uniquely human property: the masterful use of technology. The subtitle of Shelley's novel is *A Modern Prometheus.* Victor is this new Greek god, "capable of bestowing animation upon lifeless matter,"[29] sharing with the rest of humanity the forbidden fruits of scientific knowledge (as Prometheus had done with fire). The elevation of *human* nature returns with a vengeance. Of course, Shelley's novel is not a blanket endorsement of Victor's actions and project (her protagonist loses everyone he cared for), but a cautionary tale about human hubris, about the pretention to mimic, if not displace, God through Victor's "creation of a human being,"[30] or rather, through his creation of a posthuman being—about unfettered scientific progress and the fantasies of rational humanism.

Ambivalence characterizes Shelley's modern Promethean myth: it warns against the abuses of technology, exposing the potential ills of scientific curiosity, *and* repositions Cartesian humanism at the center of creation, soliciting, as it were, a more responsible and responsive Victor to come. But, as N. Katherine Hayles would point out, Victor, as a paradigmatic scientist, a scientist of the posthuman, "is not abandoning the autonomous liberal subject but is expanding its prerogatives into the realm of the posthuman."[31] Cartesian dualism—the knowing mind masterfully orchestrating matter in the world—persists. Humanism's powers of adaptation/distortion are remarkable; as Neil Badmington perceptively notes, "humanism survives the apparent apocalypse and, more worryingly, fools many into thinking that it has perished. Rumors of its death are greatly exaggerated."[32]

Cartesian humanism continued to essentialize the line separating the *anthropos* from the rest of the *cosmos*. It hummed and proceeded as usual even when its essentialism was frontally challenged by Jean-Paul Sartre and other existentialists, when the *cogito* was desubstantialized, disclosed as foundationless, all-too-contingent, *de trop*.[33] In claiming that "existence precedes essence," Sartre radicalizes Erasmus's humanist motto, stressing the subject's radical freedom and its nausea-inducing reality, the lack of an intrinsic meaning to man, while also positing human consciousness as the source of meaning in the world: the freedom of the *pour-soi* (for-itself)—a region of being unavailable to nonhumans—or the power of transcendence, as the exclusive property of the human. In *Existentialism Is a Humanism*, Sartre defines man in terms of his actions and projects; there is no destiny for him—what is given is only his nothingness: "If man as the existentialist conceives him cannot be defined, it is because at first he is nothing. He will not be anything until later, and then he will be what he makes of himself."[34]

Yet a new generation of French intellectuals, spurred by the tumultuous events of May 1968, broke with Sartrean existentialism and its model of humanism. While they upheld the transience and contingency of meaning (the world does not possess any inherent, stable meaning), they radically questioned the powers of consciousness, the elevated status of the human, and of the subject as a *constituting* force, that is, a force capable of securing meaning. Louis Althusser was first to level a devastating blow to Sartrean humanism. The subject, he showed, is *constituted*; the individual is subjected to impersonal and anonymous forces, to the autonomous play of language or power. The human individual as subject is an ideological construction, the effect of what Althusser calls "interpellation." You are first an individual, then you become a subject endowed with agency: "*all ideology hails or interpellates concrete individuals as concrete subjects.*"[35] Your emergence as a subject is predicated on your recognizing yourself as a subject when you are hailed by another (Althusser's paradigmatic example is the police officer who calls out to you, *demanding* your response/confirmation). Ideology through interpellation *humanizes* the social world[36]; it discloses a meaningful world, in which there is a place for you, where you count and your voice matters.

Jacques Derrida challenged Sartrean humanism at an even deeper level by exposing Sartre's distortion of Martin Heidegger's notion of *Dasein*. Sartre, like many of his contemporaries, made use of Henri Corbin's mistranslation of Heidegger's *Dasein* (literally being-there) as *réalité-humaine* ("human reality"). In "The Ends of Man," Derrida described Corbin's rendering as a "monstrous translation"[37] and in Sartre's work this mistranslation contributes to dehistoricization and a return to metaphysics, precisely what Heidegger aimed to eschew.

Derrida decries Sartre's failure to adequately problematize the conceptual apparatus that renders possible "the unity of man": "the history of the concept man is never examined. Everything occurs as if the sign 'man' had no origin, no historical, cultural, or linguistic limit."[38] As Anson Rabinbach observes, "Whereas the Heideggerian *Dasein* is bound to a situation that is anterior to the framing of such categories as subject and object, Sartre simply substitutes one ideal of man's perfectibility for another."[39] Cartesian humanism seamlessly gave way to Sartrean humanism. The existentialist rupture—its break with metaphysical humanism, with the essence of man—was thus only apparent. *Plus ça change, plus c'est la même chose.*

As a movement, anti-humanism reached its theoretical apogee in *The Order of Things,* in which Michel Foucault argues for doing away with philosophy's cherished universal or ahistorical subject when he boldly declares "the death of man" in the concluding pages of his penultimate chapter "Man and his Doubles."[40] Language precedes man. Derrida credits this structuralist insight for enabling philosophy to think about itself differently, to consider "the structurality of structure,"[41] that which conditions all forms of representation and displaces the subject/consciousness at the center of discourse. To speak of the "death of man" is thus to recognize that language structures the reality of human beings, and not simply the other way around. "The subject doesn't speak," Žižek writes, "he 'is spoken' by the symbolic structure."[42] Simply put, with theoretical anti-humanism, human beings lose their Adamic privilege; they have been stripped of their God-given authority.[43]

But Foucault also insisted, in his later essay "What is an Author?," on the ways the humanist subject lives on in people's perceptions, even after its metaphysical death. It is not enough to declare, with Roland Barthes, "the death of the author."[44] This postmodern slogan can occlude the persistence of the author. Foucault points to its

continuing presence in the discourse of literary criticism, to the ways
the "author" operates as a "principle of thrift" or shorthand in the
interpretive reception of a work.[45] So, on the one hand, we can reject
the idea of the Author as God, seeing it as an old relic, and, on the
other, still be invested in a different—and arguably more insidious—
form of authorship, whereby submitting a work to what Foucault
dubs the "author function" involves seeing the work as fitting into
the larger, coherent thought of a unified author, namely the humanist
author at the center of all his works.

From Correlationism to
Flat Ontology (*and Back*)

If anti-humanism emerged on the scene under the banner of the
"linguistic turn," posthumanism, we might say, flourishes under
that of the "ontological turn," a turn which shifts attention back, in
the words of Quentin Meillassoux, to "the great outdoors [*le grand
dehors*]."[46] While a posthumanist sensibility surely preceded the
contemporary ontological turn, its preoccupations and full challenge
can retrospectively be articulated at the ontological level, and in
ontological terms. Against the anti-realism pervading theoretical
anti-humanism, the ontological turn urges a renewed attachment
to the external world. Meillassoux is often credited for giving the
push for this philosophical uprising against the linguistic turn. In
his 2006 *After Finitude*, Meillassoux takes post-Kantian philosophies
to task, lamenting the "Kantian catastrophe," its unmitigated
responsibility for bringing into existence a dreadful "Ptolemaic
counterrevolution."[47] From Marxism and phenomenology to
psychoanalysis and deconstruction, continental thought has
suffered the limitations of what Meillassoux calls "correlationism."

Correlationism maintains that "we only ever have access to the correlation between thinking and being, and never to either term considered apart from the other."[48] Since we do not have a rational access to things-in-themselves, all we have after Kant, all we are allowed to discuss philosophically, are the transcendental conditions for human knowledge.[49] Any claim of knowledge is immediately followed by a qualification: by "for us," that is, *for us finite beings*. As a result, Meillassoux argues, we have forsaken ontology, settling for a toothless epistemology still wedded to, and hamstrung by, a less-and-less-relevant humanism.

On Meillassoux's account, deconstruction and psychoanalysis would be the latest avatars of correlationism, remaining all too preoccupied with these Kantian concerns, removing us further and further away from a posthuman ontology. Meillassoux singles out Derrida's infectious impact on philosophy and the materialist tradition:

> Ever since Derrida in particular, materialism seems to have taken the form of a "sickened correlationism": it refuses both the return to a naïve pre-critical stage of thought and any investigation of what prevents the "circle of the subject" from harmoniously closing in on itself. Whether it be the Freudian unconscious, Marxist ideology, Derridean dissemination, the undecidability of the event, the Lacanian Real considered as the impossible, etc., these are all supposed to detect the trace of an impossible coincidence of the subject with itself, and thus of an extracorrelational residue in which one could localize a "materialist moment" of thought. But in fact, such misfires are only further correlations among others: it is always for a subject that there is an undecidable event or a failure of signification.[50]

On this reading, the theoretical anti-humanism of Derrida et al. never comes to full fruition, never opening onto a "proper" posthumanism:

an eclipsing of the subject *and* a return to objects. What is missing from this anti-humanism, what would effectively promote a posthumanist ethos, is what Manuel DeLanda names a "flat ontology."[51]

According to anthropologist and sociologist of science Bruno Latour, a flat ontology tries to remedy the asymmetry of the relation between humans and all other beings by broadening our understanding of subjects, of who or what can act and ultimately speak. This means that animals, plants, and machines all are reconceived as sharing the same ontological playing field as humans. The modern distinction between nature and culture often used to legitimatize our hierarchical relationship to nonhuman others is at the source of the problem.[52] This distinction severely limits our imagination of agency and the inanimate world, of what it means to be an actor. Latour offers an expansive definition of actor, locating agency not in intentions (and the capacity to act on these intentions, to bring them about), but in the effects of action: "There is no other way to define an actor but through its action, and there is no other way to define an action but by asking what other actors are modified, transformed, perturbed, or created by the character that is the focus of attention."[53] All beings are agential objects; their ontology exceeds their epistemological rendering as objects-for-us. Objects escape our grasp and resist our interpretations, our hermeneutic habits. Agency is thus not an ontological privilege restricted to humans, but is far more widespread in the world. Indeed, once we unmake humans the central focus of our discourse—once we demodernize the human— we can finally register objects or hear them speak.

Posthumanism's flat ontology contests humanism's long-lasting commitment to transcendence. Flat ontology is an ontology of immanence. It prefers Spinozist monism over Cartesian dualism: there is only one kind of being, which in effect rules out the elevation and privileging of one being—the human—over all others. Accordingly, flat ontology invalidates humanism's solipsistic and narcissistic belief in transcendence, in the possibility of adopting a critical, and self-serving, position from nowhere, an external standpoint immune from the social field, uncontaminated by ideology. Flat ontology also declines to answer philosophy's "timeless" question of what is proper to man, dismissing all the various answers thinkers have proposed: language, thinking, trickery, laughter, awareness of death, tool use, mourning, the face, and so on.

And yet immanence's relation to transcendence, just like posthumanism's relation to (anti-)humanism, may not be so cut and dried. *Being Posthuman: Ontologies of the Future* argues in favor of rereading Derrida's "sickened correlationism" in a different light. For the partisans of the ontological turn, what sickens theoretical anti-humanism is its attempt—though ultimately inadequate—to get outside the circle of correlationism, to break free from its "transparent cage": "it is always *for a subject* that there is an undecidable event or a failure of signification." The subject of humanism lives on—compromised, to be sure, but still viable. *It is still about the subject.* For many posthumanists, one can only truly break with humanism and anti-humanism by embracing immanence. Immanence is the proper of posthumanism.

Being Posthuman's rebuttal is that while being is indeed all there is—there is no outside of being—being itself is never simply one; its future is undetermined. A psychoanalytic supplement to posthumanism insists that being is divided, inconsistent, and forever incomplete, or "non-all" (*pas-tout*), as Žižek puts it, following Jacques Lacan.[54] Lacan introduces the notion of the non-all in Seminar XX, *Encore*, and implicitly draws a distinction between two modalities or orientations: a "masculine" logic of exception and a "feminine" logic of the non-all. These terms describe the ways a subject's enjoyment (*jouissance*) is organized or structured. For Lacan, the masculine logic of exception posits a subject who has unlimited enjoyment, who stands outside the law of castration that governs social symbolic existence; it is the sovereign exception[55] that proves the universal rule of castration. The feminine logic, by contrast, sees no exception to the law of castration; it declines the illusion of an uncastrated man (and with it the possibility of absolute enjoyment), but at the same time takes castration to be non-all, never complete or whole.

The non-all gives the lie to the phantasm of humanism, to its ideological pretention of wholeness. Whereas humanism subscribes to a masculine logic to the extent that it posits the human as exceptional, sovereign, unitary, self-constituted, and outside animality or mere corporeality, a posthumanism worthy of its name adopts a feminine logic that points to and insists on the split nature of beings. Such a psychoanalytic supplement reiterates but recasts flat ontology's rejection of human exceptionalism. The human is not the only being that is ontologically incomplete; rather, being itself is non-all.

If posthumanism imagines an embrace of immanence as the solution to a "sickened correlationism"—the true exit from the "circle of the subject"—it is a posthumanism that risks duplicating humanism's normative structures and masculine logic. Against the temptation to introduce a new proper of posthumanism, we might keep in mind Derrida's question: "does not everything that comes to affect the proper have the form of a virus?" Immunizing ontology against the virus of correlationism is a fool's errand. This virus of the subject (the subject as threat and the subject as compromised) enables as it disables. The virus disrupts the fantasy of wholeness and "absolute immunity." Without a "sickened correlationism," or, better yet, an "autoimmune correlationism," being would be one, and "nothing would ever happen or arrive; we would no longer wait, await, or expect, no longer expect one another, or expect any event."[56] If being were one—the posthumanist fantasized plane of immanence—no

3: Being = Exceptional ?

politics as such would be possible. As Todd McGowan rightly notes, "all political acts would simply be theater and all transformations would only be apparent."[57]

Such a decompleted and decompleting posthumanism is decidedly more interested in the improper, the ontological unruly, the epistemically disobedient, in that which escapes containment and classification, which short-circuits ranking and blurs vertical distinctions between higher and lower beings. The subject of this posthumanism also distances itself from that of anti-humanists by precisely declining to simply celebrate "the death of man" (as many postmodern thinkers do) and insisting, as Žižek does, instead on a Hegelian-Lacanian understanding of the subject: the subject is out of joint, empty and fraught, a nonsubstantial entity (lacking transparency and presence), and a locus of endless negativity: "the infinite power of absolute negativity."[58]

This posthumanist perspective works to undermine the ideological delineation between desirable/livable and disposable beings, and with it, the sovereign capacity to decide on the proper. The term thus becomes both a descriptive and a prescriptive category. If it first registers a shift, a historical rupture with the humanist order of things, posthumanism also works toward a future to come. Such a posthumanism subscribes to what Christopher Peterson dubs a "disjunctive temporality."[59] It "comes both before and after humanism."[60] For instance, we can detect a posthumanism retroactively in figures like Montaigne, who questions the mystifying rhetoric of the proper (troubling man's alleged others), and we can also understand posthumanism as future oriented, as a making of the *impossible possible*—as a *politics* of the future that can only appear as impossible within the coordinates of capitalism and humanism. This posthumanism undertakes what Foucault names "an ontology of the present," "an ontology of ourselves," a tireless questioning of the ways the "singular" and "contingent" has been made to appear "universal" and "necessary."[61] It seeks to reconfigure nothing short of the humanist symbolic order itself, by tenaciously contesting its neoliberal investments in the human (as *homo economicus*—the monadic, rational, self-transparent, and egotistical actor), soliciting and commanding new and inventive modes of relationality with the inhuman/nonhuman, modes that leave behind the phantasmatic belief in human exceptionalism, while, or rather by, simultaneously avowing, again and again, matter's "open ontology."[62]

Reading Posthumanly

Being Posthuman nuances from the start the prefix "post-." It complicates—but does not necessarily repudiate—the assumption that "*post-*" means "after" in the sense that what comes after has moved beyond or ontologically superseded what came before. According to this definition of "post-," posthumanism would entail a clean break with humanism. Here we might keep in mind Jean-François Lyotard's caution against thinking of the "*post-*" only in terms of a neat progression of events or, conversely, as an instantiation of the same phenomenon in a new guise. So if posthumanism ostensibly names a new body of knowledge, it remains to be seen how antagonistic a relation it maintains with humanism, the human, and the tradition of liberal rights.[63] Such a posthumanism, informed by a skeptical hermeneutics, might avoid some of pitfalls that have plagued posthumanist thinking by counterbalancing and leavening the aggressive or self-aggrandizing view it takes of itself, the type of thinking Peterson rightly decries which "implies a progressive narrative that ironically mirrors the Enlightenment principles of perfectibility that it would oppose."[64]

Thinking posthumanism through a consideration of the "post" thus highlights the necessity of thinking *with and against* humanism. *Being Posthuman* pursues this line of inquiry across four distinct, yet interrelated, vectors: cyborgs, animals, objects, and racialized others. These unruly figures, I argue, exert interpretive and material pressure on the "Human," troubling its individualism and privileges, its metaphysical underpinnings, and the ideology of its "exceptionalism" (human speciesism). The hybridity of cyborgs threatens the borders of the human, introducing a sense of the incalculable and unpredictable, forestalling, if not invalidating, dreams of human perfection; the proximity of animals contests our libidinal attachment to the singularity of humans, while their persistent and irreducible otherness solicits responsibility and new modes of relationality; objects in their opaqueness disobey human control and comprehension, disclosing a world where meaning never fully congeals, where mediation is never total; and racialized others contest the alleged universality of the human, simultaneously exposing the human's close alignment with whiteness and scrutinizing Western modernity's construction of the non-European as less than human. Reading these figures together demonstrates the need to infuse posthumanist discourse with a psychoanalytic lens, especially as it pertains to subjectivity. Such a reading unsettles modern philosophy's anthropocentric and masculinist investment in the proper, in the judgment, containment, and classification of nonhuman others.

Chapter 1, "Cyborgs," explores the new reality proffered by the figure of the cyborg. Unlike Descartes's story of mastery—over the self and others—this new story tells us that humans are no longer—and perhaps never were—"masters and possessors of nature," deploying the tools of science solely for their advantage and progress. Rather, the new posthumanist narrative reconceives the human as fundamentally relational and dependent, vulnerable and impure, constituted by a variety of technologies. Downgrading the mind means downgrading *Homo sapiens*'s privileged status in the humanist hierarchy, which places humans at the pinnacle, above animals, plants, and inanimate matter. For Haraway, the cyborg is queer, an aberration, a monster, some*thing* out of joint with the humanist order of things. It perverts society's binary oppositions between human and nonhuman, natural and unnatural, animate and inanimate, man and woman (Frankenstein's creature, for example, is a hybrid, the unnatural combination of body parts), while stubbornly rejecting all temptations of wholeness and closure. At odds with masculinist interest and thought, the cyborg subscribes to an incomplete ontology, declining the West's fantasy of full presence, sovereignty, and wholeness.

In the eyes of transhumanism, however, the figure of the cyborg points to a radically different reality and futurity. The cyborg is evidence that human beings can effectively transcend the limitations of their ontological given. On this view, technological innovation (becoming cyborg) does not disclose human vulnerability and impurity; rather, it renders possible the long-standing utopian humanist desire for immunity and purity: the unentangled mind, the *cogito* upgraded, and the mind without the (frail, porous) body, able to secure knowledge and gain more agency. The Netflix series *Black Mirror* offers a critical dramatization of the promises of transhumanism. Set in the near future, *Black Mirror* not only paints a dystopian vision of our neoliberal lives as cyborgs but also foregrounds the persistence and problem of desire, exceeding the interpretive paradigm of transhumanism along with its investment in the willful subject of humanism. New technologies do not deliver us from our weaknesses; they do not limit our vulnerabilities, but intensify them. What *Black Mirror* arguably solicits is a posthumanism supplemented by a psychoanalytic framework—where desire is understood as a desire for the other/Other, where the object (and subject) of desire is constitutively doubled. Read as an allegory for our posthuman condition, *Black Mirror* stages desiring cyborgs not as immunized subjectivities (the dream of transhumanism), nor as post-subjectivities (the dream of some posthumanisms) but as subjectivities whose ontological otherness—their inherent inhuman excess—is put on full display.

Chapter 2, "Animals," takes up posthumanist (re)turns to the animal. Thinking of the human not as a rational master but as a being existing in relationships with other beings implies profoundly reconceptualizing the way we think of human and nonhuman animals, and their shared ontologies and worlds. Humanist thought silences animals by appropriating the power to name them and to designate them as inferior and available for mastery and consumption, for domination and murder. In his metafictional novella *The Lives of Animals*, J. M. Coetzee's protagonist Elizabeth Costello describes the systematic violence inflicted on animals as an animal Holocaust, drawing a provocative and polarizing parallel between the Jews of Treblinka and the animals of modern factory farming—provincializing, in turn, the tragic event in European history by questioning the exceptionalism of the (Western) human. But even when humanists address the suffering of animals, when they gesture toward a recognition of the latter's moral worth, they typically resort to animal rights discourse (modeled on *human* rights discourse), unwittingly sustaining the animals' status as objects, as mute beings who cannot speak and must instead be spoken for. The animal as *other-than-human* can only appear as a frightening otherness, as a significant disruption of my hermeneutic comfort, my sense of the world.

Of particular interest are Derrida's posthumanist forays into animals. Cognizant of the homogenizing potential of the single category of "the animal"—of the violence in being named, in being inscribed in the socio-symbolic network—Derrida coins the anti-speciesist term "animot," which at once evokes the idea of multiplicity (as a homonym of the French plural term "animaux" [animals]), and foregrounds its linguistic character: it is a word ("mot" means "word" in French) not to be confused with the thing, the nonhuman materiality, that it represents. *Animot* enables Derrida to establish a "relation without relation" with his cat. The word applies to his cat, thematizing this nonhuman animal, but it also reflexively interrupts that designation, simultaneously registering the radical alterity of his cat, the unreadability of her gaze, treating their encounter as nothing short of an event, provoking a linguistic, existential, and ethical crisis. Derrida follows here in the footsteps of the pre-Cartesian or anti-Cartesian Montaigne (or, we might say, the posthumanist Montaigne), who also challenges human exceptionalism by musing on his cat's understanding and affectivity. In psychoanalytic terms, Derrida's cat is always more than her symbolic and imaginary rendering; she is also real, irreducible either to his phantasmatic projections or to society's gentrification of the cat into a "pet." As Derrida discovers, his cat remains a "monster," capable of provoking a radical disruption in his hermeneutic comfort. Derrida's cat is both a pet and a monster. Her ontological difference, her radical alterity, is never fully contained within the symbolic order. She is capable of producing events, of reminding us that she can't quite be categorized or explained in human(ist) terms.

Chapter 3, "Object Fever," critically investigates alternative approaches to social theory, that is, to human-centered frameworks (from humanism to poststructuralism). Latour's actor-network theory (ANT), object-oriented ontology (OOO), and new materialism (NM), all engage in the democratization of beings. While they converge on the posthumanist insight that objects matter—that they are imbued with agency—they diverge on the relevance of relationality, downplaying its pertinence in the case of OOO, favoring instead the *essence* of objects themselves, their irreducibility, and their withdrawnness. Against the tyranny of human intersubjectivity, these approaches espouse ontological humility and love for objects (with NM calling for the re-enchantment of the world after its disenchantment by the anti-humanists and suspicious/paranoid critics); they only seek to restore the dignity and grandeur of real objects, emancipating them from the persistent humanist subject/object prism.

The chapter turns to two case studies for testing the usefulness and limits of the aforementioned approaches. The first is Ari Folman's 2008 *Waltz with Bashir*, an Israeli animated docu-film that deals with the trauma of the 1982 Sabra and Shatila massacre. *Waltz with Bashir*, with its expansive treatment of trauma (the film, with its mixture of human and nonhuman actors, democraticizes the victim of trauma, performing a flat ontology), seems ideally situated for a Latourian reading. I first sketch out such a reading, highlighting elements of the film most receptive to a Latourian approach, contrasting it with a critique-oriented reading, and then return to the stubborn questions of ideology and suspicion, of guilt and disavowal. The second is Jean-Paul Sartre's 1938 novel *Nausea*, in which Roquentin, the anti-hero, might be said to experience flat ontology as an unsettling rebellion of objects. What is at stake in pairing OOO with *Nausea* is the status of the "Real." An OOO reading would undoubtedly celebrate Roquentin's decentering— yet it would do so in a narrow and ultimately unsatisfactory way. For OOO, along with ANT and NM, Roquentin's emancipation from an anthropomorphic and anthropocentric framework coincides with his recognition that language distorts the external world by imbuing its objects with a violent humanist meaning—that subjugates and instrumentalizes objects, ignoring their permanent opacity and denying them the same status of actants. What such a reading misses is that language is not simply an external instrument mediating Roquentin's relation to the world. In its eagerness to jettison the insights of the linguistic turn, OOO fails to observe that language is from the outset constitutive of reality as such. This Lacanian reframing of psychic turmoil allows us to ponder a new beginning for Roquentin's posthuman bouts of nausea.

Chapter 4, "Black ~~Being~~," addresses posthumanism's general neglect of race and racism. If the Jewish Holocaust attests to modernity's trauma (Agamben's paradigmatic example of the devastation wrought by the modern anthropological machine), to the psychic blow to its (white) humanist self-image (the death of the humanist subject), racial slavery provides an alternative analytical model that speaks to the differing concerns and existential lives of blacks. It is not to enough to say that biopolitics under National Socialism takes a turn for the worse. What is the relevance of biopolitics when blacks were unqualifiedly relegated to what anti-colonial theorist Frantz Fanon called the "zone of nonbeing"? Blackness *is* nothingness, an ontological void signified by the barring of ~~being~~, attesting to the absence of Being, to the privation of transcendence and metaphysical agency for blacks. Posthumanism misses its mark if it downplays these existing racial structures of domination (by emphasizing the Anthropocene exclusively, for instance), or if it fails to recognize that the category of the human as such was never available for a whole population of racialized bodies. Celebrating flat ontology—and its posthumanist promise/fantasy of democratizing and leveling the field of beings—proves inadequate when dealing with the racially objectified since it neglects the material conditions that produce subjects who matter and others who don't, bracketing, as it were, the unequal distribution of vulnerability.

Critics in black studies point out that blacks served a humanist function, thematizing the ontological difference between the human and the slave. Antiblackness takes on meaning in relation to the "human," which operates as a "master signifier" or "quilting point" anchoring it; though in itself meaningless, the master signifier "human" quilts the field of meaning, around which other signifiers (whiteness, blackness, animality, etc.) can stabilize. What follows from this assessment of black ~~being~~ (antiblackness as constitutive of white civil society) is nihilism and pessimism. Posthumanism, like humanism, will repeat society's antiblackness unless it confronts and transcends the fantasy of the (white) human. Yet Boots Riley's 2018 *Sorry to Bother You* declines a self-defeating nihilistic and pessimistic response to the crushing existence of antiblackness. The film offers its audience what we might describe as a "weird posthumanism." Its main character, Cassius "Cash" Green, an underemployed telemarketer, tries to cope with his racist society, with the absurdity of being black. The film's weird posthumanism reaches its apogee when Cash discovers his employer's plan to inject his workers with a formula that turns them into more vigorous, productive, and sexually potent horse-human hybrids. *Sorry to Bother You* turns the trope of dehumanization on its head, both acknowledging the voracity of capitalism's labor machine and offering a posthuman model of solidarity as a means of throwing a wrench into this seemingly intractable force.

1

Cyborgs

Cyborg unities are monstrous and illegitimate; in our present political circumstances, we could hardly hope for more potent myths for resistance and recoupling.

DONNA HARAWAY[1]

When we hear that modern science and technology pose a threat to our human identity, the first thing we should do is to raise the elementary philosophical question: which notion of "human," of the specific human dimension, guides us; which notion are we presupposing in advance as an implicit measure of being-human when we formulate such threats?

SLAVOJ ŽIŽEK[2]

Science has transformed the very notion of perfection, redefining the means by which it can be achieved. In the West today, it is often science—like the spiritual imitation of Christ, or the philosophical imitation of Socrates, which were dominant ideas at other moments in Western history—that promises to perfect humans. Gene therapy, cosmetic surgeries, prosthetic enhancement, and pharmaceutical solutions are all options available to humans in the here and now, who refuse to settle for what *is*. Science is also catching up with science fiction: artificial intelligence, nanotechnology, and the possibility of uploading human memory into computers await us. These technologies have all impacted the way in which characteristics sometimes taken as givens—age, sexuality, sex assignment, health— are redefined as malleable, and thus perfectible.

The partisans of a scientifically mediated posthuman go by the name of transhumanists. They have celebrated the new conceptions of humanity and agency that cyborg technologies have helped open up. Transhumanists see in the "cyborg"—a term that combines cybernetic and organism—the future of humanity itself, a *Humanity Plus* (captured by the symbol H+).[3] Transhumanists view the "posthuman" teleologically: the cyborg is *post*human insofar as it is the human fully realized, the human minus fleshly vulnerability. Unlike traditional humanists, transhumanists conceive of human nature as a process, a work-in-progress, rather than a static or timeless essence. Transhumanist discourse revives the Renaissance ideal of *perfectio hominis*; we might say that it ushers in the ideal of *perfectio hominis* 2.0. What comes after the human—what comes with the advances in bioscience and technology—is not less agency but more of it. In his 2005 article, "In Defence of Posthuman Dignity," Nick Bostrom, a leading figure of the transhumanist movement, writes:

> Transhumanism is a loosely defined movement that has developed gradually over the past two decades, and can be viewed as an outgrowth of secular humanism and the Enlightenment. It holds that current human nature is improvable through the use of applied science and other rational methods, which may make it possible to increase human health-span, extend our intellectual and physical capacities, and give us increased control over our own mental states and moods. Technologies of concern include not only current ones, like genetic engineering and information technology, but also anticipated future developments such as fully

immersive virtual reality, machine-phase nanotechnology, and artificial intelligence.[4]

Giving primacy to rationality, transhumanism privileges and elevates the mind while the body is devalued and treated as a limitation, whose vulnerability technological innovation seeks to reduce, if not eliminate.[5] Transhumanism fully enacts "the scientific-technological realization of the Gnostic dream of the Self getting rid of the decay and inertia of material reality."[6]

Transhumanists claim the cyborg as an example of posthuman progress, of a futurity beyond humanity: with the advances of biotechnology, the posthuman is stronger, its bodily precariousness minimized (and potentially surmounted altogether in the future). The cyborg, in the eyes of transhumanists, has transcended many of the given limitations surrounding the original mortal body of the human. The human as would-be victim, plagued by his or her mortal body, now gives way to a heroic, masculinist posthuman. Mastery, perseverance, and the promise of technological immortality typify the cyborg of transhumanism.

In contrast to this aggressively utopian and optimist rendering of the cyborg, we might keep in mind Donna Haraway's seminal account of this locus classicus of the posthuman in her 1985 "A Cyborg Manifesto." In it, Haraway foregrounds the interpenetration of humans and machines, the hybridity and impurity of the human, its coexistence or fusion with the machine in the sci-fi image of the cyborg. This posthuman figure comes to stand for all that disrupts and contaminates binary oppositions (including human and animal, organism and machine, the physical and the nonphysical), embodying her socialist-feminist vision of and for the subject. George Myerson attests to the cyborg's transformative and inventive presence: "You can tell you are in the presence of a cyborg figure when you feel a new world coming into being around you."[7] At the same time, the cyborg illustrates and enacts the hopes, anxieties, and ontological and ethical dilemmas bound up with science and its potential to alter being itself.

Pace the transhumanists, Haraway's cyborgs do not represent the achievement of a "dematerialization of embodiment"[8]—that is, a perfect, static ideal of the subject—but rather the entanglement of the human with other forms of life, an entanglement that accentuates, rather than escapes, questions of power, responsibility, and relation. The cyborg, as Haraway deploys it, downgrades the mind, and downgrades man's privileged status in the humanist order of things, in the hierarchy that places humans at the pinnacle, above animals, plants, and inanimate matter. Moreover, this shift away from the hegemonic model of the undivided, sovereign subject, Haraway insists, has already happened: "By the late twentieth century, our time, a mythic time, we are all chimeras, theorized and fabricated hybrids of machine and organism—in short, cyborgs. *The cyborg is our ontology*; it gives us our politics" (7, emphasis added). Whereas ontology is traditionally about the classification and categorization of beings, the cyborg's ontology—our queer ontology—lies in its impropriety, in its refusal to be put in its natural or proper place. The figure of the cyborg illustrates and enacts Haraway's ethico-political imperative to queer the "natural": "Queering what counts as nature is my categorical imperative."[9] The cyborg is not only a menace to the humanist order of things ("the organic, hierarchical dualisms ordering discourse in 'the West' since Aristotle" [32]) but being cyborg also perverts "Man" (from the Latin *pervertere*, meaning to subvert, to turn upside down), taking pleasure in "taboo fusions" (52). Nothing is more foreign to the cyborg than desiring perfection, a permanent state of stasis—for this reason, "the cyborg would not recognize the Garden of Eden" (9), that is, it would not perceive it as something desirable. Indeed, the cyborg jams *all* fantasies of closure, having "no truck with bisexuality, pre-oedipal symbiosis, unalienated labor, or other seductions to organic wholeness" (8).[10]

On Haraway's model, transhumanists are producing their own fantasy of closure. The transhumanist cyborg dream is a dream of pure transcendence, which is after all nothing but a renewed humanist desire to escape mortality, corporality, and/as animality. Haraway's own version of the cyborg is decidedly not amenable to such transhumanist co-optation. But is this liminal figure any safer from the more progressive camp of the posthumanists? It obviously depends on the posthumanism that is being proffered. Again, this brings us back to the ontological status and understanding of the human in posthumanism and in relation to the posthuman.

Unlike transhumanism, which embraces the humanist goals of individual perfection and self-determination, posthumanism, as defined by Cary Wolfe, proceeds by radically questioning and redefining what it means to be human in the first place. According to Wolfe, the posthumanist project must genuinely trouble the place of the human: "Posthumanism means not the triumphal surpassing or unmasking of something but an increase in the vigilance, responsibility, and humility that accompany living in a world so newly, and differently, inhabited."[11] It is thus clear that Wolfe's posthumanism is fundamentally at odds with transhumanism, which is merely "an intensification of humanism" through technological means.[12] And when you combine such advancements with a dominant neoliberal ideology, you get a disastrous sociopolitical outcome; human transformations are treated as commodities to be bought and sold. In this posthuman new normal, the rich purchase their ontological upgrades, becoming more and more posthuman, while the poor are stuck in the ontological equivalent of coach, remaining, as it were, more and more human.

Haraway's cyborg seems more hospitable to the label of posthumanist identity: an identity that overcomes human(ist)

identity. And yet it is this type of interpretive reasoning that compels
Haraway, in *When Species Meet*, to qualify, if not altogether decline,
the label of posthumanist:

> I never wanted to be posthuman, or posthumanist, any more
> than I wanted to be postfeminist. For one thing, urgent work
> still needs to be done in reference to those who must inhabit the
> troubled categories of woman and human, properly pluralized,
> reformulated, and brought into constitutive intersection with
> other asymmetrical differences.[13]

Relationality trumps de-subjectivization. Making kin, becoming-
with, is both more rewarding and more urgent than simply
critiquing the human subject. Abandoning subjectivity—a *sine
qua non* of posthumanism—is thus not a viable solution. For
Haraway, the cyborg was crucial in its challenge to essentialism
and Cartesian humanism, but almost two decades after writing her
"Cyborg Manifesto," she finds it urgent to shift attention away from
the trope or fantasy of the cyborg—away from questions of social
constructionism, spurred by the linguistic turn—and toward ethical
considerations of nonhuman otherness, especially "real" dogs, for
example. Haraway was, of course, not alone in making this move.
Theory more broadly experienced this paradigm shift: whereas the
linguistic turn is said to have paid too much attention to mediation
and representation, the ethical turn attended to material reality,
to our exposure to the other, to the ways the other (human or
nonhuman) interpellates us and "calls us to ethical accountability."[14]
It is the flesh of animals, their "vulnerability and pain,"[15] that
occupies her thoughts. In this new ethical horizon, the cyborg still
has a place but it is one dominated by Haraway's companion species:
"I have come to see cyborgs as junior siblings in the much bigger
queer family of companion species."[16]

In dealing with the question of the animal (to which I will return in Chapter 2), Haraway expresses her suspicion over posthumanism's exclusive critique of subjectivity, when what is needed is a better appreciation of our relation to animals or companion species, which is itself preconditioned on a kind of epistemic queering of the subject:[17] a defamiliarization of the human, rendering it less comfortable, less familiar, less known to itself. Yet the cyborg, I would add, played and, more importantly, continues to play an invaluable role in this queering of the human, and thus merits continued attention and exploration, not least because of the importance of this figure for transhumanists, posthumanists, and bioconservatives who are invested in preserving human nature against the encroachment of bioscience (such as biogenetic enhancement), but also for the pull or fascination it exercises in popular culture—as in the Netflix series *Black Mirror*. *Black Mirror*'s cyborg examples ironically do not conform to the utopian or normative aspirations of either transhumanists (the dream of pure transcendence, living without corporeal entanglement) or posthumanists (the dream of post-subjective existence, dwelling in the plane of immanence), nor do they unproblematically acquiesce to the nostalgic impulse of pre-cyborg reality. Haraway herself ends the cyborg manifesto with its most memorable line: "I would rather be a cyborg than a goddess" (68). It is crucial to insist on the still emancipatory force of this line. Why is it better to be a cyborg than a goddess? What do cyborg and goddess mean in the context of the ontological turn? Or better yet, what kind of beings are they? What are the politics of each figure?

Haraway with Žižek

In "A Cyborg Manifesto," Haraway aligns the figure of the goddess with an idyllic time, a matriarchal past, a utopian feminism untouched by men, grounded in nature, the organic, and all that evokes purity and transcendence. But, as she writes, "it's not just that 'god' is dead; so is the 'goddess'" (30). The cyborg, by contrast, is a thing of this world; its body does not "end at the skin" (61); it is suspicious of "holism," but hungry or "needy for connection" (9). The cyborg is not innocent; indeed, it is the product of power, "a deeply compromised figure,"[18] a problematic child of "militarism and patriarchal capitalism, not to mention state socialism" (9). The cyborg, however, doesn't believe in destiny; it prefers beginnings (which are always historical and multiple) to origins (which are divine and exceptional).[19] The manifesto that gave us the cyborg is not the "ramblings of a blissed-out, technobunny, fembot."[20] Against recuperative readings of the cyborg, Haraway stresses the unruliness of her posthuman progeny, "often exceedingly unfaithful to [its] origins" (10). Haraway's cyborgs avow their illegitimacy and consider "their fathers . . . inessential" (10). An iconoclast, the cyborg is a deviant, a blasphemous trickster, with a penchant for dissensus and breaching boundaries. Its predilection is for *serio ludere*, "serious play" (5). Indeed, the cyborg delights in "irony" and "perversity," and readily avows its partiality, making no pretension to completeness and mastery (9). Its "power to signify" (55) is of a different order.

What is at stake in the paring of cyborg and goddess, however, is not—or does not have to be—simply the choice between culture (the manufactured) over nature (the given). Being for culture in this way would return us to a binary opposition—culture versus nature— that the manifesto sought to undermine.[21] Drawing on Žižek's ontologization of Lacan's formulae of sexuation, we can instead productively reread "cyborg" and "goddess" as competing orientations and modalities of critique: the goddess is governed by the masculine logic of exception, while the cyborg follows the feminine logic of the non-all.

As Lacan argues, the "relation between the subject and the phallus . . . forms without regard to the anatomical distinction between the sexes."[22] "Masculine" and "feminine" do not refer to anatomical differences, but to a subject's relation to the phallus. On the masculine side, we find two formulae: (1) there is at least one x that says "no" to the phallic function and (2) all x are subject to the phallic function. Together these state the masculine logic of exception—of law and its necessary transgression. While all men are symbolically castrated (they are all subject to the phallic function, the law, the big Other) due to their entry into the symbolic order, into the realm of the signifier (the substitution of things—including oneself—by words), there is always one "Man" who does not sacrifice his enjoyment, one Man who must remain immune to the law of castration, holding on to the promise of a phantasmatic return to the full plenitude of a pre-symbolic enjoyment. For Lacan, the mythical primal father of Freud's *Totem and Taboo* exemplifies such a figure. While the primal father—who enjoyed all women at will, "achieving complete satisfaction"[23]—had to be killed for the symbolic order to emerge, his exceptional subject position persists in the cultural imaginary. An anatomical woman might very well occupy this position of the primal father as well. Such is the case, as Žižek proposes, of the merciless Lady of courtly love, the "capricious Master who wants it all, i.e., who, herself not bound by any Law, charges her knight-servant with arbitrary and outrageous ordeals."[24] This Lady—in comparison to all other women—operates, or rather is imagined operating, outside social norms, whimsically transgressing society's moral codes.

Much of Žižek's innovative reading of the formulae of sexuation emerges in his commentary on the feminine side of Lacan's formulation. Here too we are confronted with two formulae: (1) there is no x that says "no" to the phallic function and (2) not all x are subject to the phallic function. Unlike the masculine side, there is no claim of universality rooted in exception here, suggesting that woman (unlike Man) does not constitute a totality. If there is no exception that stands outside the system, then the system *as such* is never whole or complete. And because there is nothing of woman *outside* the Law (no constitutive exception), woman is also non-all *inside* of the symbolic order. Though describing the non-all as feminine evokes a biological register, it is, importantly, a logic and structure of enjoyment, and one that potentially applies to all subjects. "*Subjectivity as such . . . is feminine*,"[25] Žižek writes. The question, of course, is whether or not individuals avow this ontological reality, the unsettling reality of "the void of the 'barred subject,'"[26] whether or not they decline their interpellation as an undivided, sovereign subject (Montaigne, for example, avows this non-all when he perceives himself as monstrous, as an unknowable and unrecognizable self).

The problem with the goddess then is not that it looks ineffectually backward toward a mythical past (while the cyborg progressively looks to the future), but rather that it relies on a logic of completeness, fostering belief in the healing powers of the feminine, in a phantasmatic return to the full plenitude of unsullied enjoyment (the mystical time of matriarchy). This type of logic furthers the workings of ideology, projecting the fantasy of social and personal wholeness, and thus covering up the symbolic order's inherent instability. And what is desirable about the cyborg is its insistence on social reality's incompleteness and dividedness, its ironizing of the "structural inconsistency"[27] of the Symbolic—a reality that the goddess distorts in its attempt to resolve the constitutive alienation. The goddess generates the illusion of whole or all by locating the cause of feminine alienation *exclusively* in patriarchy, or some other cause that can also, in principle, be overcome: feminists reduce alienation to a disruption of reality, rather than seeing it as one of its main features. The difference in the cyborg lies in its refusal to fill the *gap* between all of reality and women's experience of it (by explaining the inconsistencies in reality away). The cyborg's identity is precisely *not* sustained by a nostalgic yearning for a lost/absent ideal, the embodiment of woman's true nature/ontology (with an ecofeminism to match); this truly emancipatory figure does not cover its imperfection and maladjustment—its "pure void of subjectivity"[28]—but identifies with its monstrosity.[29] It opts "to lose the loss, which means both to let it go and to recuperate it as being constitutively a ghost."[30] This "*withdrawal*"—losing the loss, negating the negation (if the notion of "woman" is a subject who, under patriarchy, lacks fullness, is alienated, a cyborg redoubles the alienation, transposing it into reality itself without this double negation producing a new *positivity* of woman)—"constitutes the opening for a new field of experimentations"[31] for imagining future communities and posthuman subjectivities.

Why not humanism again?

Against Cyborgs

The cyborg's very openness, its ontological incompletion, comes with no guarantees. That the cyborg can birth many possible futures makes it a source not only of hope but also of alarm, notably for bioconservatives who have turned attention to the techno-dystopian modes of relationality that any new experimentations in posthuman mutability might breed. The cyborg is a Rorschach test; critics will see in it what they want. Haraway herself is under no illusion that cyborgs are *a priori* emancipatory. Conversely, cyborgs ought not be *a priori* condemned, conforming to "an antiscience metaphysics, a demonology of technology" (67). Haraway implicates cyborgs in "scary new networks" and aligns them with "informatics of domination" (28). Simply put, our ethical and political judgments of cyborgs cannot be determined in advance: *cyborgism is not destiny.*

The political spectrum of bioconservatism is significantly wide, ranging from champion of liberal democracy Francis Fukuyama to critical theorist Jürgen Habermas. Paranoia characterizes their mode of reading. What the bioconservatives find most problematic are the technologies that most directly target the body—gene therapy, along with cloning—which have set off alarm bells among liberal humanists and neo-Enlightenment philosophers who see biotechnology as threatening to change humanity at the ontological level, bringing about the deterioration of human *beings.* "What will happen to political rights," Fukuyama alarmingly asks, "once we are able to, in effect, breed some people with saddles on their backs, and others with boots and spurs?"[32] If liberal democracy hoped to usher in "the end of history" (the end of the Cold War signaled the end of a genuine alternative to capitalism), the cyborgization of the human— the introducing of the unnatural in the natural human—is now not only threatening this utopian idea but also potentially ushering in the end of humanity.[33] We are witnessing the creation of a new class divide between the genetically poor and the genetically rich.[34] What is capitalism without its faithful humanists steering it? Transhumanism's posthuman subjects threaten a moral and political regression.[35]

Like Fukuyama, Habermas assesses this posthuman world in the making in alarmist and apocalyptic terms. What concerns Habermas is literally the future of the human, "the end of the human species as such."[36] Reminiscent of Heidegger, who warned of technology's instrumentality and colonization of the lifeworld (how it insidiously regulates and controls our modes of being, where things and relationships are "enframed," disclosing themselves exclusively as resources to be optimized),[37] Habermas urges an immediate protection *of* what is, who we are, of what it means to be human, and a protection *from* bioscience's overreach, from its myopic reprogramming of our ontological being:

> This perspective inevitably gives rise to the question of whether the instrumentalization of human nature changes the ethical self-understanding of the species in such a way that we no longer see ourselves as ethically free and morally equal beings guided by norms and reasons.[38]

Against genetic enhancement in particular, Habermas calls for a legal right to remain human, to protect future generations from decisions made by the current misguided generation, expressing it as a "right to a genetic inheritance immune from artificial intervention."[39] Fukuyama and Habermas's objections to human augmentation are basically moral in nature;[40] they follow a predictable humanist script grounded in a belief in "the 'inviolacy' of human beings in their present biological state"; accordingly, on such a view, "any attempt to alter the human constitution is regarded as 'inhumane,' 'dehumanizing,' or an affront to 'human dignity.'"[41] For bioconservatives, then, the transformation of humans envisioned and performed by bioscience is profound, altering the human at the ontological level, endangering, in turn, the long-cherished privileges of agency and self-determination.

Pace the humanists Fukuyama and Habermas, who argued for the need to *immunize* human identity—mythologizing, in turn, human nature[42]—from the perils of biogenetic enhancement, transhumanists easily counter that they are the ones who are in effect immunizing their being by precisely making it less vulnerable. They agree that any racist misuse of the science must be avoided—such as eugenics programs. And though conceding that the ontological character of our nature may change, "that subtle human values could get eroded by technological advances,"[43] transhumanists contend that the payoffs of these advances are far too great to give up. Humans are never satisfied with what *is* but seek to "expand the boundaries of their existence."[44] Moral hesitations must give way to scientific leaps. Making us permanently less precarious is worth the potentially small moral cost.[45] Moreover, transhumanists locate the threat to being-human in humanity itself, in our flawed design—our finitude and corporeal exposure. The problem is not genetic engineering but human frailty and weakness—*humans as traumatizable subjects*. Transhumanism's traumatophobia, its fear of trauma, taints its vision of the bare human, the human without the protection of science, the human as given by insufficient nature—whence the transhumanist injunction: always improve human nature by adding to it. The supplement to nature is, of course, nothing new. We know from Aristotle to Montaigne and Hegel that habit (culture) is second nature. Transhumanists, we might say, are updating this adage: science is second nature. Bioscience and technology can endlessly rewrite our ontological profile, with each intervention diminishing our (actual or virtual) disabilities, our exposure to illness, and the destructiveness of time. Who would object to less and less trauma in one's (post)human life? Objecting to our perfectibility is inexcusable, tantamount to willful ignorance, if not suicide.

Desiring Cyborgs, or beyond the Calculating Subject

The transhumanist subject is a calculating subject. Its interests are transparent and self-evident. Yet is the human truly reducible to a calculating mind? The Netflix series *Black Mirror* dramatizes what we might describe as the blind spots of transhumanism. The series complicates transhumanism's understanding of the subject by staging its limitations and creating doubt about some of its core beliefs: the benefits of biotechnologies in everyday existence and the desirability of invulnerability. It does so in part by setting its stories not in a distant reality, but rather in a very near future, in a familiar universe in which the development and commoditization of technology has moved just one or two steps beyond the 2010s, the world of the audience that the show "mirrors" back to them darkly. *Black Mirror* produces what Stefan Herbrechter calls "science faction": "a mediating (and popularizing) force between science and everyday life practice." It unsettlingly "floats in a simulative space, in between realism and fictionality."[46] Each episode in the series, which recounts a different story, also focuses intently on the interpersonal, social, political, and individual psychological dimensions of technology use—on the ways, in other words, that technical advancements shape and are shaped by a complex, dynamic, and entangled world, a world not only of minds but also of desires and fantasies, affects and bodies. "*Black Mirror*'s signature move," as Donovan Conley and Benjamin Burroughs contend, "is notable for the potency with which it blends the disruptive powers of affect with the cohering powers of critique."[47]

Two episodes in particular treat in a sustained and provocative way the complexities of subjectivity and the remainders of the human in posthuman life. "The Entire History of You" (Season 1, Episode 3) stages a world in which the shortcomings of "organic" memory have been overcome by implanted audiovisual recorders, called "grains," which can play back experience internally (in one's eyes, as a relived memory) or externally (on a screen) on demand. "Arkangel" (Season 4, Episode 2) explores the longing for invulnerability, for total immunity from harm, through the characters' use of digital technology, a biometric tracking and censoring system that allows parents to micromanage their children's lives and blur out potentially upsetting sights, ostensibly to protect them from distress and physical harm. Both episodes interrogate the function of technology and its putative purpose: to compensate for humans' epistemic lack, to make possible a knowing subject capable of managing/disciplining the elusive otherness in his or her life.

"The Entire History of You" sets up a fairly familiar storyline of jealousy. Liam (Toby Kebbell) is beginning to suspect that his wife Ffion (Jodie Whittaker) is cheating on him with Jonas (Tom Cullen). What is different in this not-so-distant future is the cyborg technology of the grain, which, while perfecting surveillance, opens up the possibility of confirming an affair with certainty. The benefits of the grain are both suggested but almost immediately qualified right from the start of the episode. In the opening scene, Liam is undergoing an appraisal by his employer. This appraisal is set in the context of the firm's interest in pursuing a new area of litigation involving adult children disappointed in life lodging claims against their parents. Not only do we learn during this opening scene that replaying one's grain recordings to prove one's suitability for hiring and promotions has become a normal part of work life, but we also see how the capacity for viewing "re-dos," as the characters call them, intensifies all emotions and creates new stakes for social interactions. Leaving the meeting, Liam senses that the session did not go well, and obsessively replays the re-do, interpreting and reinterpreting in particular one supervisor's intonation when he ends the meeting with the somewhat hedging comment, "This has been really great! Um . . . um . . . look, we're . . . Really hope to look forward to seeing you again!" The grain "can have psychologically crippling consequences."[48] Indeed, the technology creates more anxieties than it reduces, leaving Liam insecure, frustrated, and exposed to further scrutiny when he arrives at a dinner party and is goaded by Ffion's friends to show the appraisal re-do for their voyeuristic entertainment and less-than-sincere analysis. Liam's reluctance to acquiesce—to being reduced to a pleasure object of witnessing—creates a moment of social tension that appears to reinforce his feelings of inadequacy and resentment, which then turn into anger and suspicion toward his wife, whose fidelity he begins to doubt.

The ambivalence about the grain's benefits with which the episode begins is deepened during the dinner party when another guest, Hallam (Phoebe Fox), is outed to the group as a person without a grain. She then explains that after her grain was gouged out (stolen, she speculates, for voyeuristic reasons), she decided to give up the cyborg technology and is happier for it. The other guests are almost speechless, puzzled by the decision to "go grainless" and unsure how to respond to this quasi-act of self-marginalization (this would be analogous to someone, in our world, going smartphoneless, giving up what has become a prosthesis of the posthuman body). The host tries to defuse the situation by describing her choice as "brave," yet grain developer Colleen (Rebekah Staton)—who initially rudely remarked that going grainless was "huge with hookers"—offers a blunt critique, pointing out how wrong Hallam is for declining this technology. Her objection is couched in strikingly transhumanist terms: "You know half the organic memories you have are junk? Just not trustworthy . . . With half the population you can implant false memories just by asking leading questions in therapy." Not only is the grain more trustworthy than others (confirming or disproving their perception and interpretation of reality) but it is also more reliable than the organic self.[49] Who would willfully choose falsehood over truth? In this *monde à l'envers*, Hallam as a "pure" human is the actual threat to the status quo, the one menacing cyborg normality. Yet the cognitive argument fails to persuade Hallam. The good life, a life fully optimized, that the grain is supposed to promote—preventing deception, the manipulation of memory, and injustices—is not actually experienced as a better life, a more desirable life. Hallam declines to justify her position; the episode however offers Liam as an enactment and embodiment of the dangers of this technology.

Liam's lackluster performance at his appraisal affects his fantasies at multiple levels. It disrupts the fantasy of his private life on at least two fronts: first, and explicitly, in his working life, the fantasy that he is a successful employee, counted on and appreciated by his bosses; second, and implicitly, in his married life, the fantasy of a happy couple with no secrets or problems. His employment woes position him as a paranoid subject. Unsettled by the uncertain future of his work, not feeling at home with Ffion's friends, Liam focuses his frustrated energies on Jonas, who becomes the exclusive object of a "dirty fantasy," "whose fundamental form," Žižek tells us, is "jealousy."[50] Jealousy is not new for Liam—he had had an earlier bout of jealousy that had put his marriage in jeopardy—but this particular obsession is paradoxically intensified rather than attenuated by the cyborg technology of the grain.

What role exactly does the grain play, and why does it not fulfill its promise? For transhumanists, the problem with Liam is that he remains human—all-too-human. Any benefit brought by the grain is counterbalanced by his childish insecurities. More cyborg technology, more biogenetic enhancement, is the predictable transhumanist solution. Conversely, a Habermasian reading of "The Entire History of You" would locate the problem with Liam in the colonization of the protagonist's lifeworld by the same cyborg technology. It is the estrangement from his wife caused by the grain that precedes and precipitates his jealousy, and not the other way around. As evidence, it can point to the couple's lack of sexual intimacy. Lovemaking between Liam and Ffion has been denaturalized, involving less and less physical touch and direct eye contact; actual contacts are increasingly replaced by virtual ones, a digital archive, via the re-do of a prior real memory of sexual intercourse: the Platonic form of the couple's copulation. Being posthuman and having a "healthy" romantic relationship are mutually exclusive.

Such a humanist reading, however, is irremediably nostalgic and ethically problematic. Who determines what normal sexual intimacy looks like? Why should our understanding of intimacy rely on existing models or a static view of human nature? Why should we simply assume the ontological difference between humans and machines? A psychoanalytic rejoinder to transhumanism (and Habermasian humanism) returns to Liam as a subject of fantasy, as a *desiring* cyborg—a machinic subject with a libido.[51] The desiring subject is precisely what transhumanism ignores in its assessment of the human condition. It reduces the subject to its rational makeup, manifested in purely instrumental terms, without the messiness of desire, the libidinal economy of sexual relations. The rational subject is grounded in reality, leaves fantasies and biases behind, knows what it wants and what is in its interests, and acts accordingly. In psychoanalysis, however, fantasy is more than a distortion of reality; it in fact supports reality: "Everything we are allowed to approach by way of reality remains rooted in fantasy," writes Lacan.[52] And fantasy's role in the cultivation of desire is of paramount importance: "It is only through fantasy that the subject is constituted as desiring: *through fantasy, we learn how to desire*."[53] An inquiry into Liam's fantasy foregrounds then the logic of his desire, which also marks his exposure to the symbolic order, to the capitalist system (of which Liam's neoliberal firm is a metonymy). Desire is never a purely subjective or private affair; it is a desire for the other/Other. The object (and subject) of desire is constitutively doubled. As Žižek puts it, "the problem with human desire is that . . . it is always 'desire for the Other' in all the senses of the term: desire for the Other, desire to be desired by the Other, and especially desire for what the Other desires."[54]

With the appraisal not having gone according to plan, Liam is struggling to meet the desire of the Other. His "dirty fantasy" of jealousy teaches him to blame Jonas for his existential ills, to interpret his acts of kindness as fake (Jonas convinces the other guests at the dinner party to let go of their demand to watch Liam's re-do of his appraisal), to see him as enjoying life to its fullest, and stealing his own enjoyment by becoming the love interest of Ffion (in a bout of rage, Liam makes Jonas delete his erotic memories of his time with Ffion, taking back *what* he thinks belongs to him—treating his wife's current and prior life as his exclusive property). Liam's epistemology of exactitude—his obsession with determining the facts of a given situation—echoes but also departs from that of Lacan's delusional husband. Like the delusional husband, Liam develops an increasingly detailed and elaborate narrative of his wife's supposed infidelity. Yet "the delusional exempts himself from any real references"[55]—he has no need of coherent evidence, for he is completely disconnected from the reality principle. "As he climbs the scale of delusions," Lacan continues, "he becomes increasingly sure of things that he regards as more and more unreal,"[56] increasingly certain of the truth of his own delusional visions. Liam, by contrast, obsessively pursues empirical proof of his wife's guilt or innocence, scrutinizing video time stamps, background images, facial expressions, and vocal intonations. The reality principle is literally implanted in his head and immediately accessible. Nevertheless, the cyborg technology, this enhanced reality principle, cannot give him satisfaction. Liam remains unable to secure knowledge despite his technologically assisted access to an abundance of facts. His dissatisfaction points to the incompleteness of facts, to the truth that facts are non-all—that facts always need a critical interpretive supplement. In his call for an ideology critique that moves beyond a fact-driven form of demystification, Žižek argues that "if you don't change the ideological background, facts alone don't do the job."[57] In the case of Liam, if he doesn't confront and change his "dirty fantasy," scrutinizing why he needs Jonas as a foil, facts about Ffion's behavior alone don't suffice. The roots of Liam's "pathological jealousy" lie *not* in his cognitive errors (in any misapprehension of facts) but in the ways "these facts are integrated into the subject's libidinal economy."[58] There is indeed a perverse pathological satisfaction in finding out that his wife was cheating on him: "You know when you suspect something? It's always better when it turns out to be true."[59] This is why Žižek, following Lacan, says, "even if what a jealous husband claims about his wife (that she is sleeping around with other men) is true, his jealousy is still pathological."[60]

The cyborg technology powerfully confirms Lacan/Žižek's insight that the subject's libidinal economy trumps the primacy of facts. If transhumanism (represented within the episode by the character of Colleen) is more invested in accumulating data as a means to achieve knowledge, psychoanalysis remains focused on the subject's fantasies and desires: Liam's jealousy sabotages his self-interest (his employers expect a re-do of his week, which includes a host of behaviors that can easily be flagged, including drunk driving and an assault of Jonas). And unlike Habermasian humanism, psychoanalysis is by no means inhospitable to technological or biogenetic innovations. On the contrary, such new conditions, for Žižek, "*compel us to transform and reinvent the very notions of freedom, autonomy, and ethical responsibility* (emphasis in original)."[61] Psychoanalysis counters the exaggerated fears of the cyborg—or of engineered life, more generally—not by assuaging the concerns of humanists (not, that is, by arguing that cyborgs are an Enlightenment creation and that transhumanism is a continuation of the humanist project, clearing the path to liberation), but by foregrounding the inhuman already at work in the human: "It is not so much that with biogenetics we lose our freedom and dignity. Rather, we experience that *we never had them in the first place*."[62]

As we have already seen, "I'd rather be a cyborg than a goddess" compels us to reread the alienation of human beings. Whereas Heidegger, Fukuyama, and Habermas lament technology's negative impact on humans, Žižek reframes the problem of contemporary alienation not as an occasion for nostalgia or paranoia but as a moment ripe for critique. As Fabio Vighi puts it, "experiencing ourselves as radically alienated in the world, aware of our traumatic finitude, may be our best chance to break with our ideological constellation and open up the potential for a new symbolic order, a new understanding of what it means to be human."[63] The critique of technology as ideology is by no means shelved, having run its course; it is still very much needed. But Žižek gives its familiar conclusions a new twist:

> The main consequence of the scientific breakthroughs in biogenetics is the end of nature. Once we know the rules of its construction, natural organisms are transformed into objects amenable to manipulation. Nature, human and inhuman, is thus "desubstantialized," deprived of its impenetrable density . . . Biogenetics, with its reduction of the human psyche itself to an object of technological manipulation, is therefore effectively a kind of empirical instantiation of what Heidegger perceived as the "danger" inherent to modern technology. Crucial here is the interdependence of man and nature: by reducing man to just another natural object whose properties can be manipulated, what we lose is not (only) humanity but *nature itself*.[64]

Without (the fantasy of a pure) nature, nostalgia and paranoia lose their affective appeal. There is no return to the human; there is no substantial proper of the human: all there is is the (in)human (the subject as void[65]), with its meaning to be decided.

Freedom and dignity are thus not to be protected and preserved but reinvented outside of their humanist parameters. For Žižek, psychoanalysis is particularly adept at diminishing humanist authority. The psychoanalytic notion of the death drive corrodes the very possibility of a humanist solution to the dilemmas of cyborg technology:

> The true opposite of egotist self-love is not altruism, a concern for common good, but envy, *ressentiment,* which makes me act against my own interests. Freud knew it well: the death drive is opposed to the pleasure principle as well as to the reality principle. The true evil, which is the death drive, involves self-sabotage. It makes us act against our own interests.[66]

Not unlike envy and *ressentiment,* jealousy discloses this inhuman (evil) within the human: human existence itself is a problem, and a self-generating problem at that. The death drive, the drive to self-sabotage—characterized by Žižek as a "genetic malfunction"[67]—renders problematic any (trans)humanist project of self-transformation, invalidating the putatively self-evident concept of the "human" that can be deployed "in advance" as the arbitrator of what acceptable and what is discouraged in the realms of modern science and technology.[68]

In the final scene of the episode, we see Liam preparing to remove his grain with a razor in his bathroom. His emptied house bears no sign of Ffion and their child; all he is left with are his re-dos of happier times, which he is about to excise from himself. The ending of the show thus leans in a bioconservative direction, suggesting that cutting out the grain, returning to a prior, purely organic state, is necessary in order to escape the torment of loneliness and the cycle of dissatisfaction, even if it also means giving up a particular epistemology, as well as the ability to replay comforting images from the past. Ironically, however, reactions to the episode's conclusion have revolved to a significant extent around the gap in the visual narrative and the ambiguities it creates, pointing to the sway that transhumanist promises of verification hold. Viewers reproduce the structure of desire displayed by the characters, wondering on message boards what happened to Ffion and the baby. Did Liam kill them? Did Ffion leave after revealing in the re-do that she didn't have protected sex with Jonas, intimating that Liam is not the child's biological father? Did she leave despite confirming to Liam that the baby is his? In response to these questions, Charlie Brooker, the series' creator, "clarified" the ending by confirming that there was no foul play and that the re-do showed that Liam is indeed the father:

> Sometimes people think Liam's killed Ffion, but the reality is she's simply moved out. Or they think that he's not the dad. But Liam *is* the father of the child, so he's ruined his life. The moral, if there is one, is he shouldn't have gone looking for something that was only going to upset him. His wife loved him and there were secrets in the past, but he should have let them lie.[69]

This authorial intervention downplays or negates the pathological character of Liam's jealousy, the extent to which his "dirty fantasy" is immune from truth.

In this tale of cyborg dystopia, the (humanist) desire for immunity returns as an ironic silver lining of hope. Liam's solution to his predicament is self-mutilation, a *strike at himself* in an attempt to radically transform himself—to regain his humanity and freedom and be happier, like Hallam. Unfortunately, this change is more conservative than emancipatory. Liberation means liberation from technology. The "phantasmal stuff" of which Liam's ego is made remains untouched.

Immunizing the Self, or the Autoimmunity of the Cyborg

In "Arkangel," single mother Marie (Rosemarie DeWitt) turns to cyborg technology as a means to protect her young daughter Sara. If "The Entire History of You" hints at the ways technology relates to the formation and well-being of children (to recall, in that episode, adult children can sue their parents for their failure to adequately raise them to become successful adults, with the grain serving to document their shortcomings as parents), "Arkangel" (whose character and tech-company names evoke a Christian religious framework) foregrounds the protection of the child in the here and now through cyborg technology. If the grain developer's desire to seek justice for children might strike the viewer as disingenuous or, at the very least, opportunistic, Marie's desire, by contrast, seems far more authentic; she is truly invested in Sara's security and happiness, particularly after experiencing panic when her daughter disappears from sight in a park. Yet both episodes partake in what Lee Edelman powerfully describes as the trope of the child, "the perpetual horizon of every acknowledged politics, the fantasmatic beneficiary of every political intervention."[70] The child's ideological appeal is twofold: it refers to a pure existence, before the fall into symbolic existence, with its ills of mediation, dissatisfaction, alienation, and so on, and it also points to a more desirable futurity, a more authentic social order promising subjective holism, where the Symbolic is effectively transfigured and redeemed, where the transcendent innocence of the child is regained. As the "emblem of futurity,"[71] the child is fertile ground for transhumanist investment. Perfectibility of the (post) human must pass through the child.

Perfection of the child in "Arkangel" is intimately linked to the overcoming of Sara's vulnerability: to her protection from excessive stimuli or trauma. Marie's traumatophobia and her worries about future dangers Sara may face play into the hands of the slick tech company Arkangel, whose offer of a limited-release free trial she cannot turn down. The Arkangel neural implant allows Marie to track her daughter's movements, see what Sara sees, receive alerts about her daughter's health, and, most importantly, to turn on an "obscenity filter" function that pixelates any images and muffles any sounds that produce a rise in cortisol levels in the child. With the help of this digital technology, Marie seeks to optimize her daughter's life, a goal that is defined in biometric terms: maintaining a perfectly balanced blood chemistry and a heart rate that never rises or drops outside the set parameters. This striving for *ataraxia*—a trouble-free existence—is irreducible to a bad case of "helicopter motherhood"; rather, Marie's yearning for her child's security *and* her own peace of mind as a mother resonate with a long humanist tradition of self-fashioning. Shielding and immunizing the self against the unknown and unpredictable was part and parcel of the humanist project of self-mastery. Hellenistic philosopher Seneca is a case in point. For Seneca, philosophy cures and purifies the mind, seeking to prevent trauma from happening in the first place. What matters to Seneca are strategies that protect the individual's frail and vulnerable condition. Seneca's letters abound with "psycho-immunological practices"[72] aimed ultimately at correcting mistaken dispositions and reorienting one's precarious relation to self and to the world so as to achieve "a tranquil mind"[73] and a happier, more rational life. In one letter, Seneca uses the example of Liberalis, who was devastated by the unexpected fire that destroyed the city of Lyons, as an occasion to meditate on the importance of preparing oneself for the worst, of meditating on future calamities (*praemeditatio malorum*). Seneca draws the moral conclusion that since "nothing, whether public or private, is stable," then "nothing ought to be unexpected by us."[74] This philosophical practice corresponds to what Michel Foucault has called "technologies of the self," that is, techniques "which permit individuals to effect . . . a certain number of operations on their own bodies and souls, thoughts, conduct, and way of being, so as to transform themselves in order to attain a certain state of happiness, purity, wisdom, perfection, or immortality."[75] As a technique of the self, the practice of meditating on future calamities promotes the cultivation of a traumatophobic ethos, helping the would-be philosopher to indemnify the self, to attain a state of mental tranquility that would have resulted from the extirpation of his or her most intense emotions.

If Seneca's humanist philosophy urged the practice of *praemeditatio malorum* as a means of fortifying what we would call after Freud one's "protective shield,"[76] and to fashion a sovereign self by minimizing the shock of the unexpected, that is, by limiting the affectability of the contingent world (external stimuli) and thus reducing the self's vulnerability to whims of fortune, Marie, with the help of Arkangel, enables Sara to attain psychological immunity instantaneously. With Arkangel (embodying the fantasy of transhumanism), Sara gets the benefits of *ataraxia* but without the crucial work that comes with it; Marie as well, and perhaps more so, enjoys these benefits *without* having to cultivate a purposefully phobic self, without learning to curtail her immoderate curiosity to watch over Sara.

In "Arkangel," we really have two versions of the cyborg: Sara, who has a neural implant, and Marie, who has a monitoring tablet. As a child, Sara had no choice in becoming cyborg. Sara's obscenity filter turns problematic, however, when she is unable to hear her grandfather's call for help while having stroke. Growing up with this filter also marginalizes Sara at school. Irritated by not being able to see the content of a shock website, to see what blood looks like or to hear any vivid description of violence, Sara turns to self-mutilation, repeatedly pricking her finger with a sharpened pencil in order to produce blood, to prove to herself that she is more than a disembodied mind. When her mother, who is notified by the tablet of an increase in cortisol level, tries to stop her, Sara reacts violently and slaps her.

Marie takes Sara to a child psychologist, thinking her daughter might be autistic. But there is no medical sign of pathology; the psychologist locates the problem with Arkangel. Since the neural implant cannot be removed, he advises Marie to deactivate the filter and get rid of the tablet. Along the way, the doctor informs her that the program has been banned in Europe and will soon be taken off the market in the United States (the type of governmental oversight that Fukuyama calls for). Marie agrees, but rather than throwing the tablet away, breaking with it permanently, she stores it instead in the attic.

Marie's curiosity is a double-edged sword. In her hunger to know what Sara is doing, Marie ethically oversteps her role as a mother. Curiosity does not sustain the otherness of Sara but rather negates it, leading to its translation back into what Marie deems best for her child. Marie evidently cares for her child, and the spectator is invited to sympathize with her situation from the very first scene, which shows Marie giving a difficult birth to Sara (she is undergoing a Cesarean section, and when the child is delivered, she is not immediately breathing). Yet this care that sustains the mother/child relation is also killing the relation. What is depicted here is thus an autoimmune relationship as Derrida understands it.

In "Faith and Knowledge," Derrida discusses religion's paradoxical relation to technology in autoimmune terms: how religion—in its desire to remain pure, sacred—defines itself in opposition to technology (as a sign of modernity) while also needing technology to survive and spread in a global world. In the aftermath of 9/11, and the subsequent "War on Terror," Derrida enlarges the sense of autoimmunity, treating it as a "general logic of auto-immunization."[77] Autoimmunity entails a process through which, as Derrida puts it, "a living being, in a quasi-*suicidal* fashion, 'itself' works to destroy its own protection, to immunise itself *against* its 'own' immunity."[78] America's response to the traumatic events of 9/11 attests to this logic. In its desire to protect itself, to immunize itself against the spreading disease of terrorism, the United States illustrated all too well the potential "pervertibility of democracy," "los[ing] itself by itself," turning against itself, against its own self-protection, against, that is, its immune system: laws aimed at safeguarding the legal rights of its subjects, especially during states of emergency.[79] Yet while autoimmunization refers to the attempt to gain pure immunity, the attempt to wall off the self—an individual, a community, a nation— from external forces and influences, autoimmunity also names the ontological condition of selfhood and its relationality, which renders self-enclosure as such impossible.

The logic of the posthuman is an autoimmune logic to the extent that the human is always already incomplete, fraught, and contaminated from the outside.[80] As Derrida has it:

> There is no natural, originary body: technology has not simply added itself, from the outside or after the fact, as a foreign body. Or at least this foreign or dangerous supplement is "originarily" at work and in place in the supposedly ideal interiority of the "body and soul." It is indeed at the heart of the heart.[81]

The transhumanist cyborg can be read as an attempt to fix this ontological flaw in the human, a flaw that manifests itself in Sara's vulnerability to harm and Marie's vulnerability in seeing Sara harmed.

The tablet serves as a substitute umbilical cord between mother and child designed to overcome this fragility. It keeps Marie intimately involved yet at a physical distance from Sara. In the desire to immunize her daughter from harm, in the desire to keep her safe and present in her life, Marie, "in a quasi-*suicidal* fashion," undermines her relation to Sara. The betrayal begins when Marie discovers that Sara lied to her about evening plans. Rather than watching a movie at a friend's house (with parental oversight), Sara and her girlfriend meet up with some older boys at the beach. After realizing that Sara had lied to her, Marie almost immediately returns to the attic to retrieve the tablet to verify Sara's location and what she is doing. She opens on Sara having sex with her schoolmate Trick (Nicky Torchia). Marie resists confronting Sara about her sexual encounter, presumably accepting this as normal adolescent behavior or at least not wanting to reveal that she has turned Arkangel and its filtering option back on. When she next discovers that Sara has done cocaine with Trick, she escalates to active intervention, chasing down Trick's identity and whereabouts, and threatening to report him to the police for having sex with a minor (Sara is 15 years old) if he doesn't stop seeing her daughter—a demand he abides by.[82]

Sara is noticeably depressed by the sudden breakup, but Marie feels confident that her action was for the best (for Sara? for Marie?). This management of Sara's life takes an even more tragic turn when the tablet signals that Sara is pregnant. Marie decides, almost mechanically, to terminate Sara's pregnancy by crushing an emergency contraceptive pill into her breakfast smoothie without telling her she is pregnant. After Sara experiences side effects during class, the school's nurse informs her that her nausea was the result of taking this pill, but to not worry because her pregnancy has indeed been terminated, despite her vomiting. Sara pieces things together and confronts her mother, furious at this violation. During their struggle, the filter is inadvertently turned on. Sara rips the tablet from her mother's hand and knocks her unconscious with it without perceiving the consequences of her actions until the tablet is rendered inoperable and the filter removed. The last scenes of the episode show a desperate Marie screaming Sara's name in the street (recalling the earlier scene when Sara got lost in a park) then cut to Sara hitchhiking and getting into a semi-truck.

"Arkangel" is another cyborg dystopia. But as with "The Entire History of You," a humanist yearning for a blissful life without technology, a *docta technophobia*, is hardly an adequate response to the challenges that the episode poses. "Arkangel" illustrates and enacts vulnerability's *pharmarkon* character. It is poison and cure, entailing the unavoidable risk of self-loss and loss of the other, but, at the same time, it should not be exclusively feared. Rather, it must be recognized as conditioning the possibilities of what we cherish most in life. Without vulnerability, as Judith Butler points out, "we would be the kind of beings who, by definition, could not be in love, blind and blinded, vulnerable to devastation, subject to enthrallment."[83] An autoimmune cyborg avows its constitutive vulnerability; its technology (à la Arkangel) is not a pathway toward invulnerability (security and peace of mind as construed by transhumanism are ideological fantasies) but an *occasion* to trouble the human, to scrutinize, undo, and reinvent its meanings and ontology.

Cyborg Commons

Capitalism, a force underpinning technology development in both of the *Black Mirror* episodes studied here, is, of course, also engaged in its own reinvention of the human—a more compliant, more profitable cyborg would do just fine. Indeed, capitalism fully favors the posthuman—if by this we mean a figure that emerges after the evacuation of the Western subject of *human* rights. Global capitalism's unprecedented reach is introducing "a radical class division across the entire globe, separating those protected by the sphere from those outside its cover."[84] It produces the antagonism of the Included and the Excluded: "The more capitalism gets global, the more new walls and apartheids are emerging, separating those who are IN from those who are OUT."[85] Is the posthuman aligned with the Included or the Excluded? Haraway already pointed out the compromised character of the cyborg—the (unruly) offspring of power. And still she insisted that "we are all cyborgs." For Chela Sandoval, this insistence evinces a lacuna in Haraway's cyborg politics. Troubled by Haraway's trope of the "woman of color" as the paradigmatic example of the cyborg, Sandoval points out how Haraway's treatment of this "new political voice" unintentionally tends to reify the *identity of "women of color"* (17), supplying the Western critic with examples that only get fully theorized in the figure of the cyborg. What gets lost in the troping of the "woman of color" is the "approaches, methods, and skills" of differential US third world feminists, and their contribution to critique:

> Differential U.S. third world feminist criticism . . . is often misrecognized and under analyzed by readers when it is translated as a demographic constituency only (women of color), and not as a theoretical and methodological approach in its own right.[86]

Sandoval credits Haraway for acknowledging her problematic reliance on women of color and Asian technology workers as cyborg examples: "I would be much more careful about describing who counts as 'we' in the statement 'we are all cyborgs,'" she was to state later.[87] The abstraction of the "we" comes with hermeneutic violence when subject positionality is ignored in critical analysis. The statement can obfuscate the global reality that some experience technology as oppression while others live it as opportunity. In retrospect, "we are all cyborgs" appears now insufficiently cognizant of tech-privilege and the "digital divide" that exists in the world, which mirrors the contours of global capitalism. It ignores power and influence, the differential allocation of tech-accessibility, and can even come across as imperialistic: the Included lecturing to the Excluded about how much they are alike (as cyborgs one and all).

And yet, as I have been arguing in this chapter, we might be able to reinterpret "we are all cyborgs" on emancipatory universalist terms without simultaneously neglecting the differential realities of non-Western subjects. As it is worth reaffirming "I'd rather be a cyborg than a goddess"—*a* cyborg who is allergic to any form of organicity, skeptical of absolute immunity and pure transcendence, completeness and perfection, is resolutely un-nostalgic—it is worth repeating "we are all cyborgs," as long as we fully politicize the statement and inscribe it within *the global struggle for the commons*.[88] The commons is what we as human beings share, what we esteem to be social goods unavailable for corporate privatization or state control. The process of cyborgization must be open to the public. "We are all cyborgs" speaks to this "shared substance of our social being,"[89] which is currently jeopardized by neoliberalism's violent and unquenchable imperative to privatize.

In this vein of critique, Žižek, not unlike Fukuyama and Habermas, underscores the challenges of cyborg technology and the biopolitical manipulation and commodification of the genome. He does not downplay the dangers of biogenetics and its potential nefarious use for social control (the transhumanist dream/nightmare of wiring the brain to behave in a certain way).[90] Žižek gives this threat prominence by describing it as one of the four antagonisms that are unresolvable by today's capitalism: "The looming threat of ecological catastrophe; the inappropriateness of private property for so-called intellectual property; the socio-ethical implications of new techno-scientific developments, especially in biogenetics; and last, but not least, new forms of social apartheid—new walls and slums."[91] This last antagonism produces the Included and the Excluded. Without addressing it—without directly confronting the exploitative logic of global capitalism—the three other antagonisms lose their full emancipatory potential, resulting in indefinite reproduction of what *is*: "Ecology turns into a problem of sustainable development; intellectual property into a complex legal challenge; biogenetics into an ethical issue. One can sincerely fight for ecology, defend a broader notion of intellectual property, oppose the copyrighting of genes, without confronting the antagonism between the Included and the Excluded."[92] With respect to the menace of the cyborg, bioconservatives, as we have seen, adopt a stance of moral vigilance: *not under my watch will humans lose their humanity.* Accordingly, the cyborg is a problem only if it starts to ontologically alter being human, that is, our understanding of human nature.

Fukuyama might strike a political chord when he says that genetic engineering risks undermining the victory of liberal democracy, but in his analysis there is no alternative to capitalism: it is still *the end of history.* The implicit choice is between capitalism with a human face or capitalism with a cyborg face. The former clings to humanism; the latter enters the nightmarish era of the posthuman. Unregulated biotechnological developments are first and foremost an ethical issue. We, as a community of rational beings, *ought* to resist the overreach of cyborg technology and bioscience. Yet for Žižek this conservative liberal fear maintains the illusion that capitalism with a human(ist) face is the struggle of our times. It keeps the problem of new techno-scientific improvements in the private sphere of moral outrage and legality. The philosophical task is to pose the question of the cyborg in relation to the fundamental antagonism between the Included and the Excluded.

To reaffirm today the slogan "we are all cyborgs" is to tacitly accept the reality, feared by Fukuyama and Habermas, of a capitalism with a cyborg face, but also to open it up to an unexpected possibility: the cyborg as a candidate for the "part of no-part."[93] The "part of no-part" stands for the others who are systematically excluded, disprivileged, and racialized by society's laws and norms, falling outside the liberal and humanist umbrella. As a given order's constitutive outsiders, they stand for "true universality"; since their interests are not predetermined by their subject positions—there is *no identity* of the part of no-part— when they seek to remedy wrongs, they speak to universal concerns. As Žižek puts it, "in every structure of subject-positions, universality is embodied in its 'part of no-part,' in the element for which there is no proper place in the structure, the element which is forever out of joint."[94] The part of no-part attests to our cyborg (non)being, our "substanceless subjectivity": "we are all excluded, from nature as well as from our symbolic substance."[95] We might say that the cyborg is the human in its ontological rootlessness, in its noncoincidence with itself. It is never fully itself (all); it is nature open. Unlike the ideological universality of Western discourse, which masks its white, male, humanist perspective, the universality of the cyborg (as a part of no-part) is emptied of content and normativity. Not attached to the status quo in the same libidinal and ideological way, cyborgs, as vectors of the non-all, disclose the inconsistencies in the Symbolic and thus hold the promise of transformative change—of enacting politics as such. The political, as Žižek describes it, is a contestation of the established order's positivity. It is "the space of litigation in which the excluded can protest the wrong or injustice done to them."[96] The questions they raise address *all of us*—underscoring our "biogenetic commons,"[97] that is, the commons of our ontological makeup.

To insist, then, that "we are all cyborgs" does not mean to callously celebrate the reign of posthumanity, while others are still yearning to enjoy the benefits of humanity. Nor is it a rallying cry for a transhumanist intervention along the lines articulated by Tesla CEO Elon Musk for whom the urgent need confronting us (humanity) is artificial intelligence (AI) technology. On this view, affirming "we are all cyborgs" is the starting point for positioning humans as rivals to AI: "Because right now, we are already a cyborg. People don't realize we are already a cyborg. Because we are so well integrated with our phones and our computers. The phone is almost like an extension of yourself. If you forget your phone, it's like a missing limb."[98] The challenge as Musk sees it is to become better cyborgs and realize the transhumanist dream. For him, the question is basically, "Can we be able to go along for the ride with AI?"[99] To avoid being left behind ("it'll be much smarter than the smartest human"[100]), Musk's transhumanist answer is to become more like AI. In other words, "if you can't beat them, join them."[101] Toward that end, Musk founded Neuralink in 2016, a neural technology company whose principal goal is to develop "ultra-high bandwidth brain-machine interfaces to connect humans and computers."[102] Žižek rightly rejects the fantasy informing Musk's vision of a wired brain, questioning the transhumanist desire to "bypass material reality"—as if language did not play a crucial function in mediating our thoughts—and to "establish a kind of digitally mediated direct communication in the virtual universe."[103] It is true that in this virtual universe we are all connected, but what is left out of the transhumanist narrative is that we are not connected in the same ways; we must not conflate those who are the agents of technology (the Included) with those subjected to/controlled by technology (the Excluded). Predicated on the "privatization of our commons," Musk's celebration of this new technology masks its ripeness for abuse if/when it is left to "the control of private capital and state power."[104]

Against the reading of liberal conservatives and neoliberal transhumanists, to assert "we are all cyborgs" is instead to say that "we are all potentially alterable," that no one is *a priori* immune from the reach of global capitalism—and again we clearly do *not* lack immunity in the same way. The only way to avoid actually becoming, or continuing to be, the cyborg feared by bioconservatives, ignored or disavowed by transhumanists, and dramatized in *Black Mirror*, is to act preventively and confront global capitalism's digital divide, new forms of social apartheid, and insidious regulation of our lives (which we erroneously experience as free).[105] "We are all cyborgs" is a call for global solidarity; it solicits nothing less than cyborg commons: being posthuman—avowing our biogenetic commons/inheritance—is not to be ethically fetishized but politically defended.

2

Animals

The being of animals is a struggle for life. A struggle for life without ethics. It is a question of might.

EMMANUEL LEVINAS[1]

It is true that I identify it as a male or female cat. But even before that identification, it comes to me as this irreplaceable living being that one day enters my space, into this place where it can encounter me, see me, even see me naked. Nothing can ever rob me of the certainty that what we have here is an existence that refuses to be conceptualized.

JACQUES DERRIDA[2]

Thinking of the human not as a master but as a being existing in relationships with other beings implies profoundly reconceptualizing the way we think of humans and animals, and their shared ontologies and worlds. Cary Wolfe explains the importance of the animal question for posthumanism: "The animal properly understood is a privileged figure for the problem of difference and subjectivity generally, because it foregrounds how the subject is always already multiple."[3] Humanist thought silences animals by appropriating the power to name them and to designate them as inferior and available for mastery. Even when humanists want to defend animals, they typically resort to an

animal rights discourse modeled after human rights discourse—
leaving unquestioned its metaphysics of assimilation and unwittingly
sustaining the animals' status as objects, as mute beings who cannot
speak but must be spoken for.[4] Moreover, animal rights discourse
tacitly perpetuates an economy of the Same, where caring for the
animal is preconditioned on the animal resembling in some way the
human. "The animal other matters," Wolfe writes, "only insofar as it
mirrors the *human* form that is the 'source' of recognizing animals
as bodies that have sensations, feel pain, and so on."[5] Posthumanism
questions these reductions and moves to reconfigure our modes of
relating to difference.

Yet how exactly we should reconceptualize the human-animal
relation continues to be disputed. A flat ontology, for instance, shifts
the emphasis away from the singularity of the human subject by
enabling a reimagination of animal agency. Widespread in the world,
agency is something humans and animals share alike. Indeed, once
we unmake humans the central focus of our discourse—synonymous,
for Latour, with the act of de-modernizing the human—we can finally
make or hear objects speak. A different kind of de-modernization
of the human and the animal takes place in Gilles Deleuze and
Félix Guattari's writings. In their project to undo species identities,
Deleuze and Guattari introduce the concept of "becoming-animal,"
which does not mean crudely mimicking animals, "playing animal
or imitating an animal."[6] Rather, it involves changing modes of being.
Gerald L. Bruns outlines the force of this concept:

> becoming-animal is a movement from major (the constant) to
> minor (the variable); it is a deterritorialization in which a subject
> no longer occupies a realm of stability and identity but is instead
> folded imperceptibly into a movement or into an amorphous
> *legion* whose mode of existence is nomadic or, alternatively, whose

"structure" is rhizomatic rather than arborescent, that is, restless, insomniac, or in flight rather than settled, upright, at one with itself and at peace with others.[7]

The animal for Deleuze and Guattari takes multiplicity as constitutive: "A becoming-animal always involves a pack, a band, a population, a peopling, in short a multiplicity."[8] As Wolfe observes, this type of thinking complicates the comfort of humanist subjectivity, which tends to conceive of its selfhood in identitarian terms, as a whole, complete, and rooted being. In offering the notion of becoming-animal, Deleuze and Guattari aim to scandalize humanism by insisting that there is no unified "Man" but that "the subject is always already multiple."[9] Consequently, the long-cherished humanist values of autonomy, self-mastery, sovereignty, all become suspect, ideologically dubious. The concept of becoming-animal insists on the exteriority of the animal; its alterity is encountered as "contagion."[10]

Nowhere do the stakes of such a claim become clearer than in discussions of the figure of the family pet, a focal point in disputes over the proper form that a posthumanist relationality to nonhuman animals should take. For Deleuze and Guattari, the pet represents an all-too-humanized and humanizing image of the animal, an instrumentalized being, a docile animal available for human enjoyment:

> Individuated animals, family pets, sentimental, Oedipal animals each with its own petty history, "my" cat, "my" dog. These animals invite us to regress, draw us into a narcissistic contemplation, and they are the only kind of animal psychoanalysis understands, the better to discover a daddy, a mommy, a little brother behind them . . . anyone who likes cats or dogs is a fool.[11]

The animal as *other-than-human* can only appear as a frightening otherness, as a significant disruption of my hermeneutic comfort, my sense of the world. In Derrida's colorful language: "Monsters cannot be announced. One cannot say: 'Here are our monsters,' without immediately turning them into pets."[12] Indeed, even the perception of "a monster in a monster" initiates the process of epistemic domestication: "one begins . . . to compare it to the norms, to analyze it, consequently to master whatever could be terrifying in this figure."[13] Structures pacify and normalize, invariably turning raw affect into meaningful emotion, monsters into pets.

But what is so wrong with pets?, asks Donna Haraway. She criticizes Deleuze and Guattari's bias against family pets, deeming their vision too abstract, too disconnected from the lives of actual animals and, ultimately, a failure to imagine another kind of world: "This is a philosophy of the sublime, not the earthly, not the mud; becoming-animal is not an *autre-mondialisation* [an other-worlding]."[14] Haraway is more sympathetic to Derrida's reflections on animals. After finding himself interpellated and othered (his own animality disclosed, generating a sense of shame, and of being ashamed for being ashamed) by his little female cat as he was naked and coming out of the shower,[15] Derrida meditates on his feline's singularity and the inadequacies of language to account for it:

> If I say "it is a real cat" that sees me naked, this is in order to mark its unsubstitutable singularity. When it responds in its name . . . it doesn't do so as the exemplar of a species called "cat," even less so of an "animal" genus or kingdom. It is true that I identify it as a male or female cat. But even before that identification, it comes to me as this irreplaceable living being that one day enters my space, into this place where it can encounter me, see me, even see me naked. Nothing can ever rob me of the certainty that what we have here is an existence that refuses to be conceptualized [*rebelle à tout concept*].[16]

Derrida follows here in the footsteps of the pre-Cartesian or anti-Cartesian Michel de Montaigne (or, we might say, the posthumanist Montaigne), who also challenges the obsession with autonomy/self-sufficiency and human exceptionalism ("the most vulnerable and frail of all creatures is man, and at the same time the most arrogant") by musing on his cat's understanding and affectivity: "When I play with my cat, who knows if I am not a pastime to her more than she is to me?"[17] Agentiality—enacted in the cat's "capacity to respond"[18]—is on the cat's side as much as on Montaigne's.

Yet Derrida also disappoints Haraway by shifting conceptual gears too quickly, leaving his cat behind for a more sustained deconstructive mediation on "the animal" and its ambivalent place in the history of Western philosophy: its denial of the animal's face, language, and subjectivity, its determination that the animal "lacks the lack,"[19] and so on. Along the same lines, Rosi Braidotti accuses Derrida of "reduc[ing] animality to a general figuration of Alterity."[20] Similarly, Cynthia Willett writes: "Derrida's cat remains a figure and not a character in his life."[21] Rather than a wholesale assault on the sovereignty of human subjectivity, Haraway would have preferred more of a "becoming with" the animal. This is a project that she undertakes herself. As Braidotti puts it, Haraway invites us "to see the inter-*relation* human/animal as constitutive of the identity of *each*."[22] Human animals and nonhuman animals become who they are only in relation to one another, not in isolation. Unsatisfied with the sublime abstractions of "becoming-animal," and also with Derrida's staging of his encounter with his cat as an *event*, which similarly flirts with the rhetoric of the sublime, Haraway introduces her more sober concept of "companion species" as a means for thinking about new possibilities for human-animal life. The concept of companion species, which she now prefers to the figure of the cyborg, reflects the ontological and material entanglement of humans and nonhumans, foregrounding touch over abstraction in the interaction with her pet dog. Haraway rejects the idea that the designation of "pet" necessarily neutralizes the nonhuman animal: "If I have a dog, my dog has a human; what that means concretely is at stake."[23] She finds Deleuze and Guattari's statement "anyone who likes cats or dogs is a fool" at once arrogant and ignorant, and though Derrida is more open to his cat for what she teaches him about himself, Haraway also faults him for lacking curiosity about the details of animals' lives and experiences.[24]

At stake for Haraway is the danger of a posthumanism that does away with subjectivity altogether, leaving the human dispossessed, with nothing to offer nonhuman animals. This is why Haraway argues that she is not a posthumanist. The relation between humans and their companions define and shape who they are: "The partners do not precede their relating; all that is, is the fruit of becoming with: those are the mantras of companion species."[25] Haraway's suspicion of posthumanism, then, lies in its exclusive critique of subjectivity, when what is needed is a better appreciation of our relation to companion species. Simply stated, posthumanism in its poststructuralist mode always risks compounding the problem of humanism rather than effectively overcoming its self-centered metaphysics.

I wonder however whether Haraway forecloses too neatly and quickly what Derrida's thinking can bring to an alternative posthumanism, to a less solipsistic and narcissistic account of the posthuman. Materiality is never crudely opposed to figurality in Derrida's writings—and it is for this reason that the ontological turn must not be simply opposed to the linguistic turn. Derrida's posthumanist forays can and do accommodate relationality. The animal question (which is "not one question among others" but "represents the limit upon which all the great questions are formed and determined, as well as the concepts that attempt to delimit what is 'proper to man'"[26]) for Derrida exerts hermeneutic pressure precisely on the "*doxa*," as he calls it, of the "liquidation of the subject."[27] Answering—while not answering—Jean-Luc Nancy's question of "who comes after the subject?" Derrida frames his response as a series of questions. He raises doubts about Nancy's liquidated subject, preferring to conceptualize the subject as "re-interpreted, displaced, decentered, re-inscribed," and questioning the humanist and anthropocentric investment in his interlocutor's "who" by shifting the focus to the animal—delinking subjectivity from man and extending it, along with neighborliness, to the animal. For Derrida, the question of the animal is marked from the outset by what we might describe as a call to posthumanist responsibility; this responsibility affirms itself as constitutively excessive: "responsibility is excessive or it is not a responsibility."[28] Absolute or unconditional hospitality does not follow the path of business as usual, where measured or tempered responsibility is imagined as satisfying the demands of the other. This is a position that the animal is excluded from occupying; the animal is, in this respect, the other's other, for the animal's otherness is not redeemable through recognition as with marginal human groups who can, in principle, be (re)integrated in the polis.

Pace Levinas, the animal does not lack a face[29]—condemned, as it were, to a deficient, amoral existence, to a "struggle for life without ethics." A clear contrast to Levinas's view comes with Hélène Cixous's observation that "there is no greater love than the love the wolf feels for the lamb-it-doesn't-eat."[30] Here Cixous paints the wolf as an ontologically malleable subject who is open to radical transformation, since this wolf, we are assured, is capable of overriding his biological instincts: "This wolf that sacrifices its very definition, its identity as a wolf, for the lamb, this wolf that doesn't eat the lamb, is it a wolf? Is it still a wolf? Isn't it a delupinized wolf, a non-wolf, an invalidated wolf? If it were a false wolf, there'd be no interest. No, we've made no mistake, this wolf is a real wolf: right up to the last second it could eat us."[31] On a smaller scale, Derrida's cat demonstrates the animal's capacity to summon me to act, to arouse an ethical feeling. Ethics is not an interhuman affair; the human is by no means immune to the feline gaze, to the call of the nonhuman.

But what, then, are the consequences of seeing animals as fellow subjects and neighbors? What does such a vision authorize? What does it unsettle? What does it foreclose? I propose to explore these questions by turning to J. M. Coetzee's metafictional novella *The Lives of Animals*, looking at his alter ego Elizabeth Costello's apology of animals, her defense of the defenseless—the invisible victims of quotidian humanism. Coetzee's text was originally presented as the 1997–98 Tanner Lectures at Princeton University as a part of its University Center for Human Values series. Rather than delivering the Tanner Lectures as straightforward academic talks, Coetzee read a fictional work about Costello, an Australian novelist invited by Appleton College to give a couple of lectures in the United States, and who takes the opportunity to address the question of animal rights. The first lecture is titled "The Philosophers and the Animals" and the second "The Poets and the Animals." In her first lecture, Costello powerfully, though not uncontroversially, describes the daily exploitation of animals as a Holocaust, and blasts human complicity with that suffering. Not unlike the complacency witnessed in some Germans' "willed ignorance,"[32] or callous indifference, with respect to the roundup of Jews in Nazi Germany in the 1930s, Costello's contemporaries refuse to do anything about repeated animal suffering—"each day a fresh holocaust" (35). She draws a provocative and polarizing parallel between the Jews of Treblinka and the animals in modern factory farming—provincializing, in turn, the tragic event in European history by questioning the exceptionalism of the (Western) human.

While any analogy between Nazi Germany and the meat industry must avoid overgeneralized comparisons between historical conditions that are fundamentally incommensurable, the Shoah is not utterly beyond analogy, and a critical engagement with the violence of the genocide and the current human mistreatment of nonhuman animals in modern-day food production can draw out important insights that might otherwise go unseen. The analogy itself is not new. Yiddish author Isaac Bashevis Singer famously evokes it in the short story "The Letter Writer," where the protagonist, Herman, writes:

> What do they know—all these scholars, all these philosophers, all the leaders of the world—about such as you? They have convinced themselves that man, the worst transgressor of all the species, is the crown of creation. All other creatures were created merely to provide him with food, pelts, to be tormented, exterminated. In relation to them, *all people are Nazis; for the animals it is an eternal Treblinka.*[33]

And Martin Heidegger, whose complicity with the rise of Nazism makes his observation morally tainted, compared the death camps to "mechanized agriculture."[34] Derrida himself does not shy from referring to "the Judeo-Christiano-Islamic tradition of a war against the animal,"[35] from evoking "animal genocides,"[36] or from denouncing factory farming and the mechanical sacrifice of animals, but he does so with interpretive precision. The question of analogy is not *a priori* morally or politically dubious. What must always be resisted is a certain will to homogenize, to erase differences in the act of comparison: to aim, in other words, for analogical *identification* rather than evaluation.[37] Does Costello display such attentiveness? Or, to put it slightly differently, what types of relationality does she practice, and how, and to what effect, is Coetzee staging—rather than simply endorsing—an animal ethics through a less-than-unimpeachable character? How does she, do we, responsibly negotiate difference?

Posthumanist Responsibility

Costello builds her animal ethics by dismantling philosophy's long-cherished commitment to the powers of ratiocination, though she confesses her inability to break with it completely. To some extent she must, reluctantly, "bow to reason" if she is to be heard (23).[38] In the humanist discourse of the proper, reason looms large. The capacity to reason defines man. Reason introduces an ontological division between those who matter and those who don't. Needless to say, this making of man has been to the detriment of the animal. The singularity of reason is distributed thriftily to humans, housed exclusively in the minds of humans—immunizing the human, the idea of the human from any hermeneutic contamination, from any semantic breach. This is a phantasm of absolute difference, of a human identity whose traits and property ("speech or reason, the logos, history, laughing, mourning, burial, the gift, etc."[39]) are deemed precious and unshareable, something to be scrupulously guarded and jealously protected—which philosophers and humanists have, of course, long taken pains to do. But this human singularity is overblown, its "universal value"[40] highly inflated, and its self-congratulatory logic—only reason can give us "access to the secrets of the universe" (123)—a sham. Moreover, it turns out that reason is not solely the property of humans; animals possess it as well, though humans are often willfully blind to its display, failing to adequately document rational thought in animals.

Rather than pursue this line of argument, however, Costello moves to substitute reason with sympathy:

The heart is the seat of a faculty, *sympathy*, that allows us to share at times the being of another. Sympathy has everything to do with the subject and little to do with the object, the 'another,' as we see

when we imagine the object not as a bat ("Can I share the being of
a bat?") but as another human being. (34–5)

The other's availability for identification, the subject's capacity to
access another's inner being, are unproblematically asserted. Is this
a case of posthumanist responsibility? Yes and no. Costello clearly
extends subjectivity to animals, a subjectivity fully capable of enjoying
life,[41] but what gets lost in her ethical vision is the question of animal
difference. Against widespread anthropocentric indifference to the
plight of animals, Costello argues for the necessity of establishing a
relation to nonhuman others. But she passes much too quickly from
indifference to identification, from the ethical stagnation of the
subject/object relationship—where animals sit firmly on the object
side of the divide, awaiting their cognitive assessment at the hands
of philosophers—to its heroic overcoming by sympathy. Costello,
we might say, resolves an epistemological problem—I cannot know
the other's interiority, especially that of an animal—with an ethico-
ontological solution: sympathy transports us into the life of the
animal; it enables us to recognize that the animal is not devoid of
thought and, more importantly, to come to appreciate that this
thinking, along with its experiences, is part of the animal's being, its
ontological makeup (in Chapter 3, we will see how OOO qualifies
the powers of sympathy by underscoring the animal's—all objects'—
resistance to direct understanding of its thinking, inner being, etc.).

Costello outlines three possibilities when it comes to sympathy: you
have sympathy and practice it (thus you are able to imagine yourself
as someone else); you don't have it (in its most extreme form, you're
a psychopath); you have it but choose not practice it (35). She directs
her address primarily to the third group. The challenge, then, is how
to convert people who have the capacity for sympathy but fail to use it.
She is confident that there are basically no limits to what imagination

can do; indeed, "there are no bounds to the sympathetic imagination," she states directly (35). But how do you make sympathetic imaginings happen? If philosophers' bias in favor of cognition seems to impose a formal limit on their ability to meet and relate to the animal, Costello finds more hope in poets. Whereas philosophers foreclose any access to the lives of animals, poets extend "our sympathies to animals"[42] via the powers of poetic imagination. For Costello, poets trump philosophers in their inventiveness and openness to nonhuman difference. When moral deliberation is not restricted to cognitive pursuits, when it makes room for emotions or affect, for the "fullness, embodiedness, the sensation of being" (33), a different relationality between humans and animals can productively emerge.

What comes as more of a surprise, given their shared concern for animals, is Costello's attack on environmental scientists. She faults these researchers for their abstraction, as well as their commitment to and imposition of an "ecological vision" (53), which results in their inattentiveness to the struggle for *each* animal to matter, to succeed, to live. Yet, as if to block a temptation on the part of the audience/reader to hear in this assertion an echo of Levinas's disparaging comment about the animal's non-ethics, its mechanical existence, Costello dismisses any reductive reading of the impulse to survive. We humans accept that we can manage life self-consciously, "but when we see the salmon fighting for its life we say, it is just programmed to fight; we say, with Aquinas, it is locked into natural slavery; we say, it lacks self-consciousness" (54). Both Aquinas and Levinas leave no room for an *ethics* of animal survival. It is precisely against the animality of animals, their alleged lack of mental capabilities, that Aquinas and Levinas uphold human uniqueness and affirm what is proper to man—rationality, the face, and so on.

Costello's position is, however, met with objections, dismissals, and counterarguments. Her own son John and his wife Norma find her lectures badly argued and naively childish. Her vegetarianism is lived with contradictions and inconsistencies. Asked by Garrard, the president of the university, if her vegetarianism stems from "moral conviction," she answers unexpectedly that "it comes out of a desire to save my soul" (43). Self-interest, then, is the motivation behind her love for and openness to animals, tainting, to say the least, her ethical standing. But, after an awkward pause, the president generously comments:

> "Well, I have a great respect for it," says Garrard, "As a way of life."
>
> "I'm wearing leather shoes," says his mother, "I'm carrying a leather purse. I wouldn't have overmuch respect if I were you."
>
> "Consistency," murmurs Garrard. "Consistency is the hobgoblin of small minds. Surely one can draw a distinction between eating meat and wearing leather."
>
> "Degrees of obscenity," she replies. (43)

In this odd exchange, Costello displays, at once, cognizance of her contradictions and a refusal to brush them aside, avowing her complicity in the very system she indicts, at the risk of sabotaging her public image, which she also does by paradoxically declining her interpellation as a source of authority: "I don't know what I think . . . I often wonder what thinking is, what understanding is. Do we really understand the universe better than animals do?" (45)[43]

Appleton philosophy professor Thomas O'Hearne adopts a far more agonistic posture toward Costello. He insists on the need to distinguish between licit and illicit killing of animals. The former is possible, he argues, because "animals do not have immortal souls" (64), nor do they understand death in all its complexity as humans do, while the latter is possible because *excessive* cruelty toward animals is a valid condition for moral outrage.

This exchange opens up a different and potentially more productive aspect of Costello's ethics, which, in its emphasis on the possibility of sympathetic identification with all animals, somewhat paradoxically results in a radical openness to any other, to all otherness. O'Hearne's "enlightened" humanism makes allowance only for what Derrida calls "conditional hospitality": *I respect you in my human world, on condition that I can sacrifice you (without cruelty) at will.* By contrast, Costello's radical posthumanism calls for "unconditional hospitality." If, as Derrida puts it, unconditional hospitality "opens or is in advance open to someone who is neither expected nor invited, to whomever arrives as an absolutely foreign *visitor*, as a new *arrival*, nonidentifiable and unforeseeable, in short, wholly other,"[44] Costello does not want to exclude the animal from the category of the other. Derrida concurs, but goes one step further by questioning the role of sympathy (of *choosing* sympathy), of identification, in this welcoming:

> Yes *to who or what turns up* [*arrivant*], before any determination, before any anticipation, before any *identification*, whether or not it has to do with a foreigner, an immigrant, an invited guest, or an unexpected visitor, whether or not the new arrival is the citizen of another country, a human, animal, or divine creature, a living or dead thing, male or female.[45]

O'Hearne effectively says no to the animal; it is determined incapable of de-worlding his world, of puncturing his horizon of intelligibility and expectations. But if this weren't the case, O'Hearne's licit/illicit killing distinction would falter, rendering killing as such, the sacrifice of any animals, ethically problematic.

The strongest pushback to Costello's rejection of animal killing and endorsement of a posthumanist responsibility to nonhuman beings comes when she designates the animals victims on a par with the Jews of the Shoah, even exceeding them in their suffering:

Let me say it openly: we are surrounded by an enterprise of degradation, cruelty, and killing which rivals anything that the Third Reich was capable of, indeed dwarfs it, in that ours is an enterprise without end, self-regenerating, bringing rabbits, rats, poultry, livestock ceaselessly into the world for the purpose of killing them.

And to split hairs, to claim that there is no comparison, that Treblinka was so to speak a metaphysical enterprise dedicated to nothing but death and annihilation while the meat industry is ultimately devoted to life (once its victims are dead, after all, it does not burn them to ash or bury them but on the contrary cuts them up and refrigerates and packs them so that they can be consumed in the comfort of our homes) is as little consolation to those victims as it would have been—pardon the tastelessness of the following—to ask the dead of Treblinka to excuse their killers because their body-fat was needed to make soap and their hair to stuff mattresses with. (21–2)

This is a blistering critique of the rationalization involved in explaining/justifying farm factories: that it is an instance of "affirmative biopolitics"[46] since death (of animals) is "ultimately devoted to life," that is, to the betterment of the *human* community. Costello zeros in on the humanist impulse to decouple the Shoah from animal killing: one is metaphysical, a trauma to the idea/l of the human, the other a necessary feature of modern social existence. Toward the end of *The Lives of Animals*, Costello reiterates her dismay at what she sees as "a crime of stupefying proportions," the ubiquitous evidence of animal violence wherever she turns her eyes: "Am I fantasizing it all? I must be mad! Yet every day I see the evidences. The very people I suspect produce the evidence, exhibit it, offer it to me. Corpses. Fragments of corpses that they have bought for money" (69).

Costello's argument meets angry resistance early on in the text at the hands of the poet Abraham Stern. Refusing to attend an organized dinner for Costello after her lecture, Stern expresses his objections in a letter, arguing for the illogic of her dreadful analogy:

> You took over for your own purposes the familiar comparison between the murdered Jews of Europe and slaughtered cattle. The Jews died like cattle, therefore cattle die like Jews, you say. That is a trick with words which I will not accept. You misunderstand the nature of likenesses; I would even say you misunderstand willfully, to the point of blasphemy. Man is made in the likeness of God but God does not have the likeness of man. If Jews were treated like cattle, it does not follow that cattle are treated like Jews. The inversion insults the memory of the dead. It also trades on the horrors of the camps in a cheap way. (49–50)

Stern's condescending lesson repeats idealist or humanist tropes about human singularity.[47] The human is not God, but in relation to animals he is exceptional, occupying a similar place of ontological superiority. The same reasons why it is illegitimate to compare God and man are identical to the ones concerning Jews and cattle. In good humanist fashion, what is, of course, *a priori* ruled out by Stern is that cattle are made as well in the likeness of God.

Anthropocentric Resistance, or Fetishist Disavowal

Stern's resistance to Costello's analogy has been for the most part echoed in the reception of Coetzee's *Lives of Animals*. Stanley Cavell considers it "an inherently indecorous comparison, not to say offensive, and perhaps deliberately a little mad; fervent news from nowhere."[48] Haraway judges the analogy "a common, powerful, and in my view powerfully wrong approach." Haraway nuances her judgment by making clear that she is not objecting to the establishment of a relation between "the Nazi killings of the Jews and others and mass animal slaughter in the meat industry"[49] but that the "analogy culminating in equation can blunt our alertness to irreducible difference and multiplicity and their demands. Different atrocities deserve their own language."[50] The problem is thus analogical identification rather than analogical *evaluation*. The analogy is asserted without the hermeneutic labor that it requires. But David Wood cautions against turning our interpretive gaze too quickly from the analogy: "If there is a worry that the distinctiveness of the human gets lost in such a comparison, there is an equal worry that the refusal of such analogies perpetuates our all-too-human blindness to the systematic violence we habitually inflict on other creatures."[51]

The analogy puts us in a double bind. First, the relation between the Shoah and animal genocides must be repeatedly affirmed; the connection itself is an offense to the Western humanist mind, a reminder of its psychic wound, its vulnerability and lack of immunity. The analogy generates anthropocentric resistance as a form of fetishist disavowal. Second, the irreducible differences between the history of anti-Semitism and the history of speciesism must also be simultaneously affirmed. Attending to the history and pervasiveness of anti-Jewish prejudice might cause the animal question to lose focus, to diminish in its rhetorical force, or even fall back into oblivion, and thus continue to leave "our moral being . . . untouched" (35). But if we simply bypass the double bind, we inadvertently treat the Jewish question as passé while insinuating that it is the mistreatment of animals—as the "new Jews"—that now deserves our attention.[52] In this respect, the same objections made to the analogy between animals and slavery are applicable, as we will see in Chapter 4. Many animal rights activists look to the abolitionist movement as a model to emulate: blacks are now free, but animals continue to live in slavery—*as if* antiblackness were a thing of the past.

To sum up: Costello's modality of *J'accuse* aims at shocking today's bystanders out of their complacency and complicity with the mistreatment of animals. Ignorance is no excuse—we don't accept this justification for those who claim it during the Shoah, so why should we accept it in this case? Humanist privilege is no excuse either. This is tacitly evoked whenever humans claim preferable treatment: yes, animals suffer (today's humanists have moved beyond Descartes), but let us not forget that "we were 'just' talking about nonhuman animals,"[53] their suffering counts less than that of humans who stand at the top of the hierarchy of victims—provided humans can affirm their humanity, which is not a given, as the ongoing history of colonialism and racism makes abundantly clear. The analogy provincializes the Jewish Holocaust. By stating that the ongoing animal Holocaust "dwarfs it" (21), Costello is not diminishing the horror of the Shoah but troubling the anthropocentric investment in this event. The Jews' unprecedented historical suffering transforms them as a people from "victims" into "Victims" of Humanity, guaranteeing them the (timeless) status of (morally untouchable) other, giving them, in turn, a paradigmatic status in trauma and genocide studies.[54] As Cécile Winter points out:

> [T]he ideological frame mounted at Nuremberg laid the foundations for a durable edifice. The "Crime" against "Humanity," the first, the incomparable and absolute, the inaccessible, definitive yardstick of all others, elevated its victims to exemplary status. The "Victims," once jews, became "Jews." "Jew," that is, turned into a metonymical signifier for Humanity . . . "Jew" is the Victim par excellence.[55]

This rhetoric of victimhood transforms the Jew into a self-enclosed and nonrelational entity.

Costello's analogy exerts pressure on the putative nonrelationality of the Jewish Holocaust. It shares Winter's ideology critique of the Holocaust industry, but also builds on this critique by linking its sacralization to the racism of Western humanism. We can see Costello adopting and adapting Aimé Césaire's anti-colonial rebuke to the Western outrage over the Holocaust. In *Discourse on Colonialism*, Césaire exposes the subject of the outrage as "the very distinguished, the very humanistic, the very Christian bourgeois":

> What he cannot forgive Hitler for is not the *crime* in itself, *the crime against man*, it is not *the humiliation of man as such*, it is the crime against the white man, the humiliation of the white man, and the fact that he applied to Europe colonialist procedures which until then had been reserved exclusively for the Arabs of Algeria, the coolies of India, and the blacks of Africa.[56]

Costello supplements Césaire's powerful anti-racist critique with an anti-speciesist one of her own. As with racism, speciesism divides the beings of the world into one group that intrinsically matters (humans) and one that only contingently matters, if at all. Costello rejects this division and the ontological elevation of the human race above all other beings on the basis of their ability to reason (only beings who share something like human reason can come to matter in this speciesist logic).

Costello's analogy explicitly traces the entanglement of both histories of genocide since it was "Chicago [that] showed us the way; it was from the Chicago stockyards that the Nazis learned how to process bodies" (53). The horror of the Final Solution grows out of the *tolerated* horror of the animal slaughterhouse: "We need factories of death; we need factory animals" (53). Notice here how Costello's use of "us" rather than "they" (for the Nazis) implicates us all in the violence. Humanist innocence (especially in the United States where the lecture is delivered) is a phantasm that Costello works to dispel. Coetzee himself reiterates Costello's position in a talk given to open the exhibition *Voiceless: I feel therefore I am*, republished in slightly altered form in an article for *The Sydney Morning Herald*. Coetzee assesses the public unease regarding "the industrial use of animals"; they tolerate it as long as they are not directly confronted by it. They don't want to see factory farms and abattoirs—and this is doubly true for their children (whom they don't want to see traumatized by the sight of animal killing). But this tacit acceptance of their presence has had grave consequences (for us and for other animals), producing the conditions and possibilities for moral disasters to come:

> The transformation of animals into production units dates back to the late 19th century, and since that time we have already had one warning on the grandest scale that there is something deeply, cosmically wrong with regarding and treating fellow beings as mere units of any kind.

> This warning came so loud and clear that one would have thought it impossible to ignore. It came when, in the 20th century, a group of powerful and bloody-minded men in Germany hit on the idea of adapting the methods of the industrial stockyard, as pioneered and perfected in Chicago, to the slaughter—or what they preferred to call the processing—of human beings.

> Of course we cried out in horror when we found out what they had been up to. What a terrible crime to treat human beings like cattle—if we had only known beforehand. But our cry should more accurately have been: what a terrible crime to treat human beings like units in an industrial process. And that cry should have had a postscript: what a terrible crime—come to think of it, a crime

against nature—to treat any living being like a unit in an industrial process.[57]

The refusal of this postscript—an unwillingness to shift care from the universality of *human* beings to the universality of *living* beings—is what a posthumanist critique seeks at once to explain and overcome. Why the persistence of this refusal? What is it about the anthropocentric insistence on the value of human lives over animal lives? Derrida, following Freud, suggests that "the anthropocentric reinstitution of the superiority of the human order over the animal order" is first and foremost a reaction to a psychic blow, a "wounded reaction not to humanity's *first* trauma, the Copernican (the Earth revolves around the sun), nor its *third* trauma, the Freudian (the decentering of consciousness under the gaze of the unconscious), but rather to its *second* trauma, the Darwinian."[58] The irony here is that while Darwinian theory demystified the ideological exceptionalism and singularity of humans, it also produced a humanist backlash: ontologically, we concede that we are on par with animals, but in the realm of the symbolic order we are sovereign and rule over them—we are subjects who *respond*; they are objects that *react*.

Another way to frame this refusal, this resistance to the animal, is to see it as displaying the psychoanalytic structure of fetishist disavowal (*I know very well, but all the same*). Counterintuitively, Žižek sees this refusal to fully engage the suffering of animals as emblematic of ethics as such. At some profound level, every ethics enacts a fetishist disavowal, "draw[s] a line and ignore[s] some sort of suffering." He perceptively asks:

> What about animals slaughtered for our consumption? who among us would be able to continue eating pork chops after visiting a factory farm in which pigs are half-blind and cannot even properly walk, but are just fattened to be killed? And what about, say, torture and suffering of millions we know about, but

choose to ignore? Imagine the effect of having to watch a snuff movie portraying what goes on thousands of times a day around the world: brutal acts of torture, the picking out of eyes, the crushing of testicles—the list cannot bear recounting. Would the watcher be able to continue going on as usual? Yes, but only if he or she were able somehow to forget—in an act which suspended symbolic efficiency—what had been witnessed. This forgetting entails a gesture of what is called fetishist disavowal: "I know it, but I don't want to know that I know, so I don't know." I know it, but I refuse to fully assume the consequences of this knowledge, so that I can continue acting as if I don't know it.[59]

It is telling that Žižek opens his list of horrors with the industrialization of animal killing.

As liberal subjects, we want to forget about the suffering of animals, we want to remain ethical but don't want to assume the consequences: the need to radically transform society's unequal distribution of values—the determination of who matters and who doesn't. As enlightened humanists, we maintain a split attitude. We know that human beings are just like pigs and birds, that we are animals subjected to evolution by natural selection. We know that we experiment on animals, mistreat and slaughter them. We know that there is nothing special about us; we readily "acknowledge the traumatic absence."[60] We know about the trauma (of Darwin, castration, being human), but nonetheless we act as if we didn't know, as if we were special, whole or non-lacking, enthusiastically humanist through and through—and thus "without having to acknowledge its traumatic effect."[61] As Todd McGowan puts it in relation to castration, "fetishistic disavowal enables the subject to know and not to know about symbolic castration at the same time."[62] We know very well that humanism mystifies and has dirty hands, but we nonetheless believe in humanism. Humanists have their "cake and eat it."[63] Fetishist disavowal allows the humanist subject to "know" but without making that knowledge paralyzing, disruptive, or detrimental to the well-being of society. An effective posthumanist critique must confront the fetishist disavowal that neutralizes this knowledge and renders possible the smooth functioning of everyday social existence, that sustains the belief that the humanist life under liberal democracy is a life without factory farms, sweatshops, sex trafficking, slums, and so on, and that liberal democracy—itself functioning as a fetish—is all there is. Posthumanism as a critique of the humanist subject remains limited if it sees the attachment to the human only as a kind of religious or metaphysical residue, a sign of a lingering immaturity. Today's humanists are not Cartesian humanists who deny that animals actually feel pain; they are not interested in the rhetoric of *res cogitans* ("thinking thing"), the human as a spiritual, thinking substance. Indeed, they acknowledge evolution and fight for its teaching in school. Still, they are anti-speciesists in theory but speciesists in practice when it comes to *their* humanity.

Žižek asks again: "Does not *every* ethics have to rely on such a gesture of fetishist disavowal? Yes, every ethics—with *the exception of the ethics of psychoanalysis* which is a kind of anti-ethics: it focuses precisely on what the standard ethical enthusiasm excludes, on the traumatic Thing that our Judeo-Christian tradition calls the 'Neighbor.'"[64] Thinking posthumanism with psychoanalysis, posthumanism as a kind of anti-ethics, returns us to Derrida's cat, the neighbor of the human.

The Cat as Neighbor

Pace Heidegger, Derrida's cat is not "poor in world" (*weltarm*);[65] she is not enslaved to her environment. Her gaze emanates from its own *Lebenswelt*. This feline-in-the-world intersects with his. She is a neighbor to Derrida, who, unlike the philosophical tradition, feels no inhibitions in extending this cherished category to his cat. But what kind of neighbor is she? Is she the neighbor in the same ways Žižek understands the term? Yes and no. We can appreciate how the two philosophers converge and diverge in their account of the neighbor by first turning to Žižek's critical engagement with the "common sense of deconstruction" in a section from *Less than Nothing* titled "The Animal That I Am."

As Žižek puts it, deconstruction asks

> naive questions which undermine philosophical propositions taken for granted for centuries. . . . As Derrida emphasizes again and again, the point of this questioning is not to cancel the gap that separates man from (other) animals and attribute also to (other) animals properly "spiritual" properties—the path taken by some eco-mystics who claim that not only animals, but even trees and plants communicate in a language of their own to which we humans are deaf. The point is rather that all these differences should be re-thought and conceived in a different way, multiplied, "thickened"—and the first step on this path is to denounce the all-encompassing category of "the animal."[66]

Indeed, cognizant of the violent and homogenizing potential of the single category of "the animal"—such naming is both "a sin against rigorous thinking, vigilance, lucidity, or empirical authority" and "a crime"[67]—Derrida coins the anti-speciesist term "animot," which at once evokes the idea of multiplicity (as a homonym of the French term "animaux" [animals]), and foregrounds its linguistic character: it is a word ("mot" means "word" in French) not to be confused with the thing, the nonhuman materiality, that it represents.[68] Surprisingly, in a section that displays an attentiveness to the role of language vis-à-vis animals and nature, Žižek does not comment on Derrida's neologism. Rather, he focuses on Derrida's simplification of the philosophical tradition; his reduction of the philosophical tradition to "phallogocentrism" or the "metaphysics of presence."[69] For Derrida, "the whole history of humanity"[70] is premised on the violent and systemic exclusion of the animal, on the persistent and obligatory disavowal of man's animality, understood here (after Jeremy Bentham[71]) as ontological vulnerability, the *negative power* to suffer. Žižek faults Derrida for failing to "treat philosophers one by one" as Lacan and Deleuze do, while ironically returning to, and doubling down on, the simplification too quickly dismissed by Derrida ("But is not such a violent levelling a necessary feature of every critical move, of every rise of the New?"), that of the binary opposition between the human and the animal:

> Instead of dismissing *en bloc* such "binary logic," one should assert it, not only as a necessary step of simplification, but as inherently true in that very simplification. To put it in Hegelese, it is not only that, say, the totalization effected under the heading "the animal" involves the violent obliteration of a complex multiplicity; it is also that the violent reduction of such a multiplicity to a minimal difference is the moment of truth. That is to say, the multiplicity of animal forms is to be conceived as a series of attempts to resolve some basic antagonism or tension which defines animality as such, a tension which can only be formulated from a minimal distance, once humans are involved.[72]

Binaries are not *a priori* dubious, nor limitations on thought; they are an invitation for dialectical thinking to take place, so here in the human-animal binary the human must not be deemed immediately and irremediably suspect or illegitimate, accused of standing in arrogance over the animal. Read dialectically, the scrutinized human-animal distinction takes on a different meaning. The "moment of truth" for Žižek is that this initial opposition produces a new insight into the nature of identity, disclosing the ways in which human identity is precisely not self-enclosed but subject to mediation: the humanist affirmation of the human already affirms the animal in order to deny it ("the affirmation of ~A already affirms A in order to deny it"[73]). There is no animality in-itself, no humanity in-itself. It is not a question of determining the positive identity of one (the human) by negating that of the other (the animal). In "the Animal" (the abstraction rejected by Derrida), the human encounters itself in its "oppositional determination": "viewed as an animal, man is *the* spectral animal existing alongside really existing animal kinds."[74]

Like Derrida, Žižek does not subscribe to biological continuism, the notion that humans and animals are basically the same.[75] There is a "radical discontinuity,"[76] an abyssal difference that separates us from the animal domain. Derrida opts to trouble and multiply rather than efface the limits separating us and them: "Everything I'll say will consist, certainly not in effacing the limit, but in multiplying its figures, in complicating, thickening, delinearizing, folding, and dividing the line precisely by making it increase and multiply."[77] Indeed, Derrida is after "the *growth* or *pluralization* of limits, as well as of the creatures that are contained in them."[78] Žižek for his part foregrounds the becoming other of the human, where the human-viewed-as-animal symbolizes a liminal space between the human(ist) and the multiplicity of existing animals. As Oxana Timofeeva observes, "the human must still be distanced from the rest of the animal kingdom, but this time not so much in order to violate animals via language as in order to acquire their animality via its own antagonism."[79] This human fully accepts "the inhuman core of being-human,"[80] its negativity/antagonism, its constitutive animality: *Je est un animal*.[81]

Returning to Derrida's encounter with his cat, Žižek draws from it not a lesson in the other's singularity but one about the subject's own animality:

> The cat's gaze stands for the gaze of the Other—an inhuman gaze, but for this reason all the more the Other's gaze in all its abyssal impenetrability. Seeing oneself being seen by an animal is an abyssal encounter with the Other's gaze, since—precisely because we should not simply project onto the animal our inner experience—something is returning the gaze which is radically Other. The entire history of philosophy is based upon a disavowal of such an encounter.[82]

Philosophy's phantasmatic investment—Žižek is also not shy about generalizing the whole of philosophy!—in the proper, in what immunizes, reinforces, and positivizes the subject ("'Man,' 'human person,' is a mask that conceals the pure subjectivity of the Neighbor"[83]), has made it ideologically resistant to its exposure to the faceless other, the animal, the animalized human. But rather than save the other by recognizing/extending a face to the destitute, Žižek speculates about what the cat sees, placing the human(ist) not in its privileged position of the *seer* but in that of the *seen*.[84]

Pursuing this idea further, Žižek shifts gears and introduces his own feline example: "I remember seeing a photo of a cat after it had been subjected to some lab experiment in a centrifuge, its bones half broken, its skin half hairless, its eyes looking helplessly into the camera—this is the gaze of the Other disavowed not only by philosophers, but by humans 'as such.'"[85] Žižek's cat is here analogous to Primo Levi's the *Muselmann*, that living-dead, faceless figure of Auschwitz—obliquely repeating the notorious Jews/animals comparison. Žižek opposes the faceless face of the *Muselmann* to Levinas's ethics of the other, disclosing the limits of the face-to-face encounter: "When confronted with a Muselmann, one cannot discern in his face the trace of the abyss of the Other in his/her vulnerability, addressing us with the infinite call of our responsibility. What one gets instead is a kind of blind wall, lack of depth."[86]

Žižek associates the *Muselmann* with the biblical figure of the neighbor, which he considers the "most precious and revolutionary aspect of the Jewish legacy," underscoring how the neighbor "remains an inert, impenetrable, enigmatic presence that hystericizes."[87] If Greek philosophy neglected this hysterical presence ("Nothing is farther from the message of Socrates than *you shall love your neighbor as yourself*, a formula that is remarkably absent from all that he says," Žižek writes, quoting Lacan[88]), Jewish law recognizes the Real of the neighbor, the neighbor as the "bearer of a monstrous Otherness, this properly *inhuman* neighbor."[89] This neighbor as Real can only appear as an alien, a disorienting otherness scrambling my hermeneutic compass: the injunction "*to love* and respect your neighbor . . . does not refer to your imaginary *semblable*/double, but to the neighbor qua traumatic Thing."[90]

As a figure of precarity and bare life, the *Muselmann* constitutes a disquieting example of the neighbor for whom no relation *as such* is affectively afforded; this "'faceless' face," as Žižek puts it, is a "neighbor with whom no empathetic relationship is possible."[91] Stripped of its symbolic veneer, recalcitrant to one's imaginary projection, denied access to the human realm of intersubjectivity, the *Muselmann* foregrounds the neighbor as Real, in which "we encounter the Other's call at its purest and most radical," and "one's responsibility toward the Other at its most traumatic."[92] It is in this context that the ethico-political injunction to "love thy neighbor" takes on its full political force, its full posthumanist potential.

The resemblance between Žižek's account of the *Muselmann* and his recollection of the cat in the lab experiment is striking. The lab cat is a cat laid bare, symbolically unrecognizable as a pet, at odds with the imaginary, fuzzy, and cute cat of domesticity so derided by Deleuze and Guattari. Unlike the Levinasian model of the face, which a posthumanist reader might be tempted to extend to the animal (a posthumanist Levinas), a Žižekian take would argue that it is not enough to say that I can never account for the animal other as other, that phenomenologically the cat is always in excess of my idea of the cat. The "Real" of the cat is impossible but it is an impossibility that paradoxically needs to be nourished and cultivated:

> The Real is impossible but it is not simply impossible in the sense of a failed encounter. It is also impossible in the sense that it is a traumatic encounter that *does* happen but which we are unable to confront. And one of the strategies used to avoid confronting it is precisely that of positing it as this indefinite ideal which is eternally postponed. One aspect of the real is that it's impossible, but the other aspect is that it happens but is impossible to sustain, impossible to integrate. And this second aspect, I think, is more and more crucial.[93]

The experience/exposure of the cat as real happens. And such happening poses a problem for the universality of humanism. The cat as real neighbor is neither *like* other cats nor a radical alterity mysteriously exempt from symbolic mediation. The cat hystericizes me. This latter recognition implicates me—in my animality, inhumanity, monstrosity—as well:

> What if that which characterizes humans is this very openness to the abyss of the radical Other, this perplexity of "What does the Other really want from me?" In other words, what if we turn the perspective around here? What if the perplexity a human sees in the animal's gaze is the perplexity aroused by the monstrosity of

the human being itself? What if it is my own abyss I see reflected in the abyss of the Other's gaze.[94]

"*Che vuoi?*" What do the *Muselmann* and the lab cat really want from me? The question "What do they want from me?" is not merely rhetorical, unlike similar questions asked about women, as Cixous has warned:

> To pose the question "What do women want?" is to pose it already as answer, as from a man who isn't expecting any answer, because the answer is "She wants nothing." . . . "What does she want? . . . Nothing!" Nothing because she is passive. The only thing man can do is offer the question "What could she want, she who wants nothing?" Or in other words: "Without me, what could she want?"[95]

Žižek's question and rejoinder follow a different path; in fact, his answer to this enigmatic question is no answer at all. He does not reify the otherness of *Muselmann* and the lab cat; he does not keep their strangeness, as it were, at an epistemic arm's length, contained and demarcated (as the other's problem/the problem of the other). Strangeness does not only emanate from *without*; it leaks from *within*. The terrifying abyss, the irreducible alterity, that I see in their gaze, that prompt my hystericization, is paradoxically *also* my own.[96] The fantasy of wholeness, the belief in its future realizability—what fetishist disavowals seek to preserve as possibility—is precisely what is at stake in the figure of the neighbor.

Are things so different with Derrida's cat? I don't believe that Žižek's lab cat is meant to displace the former, nor is it a corrective to some narcissistic Oedipal vision of Derrida's cat as a little girl (as Deleuze and Guattari would say). Rather Žižek's cat compels us to return to Derrida's cat, and to better appreciate the interpretive labor that the concept "animot" enables when it is reread through Lacan's three registers.[97] If Žižek's account of the lab cat foregrounds what the cat sees (the human as the animal of the animal), Derrida's autobiographical example enacts an ethico-political response to the other's abyssal gaze. With the notion of *animot,* Derrida establishes with his cat what he calls elsewhere a "relation without relation."[98] What sustains the (non)relationality is a hermeneutics that avows its violence from the beginning. As Derrida famously put it in his interview "'Eating Well,' or the Calculation of the Subject": "The moral question is . . . not, nor has it ever been: should one eat or not eat . . . but since *one must* eat in any case . . . *how* for goodness sake should one *eat well (bien manger)?*"[99] Derrida's phrase *"Il faut bien manger"* can be translated into English in two ways: "we have to eat, after all" and "we must eat well." "Eating" here serves as a metonymy or an index. It points to the act of taking in food, but also beyond that to the ways in which the subject assimilates linguistic and cultural codes.

Affirming the (literal and symbolic) indigestibility of the animal other—in an effort to offset a masculinist humanism of flesh eating[100]—is a posthumanist temptation that Derrida scrupulously tries to resist. There is no escape from violence and assimilation; in order to survive, all living organisms must eat other living organisms—*we have to eat, after all.* Moreover, without a degree of assimilation and violence, no friendship, no meaning could ever form. In this respect, assimilation is not an "absolute evil" (as Derrida says of autoimmunity). As Kelly Oliver points out, assimilation is all around us: "One learns language through assimilating words, one understands others and communicates with them by assimilating traditions and values, and so forth. Both words and food move through the orifices of the body, most particularly the mouth."[101]

Derrida thus declines the choice between an anthropocentric/cannibalistic/carnivorous mode of contact or an animal-centric/

noncannibalistic/vegetarian mode of contact. Abstention from the consumption of flesh (the path of vegetarianism) is not in itself a sufficient answer to what Derrida's names "*carno-phallogocentrism*."[102] This neologism builds on Derrida's previous critique of phallogocentrism. In addition to his challenge to masculinity (phallus) and reason/speech (logos), Derrida now takes up the question of carnivorism. All three components are constitutive of the gluttonous Western subject. The *cogito* not only is a possessor and master of nature but also "accepts sacrifice and eats flesh." Carnivorism is first and foremost an expression of masculine authority and power.[103] In the imaginary of Western cultures, for instance, the head of state "must be an eater of flesh." Derrida credits vegetarianism along with environmentalism and animal welfare for compelling us to confront the subject as such, while also pointing to the potential shortcomings of the line of critique:

> I am not recalling this [philosophy's anthropocentric prejudice] in order to start a support group for vegetarianism, ecologism, or for the societies for the protection of animals—which is something I might also want to do, and something which would lead us to the center of the subject. I feel compelled to underscore the *sacrificial* structure of the discourses to which I am referring.[104]

A critical response to "carnivorous virility" must address the sacrificial structure that subtends our anthropocentric/anthropophagic culture, in which the human—the Western subject from Descartes to Levinas (the latter is also unwilling "to sacrifice the sacrifice"[105])—is constituted not only by "the implicit swallowing up of the animal," its ontological subjugation of the animal as some*thing* that can be killed but not murdered (there is no "Thou shall not put to death the living in general"[106] to protect animals), but also by its compulsion for symbolic sacrifice, which is "very difficult, truly impossible to delimit."[107] Vegetarianism is by no means excluded from the possibility of eating well—after all, it "lead[s] us to the center of the subject"; it helps to raise the subject as a problem. Moreover, he repeatedly stresses that eating meat is a choice, a "decision,"[108] de-naturalizing the consumption of meat as a biological necessity for human beings:

> Who can be made to believe that our cultures are carnivorous because animal proteins are irreplaceable?[109]

> The consumption of meat has never been a biological necessity. One eats meat not simply because one needs protein—and protein can be found elsewhere.[110]

He also rejects Élisabeth Roudinesco's attempt to justify or rationalize farm factories as an expression of France's gastronomic culture:

> There are other resources available for our gastronomic refinement. Industrial meat is not the last word in gastronomy. Besides, more and more—you're aware of this debate—certain people prefer beasts raised in certain conditions said to be more "natural," on certain types of fields, etc. Therefore, it will be necessary, in the name of the very gastronomy you're speaking of, to transform practices and "mentalities."[111]

Derrida himself is said to have claimed at a 1993 conference at Cerisy-la-Salle that he was "a vegetarian in [his] soul."[112] But a vegetarianism that comfortably coexists with our culture's sacrificial structure is not a solution that Derrida is willing to endorse. This option of ethical withdrawal—refusing to be the agent of humanist violence without fully questioning the metaphysics of that very humanism—obfuscates the ubiquity and workings of carno-phallogocentrism. Derrida insists that there is no avoiding assimilation, the eating of others. The desire for "absolute vegetarianism" or belief "in the existence of the non-carnivore in general" is misguided, and even potentially dangerous, since it downplays the extent to which the idea of symbolic sacrifice is "very difficult, truly impossible to delimit,"[113] or simply ignores the social reality of our cannibalistic culture—"vegetarians, too, partake of animals, even of men. They practice a different form of denegation"[114]—whence the emphasis must not be on *what* we eat but on *how* we eat.

Oliver pushes back a bit on Derrida's distinction between *what* and *how* to eat: "One decides how to treat other beings on the basis of presuppositions, beliefs, and conclusions about *what* they are: are they sentient, are they human, are they capable of suffering, etc. *How* one treats them—or eats them—is determined in large part by *what* they are."[115] This is a valid point. Žižek's logic of the fetishist disavowal, however, helps explain why the "what" question loses its critical edge: the "what" is often acknowledged—enlightened humanists, would-be posthumanists, are aware that *what* makes us different, what separates from animals, is fluid—but this "what" is quickly forgotten. Humanist ethics "draw[s] a line and ignore[s] some sort of suffering." Fetishist disavowal neutralizes the knowledge yielded by the "what" question, allowing, in turn, for the necessary suffering of some beings. The permanent suffering of animals is an accepted fact of our culture— "we cannot imagine that an animal doesn't suffer when it is subjected to laboratory experimentation"[116]—and still, in practice, we go about *as if* liberal democracy would never tolerate such suffering. We might read Derrida's focus on the "how" as an attempt to seek out an ethics of the other that does not succumb to fetishist disavowal but rather confronts "the traumatic Thing that our Judeo-Christian tradition calls the 'Neighbor.'" Eating well aligns with Žižek's psychoanalytic project. It is not in the service of empowering the subject, of making its life more happy, more at ease in the neoliberal world. Eating well is an (anti-)ethics of the neighbor or it is nothing at all.

Eating well is precisely at odds with a depoliticized ethics of the animal. From a Žižekian-Derridian vantage point, the routinized and ritualized call to check one's "anthropocentric privilege" (among other privileges: white, male, ableist, etc.) appears too convenient. It enables the posthumanist subject to diminish his or her guilt (*I'm* doing something personally about the commodification and suffering of animals) without taking on the sociopolitical framework of carno-phallogocentrism directly.[117] We are all implicated: "We are all mixed up in an eating of flesh—real or symbolic. . . . We are all—vegetarians as well—carnivores in the symbolic sense."[118] Eating well is not about securing the "good conscience"[119] of the posthumanist subject. It is a question of the *commons*. Building on the idea of the cyborg commons from Chapter 1, the commons here is no longer what we as human beings share, but what we as humans *and* animals share—what we esteem to be social goods unavailable for capitalist privatization and commodification. The animal neighbor's biogenic commons is at stake and it implicates us: "industrial, mechanical, chemical, hormonal, and genetic violence to which man has been submitting animal life for the past two centuries. Everybody knows what the production, breeding, transport, and slaughter of these animals has become."[120]

The task of eating well keeps me from becoming comfortably anchored in my world, making eating a private affair, a neoliberal culinary practice, if you will. It keeps me from phantasmatically closing off my world, immunizing the human—reinforcing and fortifying its boundaries, from nonhuman (animal, vegetable) contamination. *Learning* to eat well is indeed hardly an isolated, private, narcissistic practice; "one never eats entirely on one's own," says Derrida. It entails simultaneously questioning one's relation to the self and to the object, to the excluded other. Eating well also complicates the posthumanist desire to transcend the human, the subject of philosophy. Its hermeneutics has a penchant for doubt, questioning the heterological dream of mythically capturing and relating to the other as is, without mediation, without the defective tools of language.

Eating is both a biological necessity and a cultural injunction. So the question is *how* to do it, how to nourish oneself with a minimum of violence: interpreting/ingesting without the mistreatment of the other (be it human or animal, living or dead), without the reduction of others to "trophies"[121] (something gained exclusively through conquest and mastery); how to interpret while acknowledging that interpretation is incomplete, imperfect, non-all, or, conversely, how to see the non-all of interpretation not as a liability, a regrettable failure, but as the very condition for interpretation and responsibility. The *how* will always entail the risk of betrayal or failure, but this is what makes ethics more than a mechanical activity, the application of a rule, what makes ethics impossible.[122] Without such a risk there would be no ethics, nor respect for the other, no responsibility at all.

The injunction to eat well informs Derrida's use of *animot*, and we can retroactively see it at work in his relation to his cat. *Animot* describes his cat, thematizing this nonhuman animal (establishing a relation), but it also reflexively interrupts that designation, simultaneously registering the radical alterity of his cat (affirming a nonrelation), the unreadability of her gaze, her refusal "to be conceptualized," treating their encounter as nothing short of an event, provoking a linguistic, existential, and ethical crisis. In psychoanalytic terms, Derrida's cat is always more than her symbolic and imaginary rendering; she is also real (a neighbor, Žižek might add), irreducible either to his phantasmatic projections or to society's gentrification of the cat into a "pet." As Derrida discovers, his cat remains a "monster," capable of provoking shame over his nudity, creating a radical disruption in his hermeneutic comfort.

Erica Fudge puts the matter in slightly different terms:

The pet crosses over species boundaries. It is an animal—it cannot speak—but it is also an ideal human—it says what we want it to say. It is only when the pet displays its animal nature—when it pees on the carpet, brings in a half-dead sparrow, destroys the furniture—that we lose the tranquility of the relation. Then, and only then, do we really confront the existence of something beyond our control in our home.[123]

Cixous shares the ethical dilemmas involved in judging *machat* (mycat) after the latter kills a bird: "Between cat and bird I took a place, I judged, settled, deprived, decided, granted. I sided with the bird without name and without face against mycat my friend my hairy daughter my sister and my consolation. I forbade death and the life that passes through death. I behaved in everything like a human being with power."[124] Her ethical intervention, the assimilation of mycat's act to Cixous's ethical sensibilities, came with regret, a thought that maybe next time she would do otherwise, and show more respect for mycat's choices.

Derrida's cat—not unlike the aforementioned cats—is both a pet and a monster. Her alterity—the cat as real neighbor—is never fully contained within the symbolic order. She is capable of producing events, of reminding us that she can't quite be categorized or explained in human(ist) terms. But what happens after the event—after catching your cat looking at you while you are naked, as Derrida does; or after experiencing your cat as a killer, as Fudge and Cixous note; or after encountering yourself in the animal or seeing yourself as an animal from the perspective of the animal, as Žižek says—merits equal attention. What *habits* we nurture with our companion species, with our neighbors with four feet, is a question just as important (this is what I take to be Haraway's rejoinder). Sustaining the "relation without relation" with the *animots* necessitates a view of habits as perpetually subjected to critique and doubt. The feeling of "'ontological' necessity" and of an "'ethical' duty"[125] to change the relations between humans and animals is prompted and fueled by this skepticism—responding to the animal question, in turn, will call for a reevaluation of the very concepts of ontology and ethics. Maintaining such a relation also requires submitting to the laws of hospitality:

> To be hospitable is to let oneself be overtaken [*surprendre*], *to be ready to not be ready*, if such is possible, to let oneself be overtaken, to not even *let* oneself to be overtaken, to be surprised, in a fashion almost violent . . . precisely where one is not ready to receive—and not only *not yet ready* but *not ready, unprepared* in a mode that is not even that of the "not yet."[126]

The paradoxical injunction *to be ready to not be ready* is all about adopting a quasi-permanent state of out-of-jointness; only in such a state of "unpreparedness" does the subject have a chance to hear the call of the other, coming, as it does, from the most unexpected of places.

Human or Animal? Yes, Please![127]

In sum, as with Derrida's cat—who complicates any designation of her as pet or monster—we must reject the standard questions informing the dialogue between humanists and posthumanists over animality: Are we human or animal? And its corollaries: Should we remain human or embrace our posthumanity? Should we forego posthumanity and adopt a more radical postanimal perspective? To the question, "Human or animal?" we must answer "Yes, Please!"

We can detect the spirit of this answer in the original French title of Derrida's *L'animal donc que je suis*: which can be translated as both "the animal therefore that I am" and "the animal therefore that I follow." The ambiguity of the title complicates a straightforward choice between the two translations (Žižek's bold title of "The Animal That I Am" eliminates this significant ambiguity). The first can read autobiographically as an anti-Cartesian statement of Derrida's ontological animality, a radical updating and reworking of Descartes's *je pense, donc je suis* (I think, therefore I am). The second foregrounds a human—but not humanist—perspective, with the promise of a negative hermeneutics, a political mode of interpretation that, mindful of the *animot*, the neighbor, implicates his cat as much as himself—touching human and nonhuman animals alike. This hermeneutics does not give up on "*identifying* a 'proper of man,'" but it does so while remaining scrupulously vigilant about what "we humans call human," all too cognizant of that discourse's ideological track record, limitations, and deficiencies—"either because some animals also possess such traits, or because man does not possess it as surely as is claimed."[128]

In "the animal therefore that I am," we can see Derrida (read with Žižek) affirming the "inhuman core of the human," recognizing human animality, while also insisting on its difference from the animality of nonhuman animals. But this ontological distinction between the human and the animal is de-emphasized—but not obliterated—by the posthuman hermeneutics of the "animal that therefore I follow." Following the animal does not announce either a new enlightened humanism (with conditional hospitality/responsibility) or a self-congratulatory posthumanism that liquidates the human in the guise of celebrating the animal, now freed of subjectivism and anthropocentrism. To the questions that have haunted posthumanism from its inception—Are we human or cyborg? Are we human or animal?—we should answer, "Yes, Please!"

3

Object Fever

We've become so used to hearing "object" in relation to "subject"
that it takes some time to acclimatize to a view in which there are
only objects, one of which is ourselves.

TIMOTHY MORTON[1]

Objects should not touch because they are not alive. You use them,
put them back in place, you live among them: they are useful,
nothing more. But they touch me, it is unbearable. I am afraid of
being in contact with them as though they were living beasts.

JEAN-PAUL SARTRE[2]

The status of subjectivity in posthumanist ontologies is always
suspect. Indeed, its alignment with humanism is almost effortless. To
be against humanism—the philosophical face of anthropocentrism—
is to be against the subject. Eager to evacuate the subject from their
conceptual arsenal, posthumanists line up to sell it out. But the subject
persists, as does the human. So we might naively ask: What exactly
is meant by the subject? Does it always designate the sovereign and
substantial subject of humanism? And, perhaps most importantly,
for what reason or purpose must we overcome the subject? While
there are many contenders who want to sell out the subject, it is the
movement called OOO that has made the strongest push to eliminate

the subject from the humanities and the social sciences. Alenka Zupančič correctly highlights the movement's goals—which are also those of new materialism (NM)—of "getting out of the subject" and of "getting the subject out."[3] While OOO seeks to liberate thought from the cage of discursivity, from its constrictive idealism, and to reconfigure the horizon of thinking as a horizon dominated first and foremost by autonomous objects, NM moves to re-enchant the material world after its disenchantment at the hands of humanists and anti-humanists alike, correcting their interpretive and epistemic overreach—from fantasies of mastery to excesses of suspicion and paranoia.

OOO is itself an offshoot of speculative realism, whose claim to fame is to have contributed to dethroning the linguistic turn—putting "language last"[4] and replacing it with a reorientation toward the external world and inaugurating, as it were, the ontological turn. Speculative realism accuses theory or continental philosophy (under the sway of Derridean deconstruction) of being stuck in its epistemological impasses. On this account, Derrida is the last inheritor of Kantian aporia; Derrida's "there is nothing outside the text [*il n'y a pas de hors-texte*]"[5] confirms the inaccessibility of the noumena, of things-in-themselves. Bypassing theory's cognitive paralysis, speculative realism returns to ontological questions, setting its sights, once again, on "the great outdoors." Along the way, the subject gets a demotion. The demotion is arguably moderate with speculative realism since the movement is still invested in knowledge of the world, in "progressively mastering the objective world through mathematical codification."[6] It is simply no longer obsessing about the linguistic or cultural conditions for knowledge, and epistemological skepticism has given way to a taste for the ontological absolute. With OOO the subject's demotion is more severe and more pronounced. Graham Harman, one of the movement's founders, insists on Kantian finitude while giving it a radical twist, "broadening this finitude beyond the human realm to include all relations in the cosmos—including inanimate ones."[7] In other words, Harman sustains the noumena-phenomena distinction, without however limiting it to humans. The inaccessibility of objects is experienced by objects as well.

Advocates of OOO and NM find their intellectual inspiration in the works of anthropologist Bruno Latour. As an alternative approach to social theory, to human-centered frameworks (from humanism to poststructuralism), Latour champions actor-network theory (ANT), which underscores the posthumanist insight that "*any thing* that does modify a state of affairs by making a difference is an actor—or, if it has no figuration yet, an actant. Thus, the questions to ask about any agent are simply the following: Does it make a difference in the course of some other agent's action or not?"[8] What an increasing number of social and literary critics appreciate about Latour's ANT is its democratization of reading, its inclusion of "*the voices of nonhumans*,"[9] its rejection of human exceptionalism, and its bold call for a "parliament of things."[10] What would the world look like if we gave up "*defending the rights of the human subject to speak and to be the sole speaker*"[11]?

In Latour's flat ontology, human intersubjectivity, or being-with (human) others, undergoes something of a downgrade; its importance is now severely qualified. If the idea of animal intersubjectivity—of animals *responding* and not merely mechanically reacting—casts doubt on human singularity, the turn to objects exerts further pressure on the uniqueness of the *anthropos*. Latour adds, "hermeneutics is not a privilege of humans but, so to speak, a property of the world itself."[12] Objects or actants are on equal footing; all there is are objects interacting with other objects. Humans do not hold any special status when it comes to agency or hermeneutics; they delude themselves in elevating themselves to the exceptional and exclusive status of *subjects.*

Theorists are the most to blame. They dominate as gods their *object* of study—but this object (the world of objects) is left bloodless and cold, devoid of any vitality. "The Zeus of Critique rules absolutely, to be sure, but over a desert," writes Latour.[13] The imperatives to disenchant, to denaturalize, to defetishize: all have led to a weakening of the humanities. Latour pleads for an alternative model, urging critics to move away from their debunking ethos—theory's "*critical barbarity*,"[14] as he calls it—to one of caring and protection, from a feeling of superiority to one of collaboration and generosity. In short, Latour's new posthumanist critic needs to "add" to reality rather than "subtract" from it, generate more ideas rather than destroy existing ones.[15]

According to New Materialist Jane Bennett, ANT helps to enact a paradigmatic shift from "the language of epistemology to that of ontology."[16] To be for objects is to be against "thing[s] [as] always already humanized."[17] To be for objects it is to acknowledge "the inadequacy of representation," "to bracket the question of the human"[18] (what can *I* know?) so that things in the world can appear, have a chance to appear, in all their strangeness and complexity (*what* can I see?). Finally, to be for objects is to cultivate a childlike vision of the matter around us, appreciating its "thing-power,"[19] its vibrancy and agency.[20] Only such attentiveness to objects, to matter's immanent vitality, can counterbalance our anthropocentric and narcissistic biases, assimilative logic, and insatiable will to dominate—"human hubris and our earth-destroying fantasies of conquest and consumption"[21]—and demystify them:

> For *this* task, demystification, that most popular of practices in
> critical theory, should be used with caution and sparingly, because

demystification presumes that at the heart of any event or process lies a *human* agency that has illicitly been projected into things.[22]

Indeed, to be for objects is to renounce and denounce "the long dictatorship of human beings in philosophy," writes Harman.[23] Simply stated, OOO is the antithesis of a "philosophy of human *access* to the world."[24]

Harman, however, distances himself from Latour's process-oriented framework (though he describes ANT as "the most important philosophical method to emerge since phenomenology"[25]) and NM, rejecting "relationalist ontologies of every sort,"[26] and favoring instead the *essence* of objects themselves, their irreducibility and withdrawnness: "the being of any object is always deeper than how that object appears to us."[27] The risk of overemphasizing relationality (the doxa of relationism) is significant since "ANT loses objects completely, by abolishing any hidden depth in things while reducing them to their actions."[28] Accordingly, a flat ontology cannot obliterate all differences among objects, giving up on the philosophical task of "drawing rigid taxonomical distinctions between [things]."[29] Similarly Ian Bogost objects to ANT's excessive investment in relationality, coming at the expense of the things-in-themselves: "entities are de-emphasized in favor of their couplings and decouplings. Alliances take center stage, and things move to the wings."[30] In other words, ANT and NM offer too much becoming (what objects *can do*) and not enough being (what objects *are*).

Harman turns to Martin Heidegger's famous example of the broken hammer to make his point. Heidegger describes what happens when a piece of equipment such as a hammer stops functioning as expected, when it breaks. The object shifts from being "ready-to-hand" (*Zuhandenheit*) to "present-at-hand" (*Vorhandenheit*). In the former case, the subject, *Dasein*, picks up the handy hammer and uses it; it is available "equipment" (*Zeug*).[31] In the latter, the tool malfunctions, the broken hammer is thematized, serving as an object of philosophical contemplation or scientific theorization. Harman invites his readers to reinterpret the significance of Heidegger's example. The lesson to draw is not that "praxis is richer than theory,"[32] as if, in the mode of "ready-to-hand," the hammer and the subject were one, united. Heidegger's insight, even if Heidegger himself didn't fully appreciate its significance, is that the hammer is reduced to a caricature in both modalities: when we treat it as a broken object, possessing certain properties, *and* when we merely use it to accomplish a task, when we claim to exhaust its being through the act of hammering. In both instances, we are "reducing things to presence-at-hand,"[33] to human purposes. We fail to capture the real hammer—its "genuine being"[34]— nor do we appreciate the hammer's "untamed, subterranean reality,"[35] its "volcanic core."[36]

The hammer, like all other objects, is intrinsically obscure, ontologically withdrawn (from both humans and other objects), possessing a reality of its own, irreducible to its sensual being.[37] The object in-itself is the real object. Against the tyranny of human intersubjectivity, Harman's approach espouses ontological humility and love for objects;[38] it only seeks to restore the dignity and grandeur of real objects, emancipating them from the persistent humanist subject/object prism. OOO's love of objects enacts and illustrates philosophy's promise: the love of wisdom, not its possession. Doing justice to the love of wisdom requires refraining from making any "claim to be an actual wisdom."[39] We must "dehumanize[e] Heidegger's tool-analysis,"[40] that is, unlearn our dispositions toward objects and relearn to see them as "entities . . . quite apart from any relations with or effects upon other entities in the world."[41] Fellow object-oriented ontologist Timothy Morton argues for the structural repositioning of the subject as object: "we've become so used to hearing 'object' in relation to 'subject' that it takes some time to acclimatize to a view in which there are only objects, one of which is ourselves."[42]

Conversely, Bennett objects to OOO's reduction of matter to "a flat, fixed, or law-like substance."[43] She prefers assemblages, which, following Deleuze and Guattari, she defines as "ad hoc groupings of diverse elements, of vibrant materials of all sorts. Assemblages are living, throbbing confederations that are able to function despite the persistence of energies that confound them from within."[44] Any given assemblage foregrounds complexity and process, drawing its "agentic capacity" from "the vitality of the materialities that constitute it."[45] Assemblages are contingent associations of human and nonhuman entities. Assemblages do not subscribe to an identitarian logic; indeed, in contradistinction to OOO's position, the essentialization of the object/thing/body is anathema to the operation of an assemblage. As Jasbir Puar observes, assemblages "de-privilege the human body as a discrete organic thing";[46] what matters is not what they *are* but what they *do*. Moreover, assemblages produce objects that are unfinished and unstable, always ontologically open to transformation and reconfiguration.

I argue OOO, ANT, and NM all display *object fever*. I take my inspiration here from Derrida's earlier formulation, "archive fever." To have such a fever is "to burn with a passion . . . It is to have a compulsive, repetitive, and nostalgic desire for the archive, an irrepressible desire to return to the origin, a homesickness, a nostalgia for the return to the most archaic place of absolute commencement."[47] For Carolyn Steedman, the archive produces its own kind of object fever. As she notes, "The object (the event, the happening, the story from the past) has been altered by the very search for it, by its time and duration: what has actually been lost can never be found. This is not to say that *nothing* is found, but that thing is always something else, a creation of the search itself."[48] The object under consideration is not "nothing," but its materiality, its thingness, is not free of the messiness of invention (creation, fantasy).

Object fever is the passion for the outside, for exteriority, the maddening compulsion to attend to all that is nonsubject, to all that is before and beyond the subject. Not unlike the archive, the object in *object fever* is imbued with fantasy. Object fever is a fetish for the singular, an infectious drive for the nonhuman; it registers "an affective excess,"[49] a fascination for and obsession with objects, a responsibility to document and preserve their mysterious lives, reflecting an urgent need to imagine a future of objects beyond the violent anthropocentric lens of the human subject. As with the archive, the assessment of the object is "never closed,"[50] the meaning of the object, what constitutes an object (its selection and classification), is never fully exhausted or contained in the place where one expects it.

To explore this passion and probe the approaches to objects outlined earlier, this chapter turns to two case studies: Ari Folman's 2008 *Waltz with Bashir*, an Israeli animated docu-film that deals with the trauma of the 1982 Sabra and Shatila massacre, and Jean-Paul Sartre's 1938 *Nausea*, a novel dramatizing its anti-hero protagonist's disturbing encounter with indocile objects. *Waltz with Bashir*, with its rich and complex treatment of trauma, invites a Latourian approach, democratizing, as it were, the devasting effects of the war (Folman characterized his picture as an anti-war film). From a New Materialist standpoint, the film reads Sabra and Shatila as an assemblage, expressing the intricacies of the massacre by bringing to light its effects and affects, its human and nonhuman actants. But here *Waltz with Bashir's* progressive posthumanist, nonanthropocentric message is not untainted by an ideological framework: what happens with the putative subjects of the massacre—the Palestinian refugees of the camps—when their political injustice takes a back seat to a more expansive, abstract, and "ethical" outlook on the violence of war? In the second case, what is at stake in pairing OOO with *Nausea* is the status of the "Real." It is no accident that Žižek dubs *Nausea* "one of the paradigmatic literary approaches to the Real."[51] For this reason, Sartre's novel allows for an apt testing of both OOO's attempt to dispense with the subject (in the name of real objects) and psychoanalysis's commitment to the subject (in the name of the Real). Together, these case studies illuminate the uses and limitations of OOO's, ANT's, and NM's conceptualizations of posthuman subjectivity, language, violence, and the Real.

Beyond Suspicion, or the Ideology of Posthumanist Generosity

The descriptive turn reflects Latour's undeniable mark on literary studies. It is to Latour that Rita Felksi, for example, repeatedly turns in *The Limits of Critique* (2015). Latour offers Felski and others a way out of critique's anthropocentric orbit of suspicion, pointing to alternative ways to imagine literary studies.[52] Latour's often-quoted 2004 article, "Why Has Critique Run Out of Steam?" could have been titled, "Why Has (Anti-Humanist) Theory Run Out of Steam?" In his polemical article, Latour makes a series of accusations about theory's overreach, unproductive habits, and waning relevance. I stress that these are accusations, displaying a dearth of cited evidence, and thus lacking a serious engagement with any theorists. Latour decries the arrogance of theorists, and critique's excessive paranoia. For Latour, the path of critical theory—the path taken by the Frankfurt School, psychoanalysis, and deconstruction, among others—is dangerous and unsustainable, doing more harm than good. Latour himself assumes partial responsibility, making a *mea culpa* for the current state of affairs: "The mistake we made, the mistake I made, was to believe that there was no efficient way to criticize matters of fact except by moving away from them and directing one's attention toward the conditions that made them possible."[53]

Latour calls for a return to the "world": "Down with Kant! Down with the Critique! Let us go back to the world still unknown and despised."[54] While theory is "on the side of knowing" (focused, that is, on the subject of knowledge—at the cost of neglecting the world and its nonhuman objects), Latour's brand of antitheory is "on the side of the known," the objects of knowledge, the world, the given, the readily accessible.[55] Latour has little patience with the plight of theorists and their critical or deconstructive hermeneutics. He wants to leave behind the revolutionary energy of May 1968 that produced a whole generation of French anti-humanists. As Latour puts it, "we don't wish to have too much to do with the twentieth century."[56] While theorists typically foreground reflexivity and the opacity of signifiers, Latour wants to talk about things in the world, freed, as it were, from the self-defeating preoccupations of theory.

Like Latour, Eve Sedgwick presents herself as a reformed theorist in her memorable 1997 essay, "Paranoid Reading and Reparative Reading, Or, You're So Paranoid, You Probably Think This Essay Is about You." Latour and Sedgwick attribute theory's flaws to a fear of being duped or becoming compromised by the unexpected. Simply stated, theorists—proponents of critique—are by training traumatophobic. Theorists are paranoid; they want to minimize interpretive vulnerability; they are allergic to anything laden with surprise:

The first imperative of paranoia is *"There must be no bad surprises,"* and indeed, the aversion to surprise seems to be what cements the intimacy between paranoia and knowledge per se . . . because there must be no bad surprises, and because to learn the possibility of a bad surprise would itself constitute a bad surprise, paranoia requires that bad news be already known.[57]

On Sedgwick's reading, theory compels you to turn your gaze forward and backward; "at once anticipatory and retroactive,"[58] paranoid thinking works to master the past (what has happened, what lessons can we draw from this or that example) and foreclose any deviation from a projected future. A rhetoric of exemplarity soothes, as much as possible, a paranoid mind. It gives the paranoid hermeneut tools to tame temporality's alterity, to convert the "new" into something always already known.

For Latour and Sedgwick, critique's will to mastery is at the root of its demise, or at least of its diminishing value. If theory were to undergo a conversion, it would have to shed its hermeneutics of suspicion, its investment in subjectivity and ideology critique. Literary studies after the subject, under the "democratic" regime of antitheory, would be decisively more descriptive, less judgmental, and, most importantly, less anthropocentric and more inclusive in what it cares about. In treating trauma with posthuman generosity, *Waltz with Bashir* provides an excellent opportunity to test a Latourian approach. I will first sketch out such a reading, highlighting elements of the film most receptive to a Latourian ANT, contrasting it with a critique-oriented reading, and then return to the stubborn questions of ideology and suspicion, a mode of reading that, I ultimately argue, we should replace with a more salutary form of skepticism.

Waltz with Bashir opens with a pack of rabid dogs racing at night through the streets of Tel Aviv and finally gathering beneath a man's apartment window. We then quickly discover that this intensely affective scene is actually a dream that Boaz Rein, the man in the window, is recounting to his friend Ari Folman. He explains to Folman that he has been having this recurring nightmare, whose origins, he speculates, lie in his involvement in the 1982 Lebanese invasion twenty years before, where, as a less-than-willing invading soldier, he was ordered to kill dogs so as to prevent them from barking at troops entering Lebanese villages. He confesses to Folman: "They knew I couldn't shoot a person. They told me: 'Go ahead and shoot the dogs!'" Distraught by his dreams, haunted by his victims ("every face, every wound. The look in their eyes. Twenty-six dogs"), he asks Folman if he is experiencing any lingering traces of the war. Folman claims to have no memories of his military service in Lebanon. This absence of memory comes to puzzle Folman, triggering his meditation on his involvement in Lebanon, which circles back to the Sabra and Shatila massacre. Folman eventually arrives at the realization that he was a witness to the tragic event, and, moreover, that he, alongside other Israeli forces, assisted the Lebanese Christian Phalangist militia, either by launching flares or by helping to contain the Palestinian refugees while the Phalangists ran their operation. The film ends with an abrupt interruption of the animation, which is replaced with actual video footage of the aftermath of the massacre showing dead bodies and the lamentations of a Palestinian mother.

While *Waltz with Bashir* has been highly acclaimed, it has received a critical reception among literary scholars, at least from those still invested in critique and anti-racism. For example, Raz Yosef is rightfully suspicious of the turn to the video footage, claiming that it does nothing to counteract the film's depoliticized and depoliticizing narcissistic bent:

The horrifying archival images of slaughtered Palestinian men, women and children at the end of the film are . . . detached from their historical and political context and provide a kind of catharsis for the protagonist: now he remembers and is released from the trauma that had been haunting him; now he is cured and redeemed from the wounds of the past and can apparently carry on with his life.[59]

Contributing further to this detachment is the evocation of the paradigm of trauma: Auschwitz. In an exchange between Folman and his psychologist friend, Uri Sivan, the latter interprets the former's trauma in relation to his parents' traumatic experience of Auschwitz, perversely suggesting that the trauma of Sabra and Shatila is not really about the Palestinians themselves, that the "true" causes of his disturbance lie spatially and temporally elsewhere. On Sivan's reading, Folman's split identifications with both victims (the Jews of Auschwitz) and victimizers (Sivan describes Folman's behavior at the Sabra and Shatila camps as Nazi-like) displaces the putative victims of the Sabra and Shatila massacre: the Palestinians.

But for Latour and the postcritical posthumanist faction, such a reading is in the business of negating and demystifying. It tells its readers: don't be fooled by the film's ideology, its veneer of complexity. A Latourian response would claim that Yosef's reading reflects a transcendent perspective on the world, one that is premade, ready to be applied "critically" to any cultural product that does not tell the story of the Palestinians. A Latourian reading would set itself apart from Yosef and other demystifiers of the film. It would acknowledge the attachment that a spectator may have for the cultural artifact and ask a more reparative question: How does the film *add* to our understanding of trauma, guilt, and the horrors of war? It would reorient the spectator toward the film's admirable posthumanist distribution of trauma, its accommodation of nonhuman voices (enabling us to see "the killing of dogs as itself a real crime"[60]), to the ways it multiplies connections to trauma. It might stress that this is not the exclusive story of Ari Folman, a journey into his phantasmatic and solipsistic process of working through his pain. By opening with the dog scene, *Waltz with Bashir* signals that the film will take a more expansive view of trauma. Roughly midway through the film, during a session between Folman and Professor Zahara Solomon, a PTSD scholar, Solomon recounts the story of a photographer covering the Lebanese war. In the beginning, the photographer maintained an aesthetic distance between himself and his journalistic object: "he looked at everything as if through an imaginary camera." The camera gentrified the horrors of war, mediating his exposure to the Real of the war. In other words, the war on Palestinians was simply a film. But his camera faltered; it could no longer shield his psyche. Things changed after his exposure to the death and suffering of horses at the Beirut hippodrome. He tells Solomon that "his camera broke and he freaked out." The war suddenly "turned traumatic for him": "It broke [his] heart. What had those horses done to deserve such suffering?" The raw horror of animal victimization was too much to process; the affective distance between subject and objects was lost.

We can imagine a Latourian reading carefully describing the ways dogs, horses, Israeli soldiers, Phalangists, Palestinians refugees, and even the materiality of the film (its animation and documentary footage), all emerge as actors or forces in the film, some as strong actors (the Phalangists and Israeli soldiers) and some as weak actors (the dogs, the horses, and the Palestinians). Grievances are multiplied; justice for all (humans and nonhumans) is implicitly demanded. The film, with its mixture of human and nonhuman actors, performs a flat ontology. A critic's task is straightforward: they need to translate, trace out, and pay attention to the patterns of relation, the ways actors in the film do not exist in themselves, in isolation, but in their relationality and arrangement, that is, in their networks of association.

Yes, but lingering questions of ideology persist. The distinction between victim/victimizer is not the same type of division as subject/ object. While the latter is precisely what an ANT wants to overcome, it is important to stress that not all binaries are equally problematic. Folman's trauma—rooted in his realization that he could become that type of Nazi-like person—is not a sufficient condition for victimhood. Aggressors are not immune to trauma but this fact alone does not make them victims on equal ethical and political footing with the victimized. The film appears to be guilty of this dubious conflation; a flat ontology-inspired interpretation risks compounding that problem.[61]

If *Waltz with Bashir* humanizes dogs and horses, it also seems to animalize Palestinians. As with "pinkwashing"—where the celebration of Israel's gay rights simultaneously obfuscates the mistreatment of Palestinians—we might have here a case of "vegan-washing":[62] another distraction from Israel's cruel occupation that is achieved by drawing attention to Israelis' self-critical mind and their attentiveness to the suffering of animals. The film's posthumanist cues trivialize Palestinian suffering. They work ideologically by depoliticizing objections to domination: speciesism and racism are kept separate. The former is acknowledged (Folman's soldier friend is haunted by their killing, another Israeli is overwhelmed by the effects of war on horses), while the latter is attributed to others (the Phalangists are the true agents of the massacres).

But what about Latour's objection that critique has become too mechanical? As he puts it, "Are we not like those mechanical toys that endlessly make the same gesture when everything else has changed around them?"[63] In the context of the Israeli-Palestinian conflict, we may ask: What exactly has changed? From the Sabra and Shatila massacre in 1982 to the last devastating Gaza War in 2014, there is a strong continuity in the Israeli disregard for Palestinian lives. Perhaps the change lies in the attitude of *some* Israelis. This is after all a film made by an Israeli in Israel protesting against Israel's hawkish ways. We might point to Folman's interview statement that he made an anti-war film, a film obliquely critical of Ariel Sharon's leadership during the Lebanese invasion. Here Latour might caution leftist critics not to let their paranoia cloud the "positive" posthumanist message of the film. Antitheory would urge a reparative perspective, evaluating the film for what it does (its impact on other actors) rather than what it is (ideologically tainted from the start), for what it opens up rather than what it excludes. Simply stated, the slogan of Latourian antitheory is, *Opt for hermeneutic generosity rather than critical hermeneutics.*

The persuasiveness of Latour's argument relies on the validity of that choice: Hermeneutic generosity or critical hermeneutics? But again, this is a false choice. Generosity and critique are not intrinsically at odds with one another.[64] Moreover, critical hermeneutics takes more than one form. While Paul Ricoeur's distinction between a hermeneutics of faith and a hermeneutics of suspicion is well known, it is also important to remember that Ricoeur evokes two additional types of hermeneutics. There is an aborted hermeneutics—a hermeneutics of skepticism (nihilistic in its orientation)—and a projected hermeneutics, a hermeneutics of postcritical faith.

Whereas Ricoeur insisted on the difference between skepticism and suspicion, hoping for a dialectics of faith that transverses suspicion, resulting in a hermeneutics of postcritical faith, the posthumanism of ANT has tended to efface the distinction between suspicion and skepticism. A deconstructive-psychoanalytic posthumanism might be well served to return to Ricoeur's aborted hermeneutics. And I would further add that it is not paranoia but hysteria, a mode of incessant questioning, that fuels such a hermeneutics of skepticism. The theorist as hysteric is never satisfied with the master's answers, constantly contesting his or her interpellation as a would-be knower and desiring subject: What do I know? What do I want? What the critic-hysteric says about objects is always tentative, and open to expansion and revision.

But is the hysteric too enthralled by his or her own negativity, too captivated by his or her nonidentity and undecidability? Not necessarily. Skepticism does not care only about throwing humanism's cherished concepts into crisis; it can be reparative as well. Its negativity is also what incites its practitioner to want more, to know more, and to do more. A deconstructive skepticism is not any less faithful to its object than Latour's ANT. To make this point, I want to return to the final scene of the film in a way that is "reparatively critical." I read the scene, at least in part, as a rebuff of Sivan's allegorical interpretation of Folman's trauma. We must not forget that the psychologist is only a character in the film and does not necessarily represent the film as a whole. We shouldn't just assume that he is the mouthpiece of the director, as some critics have done. In any case, the saying of the Palestinian woman—which, in the Levinasian sense, designates the expression of a desire to communicate, the phatic function of language—reminds the audience that the scene of violence is (and should be) about the Palestinians. Her saying jolts spectators out of their comfortable consumption of a Lebanese war aestheticized through the subjective gaze of its protagonist. It throws the viewer back into the morally bewildering place of Sabra and Shatila.

But is this return to the reality of the massacre too late and thus incomplete? The spectator is confronted with the saying of the woman, but her saying is left without a response. Folman declines to engage with her story, her collective story. He does not directly express any sense of personal responsibility for Palestinian suffering nor collective responsibility for the Lebanese invasion, not to mention the Nakba, which brought the refugee camps into existence in the first place. As these difficult questions go unexplored, Folman leaves his spectators with a generalized sense of responsibility, but this universalization of responsibility risks reifying the Palestinians' saying by presenting it as undigested (it is left untranslated for Folman's Israeli and Western audiences), and by depoliticizing Israel's involvement: *if everyone is responsible, no particular one is responsible.* To be sure, telling the other's story, speaking for them, is a thorny interpretive adventure. Folman chooses to engage with what he knows—which is first and foremost his own experiences as an Israeli soldier. In an interview, Folman describes entertaining the possibility of "making a *Rashomon* of 1982, showing the conflict from the differing viewpoints of all those involved. But it was not for him. 'Who am I to tell their stories?' he says of the Palestinians. 'They have to tell their own stories.'"[65] But one wonders if this expression of humility serves a self-protective function instead, foreclosing contact with the other rather than making room for their voice. It is after all never a simple choice between speaking *for* others or only speaking for oneself/one's people. In any case, when it came to the Palestinians, Folman refused to engage their trauma, opting for hermeneutic fasting or withdrawal, perhaps out of a desire to respect the opacity of the other, but at the expense of prolonging a dialogue with the survivors and the memory of the victims.

If one posthumanist approach to the film reads Sabra and Shatila as an assemblage, as an anti-war object, should we understand the return to/of the Palestinians as a deviation from its posthumanist foray? Defending the film against its critical reception, Rupert Read points out that the accusations of Folman's displacement of the Palestinians are at best premature and at worst a complete distortion of the film's message. The animals in *Waltz with Bashir* serve a humanist and humanizing function. They spark Folman's reflections[66] and prepare the reader for his or her unsettling encounter with the Palestinians of the documentary footage: "The film precisely, deliberately obscures the humanity of the Palestinians and the Lebanese—the Arabs—from us, until the veil is ripped away, at the end."[67] The film instrumentalizes animal suffering (though they are not only metaphors for Palestinians) for its critical pedagogical potential, strategically soliciting from its viewer the desire to empathize with its dogs and horses only to turn this self-congratulatory experience critically back on itself: How can you feel empathy with dogs while ignoring the treatment of Palestinians as dogs? How can you lament the innocent suffering and death of horses while disregarding those of Palestinian women and children?

But must a sympathetic reading of the Palestinians necessarily be humanist in its orientation? And conversely, is a posthumanist reading of *Waltz with Bashir a priori* anti-Palestinian? Not necessarily. As we saw in Chapter 2, Žižek's notion of the neighbor holds a potential for reconfiguring, if not exploding, the humanist and posthumanist opposition. In the defaced figure of the Palestinian woman "we encounter the Other's call at its purest and most radical," and "one's responsibility toward the Other at its most traumatic."[68] The Palestinian in the humanist reading is rescued from oblivion, but it is a figure frozen in her pathos, reduced to mere victimhood. But as Žižek is fond of remarking: What happens next? Yes, the film succeeded in transforming the Palestinian woman into a proto-human, a being worthy of grievability, ending with an appeal for her recognition as a subject. But what kind of subject is she really? She is a subject only in abstraction; in practice, she remains (for the liberal Zionist/Western viewer) an *object* of would-be humanist sympathy, locked in her vulnerability. To see her as a neighbor, however, means something wholly different. It acknowledges from the start the inhuman dimension of the Palestinian other. This is why "Love thy neighbor" functions as the ultimate commandment for a posthumanist politics.

What happens after I see the Palestinian as a neighbor characterizes the situation of Israel's *refuseniks*: Israeli soldiers who refuse to complete their compulsory military service in the occupied territories. The *refuseniks* decline to serve as instruments of Israel's

brutal necropower. They seriously take up, if not fulfill, the injunction to "Love thy neighbor":

> What the *refuseniks* have achieved is the passage from *Homo sacer* to "neighbour": they treat Palestinians not as "equal full citizens," but as *neighbours* in the strict Judeo-Christian sense. And, in fact, that is the difficult ethical test for Israelis today: "Love thy neighbour!" means "Love the Palestinian!" (who is their neighbour *par excellence*), or it means nothing at all.[69]

Does *Waltz with Bashir* generate anything close to this injunction? It is unclear. In any case, a humanist reading of the film tends to foreclose this possibility since it purports to treat Palestinians on equal footing. In doing so, it adheres to the faux universality of an "equal full citizen" model, one that makes the Palestinian other grievable (no longer designated as a *homo sacer*, not-quite-human or nonhuman) on the basis of an implicit identification with the formerly excluded, now brought fully into the polity and the "privileges" of humanity, into the realm of intersubjectivity and sameness, controlled and contained under the umbrella of an inclusive humanism (i.e., a false universalism).

"The Otherness" of the Palestinian "reduced to inhumanity"[70]—the Palestinian in her "abyssal dimension"[71]—is what a humanist disavows (not only in the other but also in the subject) and what a Latourian reading neglects in favor of a decaffeinated posthumanism, a postpolitical posthumanism that dispenses with all forms of ideology critique. It is here that a reading of Sabra and Shatila as an assemblage can gain additional critical traction. By stressing the inhuman in the Palestinian, the other nonhuman actants are not deprived of their significance; quite the contrary, this posthumanist framing opens up the possibility for "interspecies connectedness"[72] between dogs, horses, and Palestinians—these inhuman objects that constitute the assemblage that is Sabra and Shatila. Unlike the assemblage generated by a Latourian reading, being posthuman here foregrounds the subject (the subject as an uncanny stranger, as a neighbor[73]) rather than doing away with it.

The posthuman subject is clearly not the subject of old. Its ontology—its being—does not follow the path of substance ontology so dear to humanists. Rather, its ontology is divided, non-all, shot through with negativity. Being posthuman and affirming a nonsubstantial subjectivity go hand in hand. Being posthuman avows the monstrous *within*—the inhuman, unruly, or untamable dimension at the core of subjectivity. At odds with the subject-producing ways of humanism, being posthuman discloses and affirms a subject in a state of out-of-jointness. Being posthuman, however, is not simply another name for humanism's foe—the anti-humanist. Objects are not denigrated or deemed of secondary importance in the struggle against the metaphysics of humanism. Being posthuman acknowledges that the subject is an object, even making the question of objects constitutive of its being. And yet it is not "an object among other objects," as OOO would have it. Turning now to Sartre's *Nausea* will help us to see how a posthuman vantage point can allow us both to scrutinize the subject's powers and historically ascribed privilege and to retain the category, reimagining it as ontologically incomplete, fraught, and grounded in negativity.

When Objects Rebel

Troubled by an undetermined cause, Roquentin decides to keep a diary in the hope that it will help him to "see clearly" and improve his unsettled condition. He adopts a now-familiar phenomenological stance. Bracketing all presuppositions about the nature of the external

world, Roquentin proceeds to observe and represent objects *as* he
perceives them, *as* they are revealed to his consciousness in their "pure"
immediacy, uncolored by any subjective investments or preferences:
"Let none of the nuances or small happenings escape even though they
might seem to mean nothing. And above all, classify them. I must tell
how I see this table, the street, the people, my packet of tobacco. . . . I
must not put in strangeness where there is none" (1, emphasis added).
An OOO reading would certainly welcome Roquentin's interest
in objects all around him, but it would also quickly point out the
limitations of his inquiry into the life of objects. Roquentin is only
assessing the objects for their epistemological worth. The emphasis on
how objects appear *to him* reflects a correlationist bias. Correlationism
maintains that "we only ever have access to the correlation between
thinking and being, and never to either term considered apart from
the other."[74] The human monopolizes too much of the relation between
itself and the external world: "The human remains 50 per cent of every
philosophical situation, receiving a full half of reality, while all of the
many atoms, frogs, schools, puppies, comets, supernovae, tectonic
plates and black holes in the universe are packed like sardines into the
other half."[75] Compare Roquentin's list of objects, "table, street, people,
packet of tobacco," with Harman's "atoms, frogs, schools, puppies,
comets, supernovae, tectonic plates and black holes."[76] The former
posits a subject, a consciousness that brings the objects into disclosure
and relevance; the latter eclipses the subject by asking us to consider
what constitutes an object as such.

The novel might nevertheless be said to be doing the work of
OOO. Roquentin may have started out as a correlationalist, a
phenomenological idealist, but as the novel progresses we discover
a Roquentin submerged in ontology, immersed in the in-itself of
objects. His exceptionalism is evaporating; his reality deteriorating.
Roquentin feels shame at the excess, *de trop*, of his body.[77] He cannot

find any justification for his existence, which leads him to align himself with objects:

> I hadn't the right to exist. I had appeared by chance, I existed like a stone, a plant or a microbe.

> It seems as though I belong to another species. (84, 158)

His investment in epistemic lucidity begins to falter as objects gain independence and are no longer constituted by their relation to Roquentin the masterful knower. If there is an emergent "parliament of things," Roquentin effectively experiences it as a coup d'état.

If Roquentin is "enchanted" by the world of inanimate objects, by their newfound vibrancy and agency, if he is indeed "struck and shaken by the extraordinary that lives amid the familiar and the everyday,"[78] he nevertheless does not associate his enchantment with the feeling of childlike wonder. Rather, his enchantment produces a series of negative affects: fear, terror, and disgust, among others. Roquentin discovers the liveliness of nonhuman matter and comes to realize—to his dismay—that inanimate objects are not "worldless" (*weltos*), as Heidegger had so authoritatively proclaimed.

Objects have started to question, or better yet threaten the authority of Roquentin's sovereignty, affirming their right to touch and be seen as occupying the same ontological plane. Roquentin questions the reasons behind his uneasiness and vulnerability in the presence of innocuous objects, like the pebble he picks up at the beach causing his first attack of nausea. As he notes with consternation, the texture of being has changed:

> Objects should not *touch* because they are not alive. You use them, put them back in place, you live among them: they are useful, nothing more. But they touch me, it is unbearable. I am afraid of being in contact with them as though they were living beasts. (10)

Perhaps the most famous example of an *objet revolté* is the root of
the chestnut tree that Roquentin encounters in the public park.[79]
This episode is typically read as the site of Roquentin's philosophic
epiphany. Roquentin himself writes down in his diary: "And suddenly,
suddenly, the veil is torn away, I have understood, I have *seen*" (126).
Roquentin announces that his illuminating experience was preverbal:

> The word absurdity is coming to life under my pen; a little while
> ago, in the garden, I couldn't find it, but neither was I looking for it,
> I did not need it: I thought without words, *on* things, *with* things.
> (129)

After this remark, the reader expects that Roquentin has succeeded
in securing knowledge of things-in-themselves, and that he will
share, clearly and distinctly, as would an epistemological realist,
his unmediated apprehension of reality, stripped of all subjective
distortions or biases. At the precise moment when Roquentin is
about to provide his reader with a lucid account of naked existence,
with direct access to the "real" chestnut root, he frustrates these
expectations by indulging instead in the production of uncanny
metaphors:

> Absurdity was not an idea in my head, or the sound of a voice, only
> this long serpent dead at my feet, this wooden serpent. Serpent or
> claw or root or vulture's talon, what difference does it make. (129)

While constantly invoking unconventional metaphors, Roquentin
appears to distance himself from his initial philosophical project
of purifying his language of all semantic opacity. The episode both
accommodates and exceeds a Sartrean interpretation. Roquentin
does not stop with the philosophical insight that it is "impossible
to grasp facticity in its brute nudity"[80] but rather translates his
"horrible ecstasy" (131) *poetically*. The "experience" of absurdity (the

absence of inherent meaning in the world) provokes a proliferation of conspicuous metaphors—"wooden serpent," "claw" and "vulture's talon"—that pull the reader's attention away from the referential reality of the event to its traumatizing *effects on* Roquentin.[81]

Alain Robbe-Grillet was one the first critics to draw attention to Roquentin's use of metaphor, which he maintains is "never an innocent figure of speech."[82] Though *Nausea* admirably highlights human contingency, Robbe-Grillet continues to argue, the novel's critique of essentialism falls short of evacuating *all* human significance from its narrative, that is, of producing a pure and neutral description of the world. For Robbe-Grillet, *Nausea*'s metaphors—what he calls Roquentin's "fatal complicity"[83] with the world of objects—have the contradictory effect of humanizing the world to the extent that they impose relations where none are present. Sartre himself would later confirm Robbe-Grillet's critique, seeing his early work as symptomatic of a deeply ingrained idealism, of a correlationalist idealism that repeatedly privileged consciousness over materiality, thinking over being: "In Platonic fashion, I went from knowledge to this subject. I found more reality in the idea than in the thing. . . . From that came the idealism which it took me thirty years to shake off."[84]

Surprisingly here, OOO might offer a defense of Roquentin's use of metaphors. A Harman-inspired reading might explain Roquentin's metaphors more generously as a case of "vicarious causation,"[85] where the sensual façade of the root is said to mediate the encounter between Roquentin and the real root. Rather than adopting a more straightforward mode of description—typical of epistemological realism—Roquentin's metaphors attest and respond to the allure of the sensual root, offering us indirect contact with the real root. The strangeness of Roquentin's metaphors thus registers the affective impact of the being of the root. This would be OOO's lesson of Roquentin's epiphanic encounter. As with Heidegger's broken hammer, OOO returns to the real object outside of its sociolinguistic context, that is, to the object that *holds something in reserve*,[86] making it always in excess of its representation. But does this OOO reading actually manage to sell out Roquentin? Does it get out of Roquentin? And does it get Roquentin out? My answer is a resolute no. The subject persists. Roquentin as subject remains indispensable for the reading of objects.

If Robbe-Grillet's objections and Sartre's belated self-critique too quickly dismiss Roquentin's metaphors, a Harman-sanctioned use of metaphors sends us back to a rather traditional anthropomorphic subject. We should keep in mind Harman's actual example of allure— the distinction between "the cypress is a conifer" and "the cypress is a flame" (with Harman's preference for the latter).[87] Such a metaphor pales in comparison to what we witness in *Nausea*. Roquentin's metaphors do establish a relation with the world of objects, yet it is an aesthetic experience that is *otherwise than humanizing*, since the metaphors themselves work to undermine the noumena/phenomena distinction. Roquentin's metaphors are not those of a sovereign subject, a mega-actant. Rather, they register his passivity, if not impotence. Roquentin is an object in an even more radical sense than OOO espouses since Roquentin's fantasy of the noumema is shattered rather than sustained (via the idea of vicarious causation). But the question is, what kind of object is the subject that is Roquentin? He is an object for whom a horizon exists. To be human is to be thrown into a transcendentally constituted reality. But this horizon is not destiny; its human coordinates are not immune to change. Roquentin breaks out of this horizon not by isolating the pure in-itself behind, beneath, or beyond the world of phenomena but by producing a *surplus of meaning*, jamming, in turn, the signifying machine of the Symbolic. In Lacanian parlance, the Symbolic is non-all, forever incomplete and inconsistent. Roquentin's metaphors jam the existing signifying order; they touch the Real, obliquely gesturing to an indigestible and irreducible remainder, disrupting his society's smooth-functioning field of knowledge.

Roquentin's unruly metaphors negate what he knows about his world and the objects in it; they overwhelm his phenomenological reduction, effectively disrupting his narrative of the event, its gentrification—pointing to the Real of being, which is not a whole substance. The Real, as Žižek puts it, is "not an external thing that resists being caught in the symbolic network, but the fissure within the symbolic network itself."[88] The Real is thus not a substantial region outside the Symbolic "but a constant companion to 'reality.'"[89] Being in-itself is always already fraught, divided, non-all. The ontological lesson of *Nausea* is that there are no noumena. Roquentin's encounter with the root of the chestnut—with the *materiality* of the root—reveals that the unknowable or unmasterable is not external to his field of knowledge (in some inaccessible, extralinguistic realm) but internal to it.

Whereas OOO proceeds to "Kantianize"[90] the Real, *Nausea* inscribes inconsistency and incompleteness in reality by foregrounding language's relation to the Real. The Real does not cause the gaps and inconsistencies in the Symbolic; the former is an effect of the latter. The presence of the Real signals these gaps and inconsistencies.[91] In his diary, Roquentin meticulously records his "becoming-unexceptional." His speech faithfully attests to his existential struggle; again, he experiences the rebellion of objects as a series of traumas. An OOO reading would undoubtedly celebrate Roquentin's decentering—yet it would do so in a narrow and ultimately unsatisfactory way. What such a reading misses is that language is not simply an external instrument mediating Roquentin's relation to the world. For OOO, Roquentin's emancipation from an anthropomorphic and anthropocentric framework coincides with his recognition that language distorts the external world by imbuing its objects with a violent humanist meaning—that it subjugates and instrumentalizes objects, ignoring their permanent opacity and denying them the same status of actants. But Roquentin as "subject" is "an *objective* embodiment of reality's contradiction."[92] The subject of theory is the subject of the signifier. This Lacanian reframing of psychic turmoil allows us to ponder a new beginning—or at least, an additional cause—for Roquentin's bouts of nausea.

Žižek repeatedly stresses that trauma is at the origins of our entry into language (symbolic castration), and that what we experience as existential turmoil needs to be given a stronger ontological understanding by relating it back to the primordial exposure to language, to the *cut into the Real*, which coincides with the emergence of the subject as such: "The relationship between psychic turmoil and its expression in speech should thus also be turned around: speech does not simply express or articulate psychic turmoil; at a certain key point, psychic turmoil itself is a reaction to the trauma of dwelling in the 'torture-house of language.'"[93] The least we can say is that Roquentin's change does not simply come from outside (the domain of unruly objects). What contributes to Roquentin's transformation is his ontological makeup, his profound lack of self-identity, his strangeness to himself. Living with nausea is living with the Real. As Žižek puts it, "The experience of nausea with regard to life as such is a primordial ontological experience."[94]

In *Nausea*, however, Roquentin does experience precious moments of reprieve whenever he hears the jazz song "Some of These Days." The creation (or so imagines Roquentin) of a Jewish composer and a black singer, whose refrain, "Some of these days/ you'll miss me honey," and euphonious melody—it has nothing *de trop*—enables him to "transcend" his nausea and cope with reality by allowing him to take momentary refuge in an imaginary realm away from the contingencies of life.[95] What attracts him to this jazz piece is the song's being (its status as being), its ideal ontological status, its teleological nature, the way in which each element has a fixed and necessary value—giving Roquentin, in turn, a sense of finality. "Some of These Days" is an object for Roquentin but it is no ordinary object. His propensity to cathect to the song sets this object apart. It is what Lacan names an *objet petit a*. This cathexis magically turns this ordinary thing into a desirable object. *Objet petit a* poses a problem for OOO. Its location is paradoxical. It is not only in the object—as the object-cause of desire; the unattainable object of desire—but also *in* the subject.[96] The desiring subject is the by-product of the Symbolic— *desire is always desire of the Other*. My desires are never purely my own; we desire according to others. Social scripts and fantasies teach me how to desire and so on. Prior to the Symbolic, antecedent to any subject/object distinction, the child is said to experience the mother directly—in the fusion of the child and the mother's breast—as a pure satisfaction. The child's contact with *das Ding*—the unmediated (m)other—is a primordial scene of unity and plenitude.

Objet petit a, then, emerges after the subject's entry into the Symbolic; it "designates that which remains of the Thing [*das Ding*] after it has undergone the process of symbolization."[97] After the proper formation of subjectivity—after the cut or symbolic castration—such a blissful experience becomes unrepeatable: all we have access to are partial objects (instances of the *objet petit a*), with only partial satisfaction. As with the Real, however, Žižek cautions against "substantializing" *das Ding*, and foregrounds the role of language in our conceptualization of *das Ding*, seeing it thus as an *effect* or fiction of the Symbolic:

What we experience as "reality" discloses itself against the background of the lack, of the absence of it, of the Thing, of the mythical object whose encounter would bring about the full satisfaction of the drive. This lack of the Thing constitutive of "reality" is therefore, in its fundamental dimension, not epistemological, but rather pertains to the paradoxical logic of desire—the paradox being that this Thing is retroactively produced by the very process of symbolization, i.e. that it emerges from the very gesture of its loss. In other (Hegel's) words, there is nothing— no positive substantial entity—behind the phenomenal curtain, only the gaze whose phantasmagorias assume different shapes of the Thing.[98]

Phantasmatically speaking, then, Roquentin encounters the jazz song as an *objet petit a*. In desiring the song, Roquentin seeks "to reproduce the initial state, to find *das Ding*, the object"[99]—an object that would satisfy his hunger for plenitude, fill the void left by the cut of the signifier, deliver on its promise of full enjoyment, and thus undo his existential alienation. Roquentin's attraction and attachment to the song persist from the beginning to the end of the novel. Despite, or because of, his chestnut "epiphany," Roquentin is still prey to the captivating forces of fantasies, to the bewildering effects of his *objet petit a*. His (anti)humanist hubris does not inaugurate a new critical consciousness, announcing the birth a mega-actant, but gives way to what Zupančič cleverly describes as an *object-disoriented ontology* (ODO): "If there is an ontology that follows from psychoanalytic (Lacanian) theory, this can only be an ontology as 'disoriented' by what he calls the *object a*."[100] If OOO is the movement of those posthumanist critics who have dispensed with the subject, ODO is the one for those who foreground the barred subject, the subject reduced to the void, the subject whose lack—only intensified by the encounters with *objets petit a*—is constitutive of his being. For ODO, this is not the subject of the anthropocentric tradition; it is an ontologically paradoxical subject, a subject perpetually at odds with itself—"*the subject is itself the wound it tries to heal.*"[101]

The Subject after the Object

The antidote to object fever is, then, not a heroic and sober return to the subject, but an affirmation of the subject *after* the object, a subject riveted and altered by its extimacy to the object, by its perpetually interrupted proximity to the object, "something strange to me, although it is at the heart of me."[102] A care for objects and an appreciation of the structural roles that ideology, fantasy, language, and desire play in our encounters with and attachment to objects of all kinds are by no means mutually exclusive. The call to place all objects on equal footing emanating from ANT, NM, and OOO functions at best as virtue signaling, and, at worst, obfuscates the workings of ideology. In other words, hermeneutic generosity risks turning into the latest ruse of ideology itself.

Against the Latourian blackmail—either you *add* to reality or you *subtract* from it—a critical reading of *Waltz with Bashir*'s posthumanist overtones does not adopt the position of the all-powerful Zeus judging and condemning others (the director, the film, the naïve spectator, and so on) for their fetishes and mystifications. To insist that ideology matters, to see *Waltz with Bashir* as ideological, is to say, first, that a certain framing, making, and marking of Palestinian suffering is fraught, that there is something problematic about construing the Israeli soldier as a *complex subject*, the self-reflexive, "'enlightened occupier' who 'shoots and weeps,'"[103] all-too-attentive to nonhuman traumas (making Folman less accountable for his crimes and thus more forgivable than the Phalangists, the "bad" Arabs), while maintaining the Palestinian other as a *static object* of pathos, mute, ossified, as it were, in her suffering. But it is *also* to insist that more is going on (in reality and in the film)—whence the labor of critical hermeneutics: the impetus to reread, to read *with and against* the film's posthumanist forays, to take up the film's provocation to begin the story of the other's trauma with the nonhuman.

  In their eagerness to jettison the insights of the linguistic turn, the various movements espousing the primacy of ontology repeatedly fail to observe that language is from the outset *"included into reality as a mode of its distortion."*[104] Roquentin—the posthumanist *malgré lui*—enacts and illustrates this Lacanian insight. Desperately wanting to name Being—that is, to regain his fantasy of sovereignty and/as dominance over objects—Roquentin can only *register* his failure, can only register Being's intransigence discursively, at the symbolic level, through his dizzying display of metaphorical excess. This is an instance of what Lacan dubbed *lalangue,* a neologism referring to "language as the space of illicit pleasures that defy any normativity: the chaotic multitude of homonymies, word-plays, 'irregular' metaphoric links and resonances."[105] What Roquentin's *lalangue,* this monstrous excess, produces is an "'inhuman' view" of things (*Waltz with Bashir* hints at the possibility of viewing Sabra and Shatila from "inhuman eyes," of seeing *the Palestinian as neighbor, as faceless object,* though Folman leaves the "subversive potential" of the assemblage approach unrealized), a view of the world of objects that can only emanate from "an (empty) subject," a subject who has dislodged himself (even if temporarily) from his human coordinates—from his symbolically constituted reality—and whose "violent abstraction" from his particular situation enables him to see himself as an object among other objects in the world.[106] But there is simply no place for a subject like Roquentin in OOO, ANT, or NM.[107]

  Dispensing with the subject is an attempt to contain such excess, either by fetishizing it as the expression of a vibrant materiality, "the 'inner' life of things,"[108] the manifestation of an object's essence, its irrepressible volcanic core, thus prolonging *object fever*, or else by returning to a more compliant, modest, postcritical subject who conveniently "covers up the cut of the Real"[109]—as with more mainstream posthumanist strands of thought.

4

Black ~~Being~~

One cannot help but sense that there is something else amiss in the call to move "beyond the human": a refusal afoot that could be described as an attempt to move beyond *race, and in particular blackness, a subject that I argue cannot be escaped but only disavowed or dissimulated in prevailing articulations of movement "beyond the human."*

ZAKIYYAH IMAN JACKSON[1]

The black is a phobic object because he or she presents me with a problem that is beyond language, that leaves me with no way to redress what this person represents. This person is the antithesis of humanity.

FRANK B. WILDERSON III[2]

In posthumanist circles, the urge to theorize "humanity otherwise"[3] is almost second nature. The "human" as a unitary category is an outdated concept. Posthumanists counter the (trans)humanist desire for immunity and transcendence with an invitation to defetishize human exceptionality, to reconsider our hybridity and our reliance on mixture and entanglement with nonhumans. The ideology of humanism is deemed responsible for many of the ills on earth; it has led us into the catastrophic age of the Anthropocene, with climate change wreaking havoc on all of us—that is, on *all living beings.*

Going beyond the human is thus not only an ethical choice but also a survival necessity. If the "human" of humanism is the greatest threat to survival, then waging war against human exceptionalism is, or must become, the mission of all serious posthumanists. Yet as Zakiyyah Iman Jackson points out, the question of racism and its dehumanizations are too often elided in these arguments. More than an omission, this disavowal, as Jackson puts it, covers over a problem for posthumanism that cannot go unaddressed if we are ever to truly break from the paradigms at the heart of anthropogenic violence.

Keen to expose the humanist blind spots of most sophisticated readers, Cary Wolfe takes up the topic of racism in a way that exemplifies the tendency toward disavowal that Jackson identifies in posthumanist thought. Wolfe articulates his critique as a friendly one, offering his thoughts as a supplement to Toni Morrison's insightful musings on the cult of American individualism and its racist underbelly (American whiteness relied on its distinction from its other, Africanism):

In Toni Morrison's eloquent meditation . . . she argues that the hallmarks of the individualist imagination in the founding of United States culture—"autonomy, authority, newness and difference, absolute power"—are all "made possible by, and shaped by, activated by a complex awareness and employment of a constituted Africanism," which in turn has as its material condition of possibility the white man's "absolute power over the lives of others" in the fact of slavery. My point here, however, . . . is to take Morrison very seriously at her word—and then some. For what does it mean when the aspiration of human freedom, extended to all, regardless of race or class or gender, has as its material condition of possibility absolute control over the lives of nonhuman others?[4]

On this view, Morrison's critique of antiblackness along with her desire for human freedom—of the type of agency that blacks have been systematically denied—is noble and understandable, but doesn't go far enough. Morrison stops short of shifting her critique from white racism to the human subject itself.[5] Wolfe argues that without fully confronting the evils of speciesism, the belief that elevates the human above all others, an anti-racist discourse that seeks the full inclusion of blacks under the umbrella of the human will continue to reproduce the humanist status quo to the detriment of the lives of both humans and nonhuman others.

In "Animals—Property or Persons?" Gary Francione takes up a similar question but approaches it from the perspective of animal rights, foregrounding the historical argument that the plight of animals is analogous to that of black slaves who *fought* for their recognition as persons:

> If we extend the right not to be property to animals, then animals will become moral persons. To say that a being is a person is merely to say that the being has morally significant interests, that the principle of equal consideration applies to that being, that the being is not a thing. In a sense, we already accept that animals are persons; we claim to reject the view that animals are things and to recognize that, at the very least, animals have a morally significant interest in not suffering. Their status as property, however, has prevented their personhood from being realized. The same was true of human slavery. Slaves were regarded as chattel property.[6]

Such a posthumanism transmutes animals into the "new blacks" in need of emancipation, placing posthumanists in the position of the "new abolitionists." Being posthuman, on this reading, is already to leave the black behind (whose personhood has already been secured) for the animal (who is still in need of help).

As discussed in Chapter 2, the analogy between the mistreatment of animals and that of some humans deemed less than human is not in and of itself dubious. Rather, it is the logics through which the analogy is deployed that are troubling for anti-racism critics. As Alexander Weheliye has vigorously objected, the tendency to substitute speciesism for racism—to displace blacks with animals and to refocus critical attention away from antiblackness to the question of animality—relies on both a false opposition and a questionable attribution of critical responsibility. "Given that Morrison mentions neither the subjugation nor liberation of animals," Weheliye ponders, "it remains unclear why her ideas about blackness and chattel slavery are summoned here, why the aspiration for human freedom would ineludibly lead to the subjugation of nonhuman others, and why black subjects—rather than, say, slave owners—must bear the burden of representing the final frontier of speciesism."[7] Why should fighting for human freedom commit you by definition to humanism at the expense of a more inclusive posthumanism?

Presumably, the posthumanist argument takes slavery to be a problem of the past, and thus sees no fundamental differences between the white and the black descendants of those implicated in the wrongs of slave society. Both are said to enjoy the privileges of humanity. The task now, then, would not be to critically look backward (at the racialization of this Africanist presence in white America) but to look forward and conceive of new models of interspecies coexistence, to cancel or invalidate that all-too-humanist impulse to subjugate the nonhuman. According to this narrative, Western modernity can self-critically assess its past and find much to critique, but what it is unable to do on its own is to fully de-attach itself from its investment in the "Human." Speciesism names this cathexis. To be posthuman is effectively to break with the speciesism at the heart of Western modernity. Yet the posthumanist narrative that posits the animal question as the next ethico-political chapter in emancipation perpetuates, in turn, a linear temporality of oppression: chattel slavery, colonialism and settler colonialism, the Shoah, and now slaughterhouses. Moreover, this self-critical understanding of the West remains deficiently uncritical—not only of the animal but also of race.

Global modernity—driven by Eurocentric humanism—is founded on racial inequality; its ontology of the human is predicated upon a matrix of racialization. Modernity invented blackness: "modernity gave birth to" black being "through dispossession and abjection."[8] The non-European other—embodied most powerfully and phantasmatically in the figure of the African—was not simply excluded from Western civilization's fold; this racialized or blackened other was needed for *white* modernity's legibility and legitimacy: "to define its own limits and to designate humanity as an achievement as well as to give form to the category of 'the animal.'"[9] And if Agamben viewed Nazism and its death camps as the dreadful moment *"when the state of exception starts to become the rule,"*[10] when modernity's nightmarish potential (the disastrous danger of state racism) disclosed itself to the world, he simultaneously neglected to account for racial slavery and colonial genocide as key and violent events in the modern ontology of the human.[11] Provincializing Agamben's European framework of the Shoah as paradigmatic trauma is a necessary—but often forgotten—step in theorizing a space beyond the human. Black being, a barred being, paradoxically names modernity's constitutively excluded other—that forgotten genealogy erased in biopolitical frameworks such as Agamben's and Foucault's. As modernity's reject, black being has been either ignored by Western philosophy (including most posthumanists) or relegated to minority discourses (allegedly bearing no universal relevance; failing to provoke, for example, a rethinking of the human, modernity, otherness, etc.).[12] With the ontological turn, however, the question of the (non)being of blackness has garnered critical attention in critical race and anti-colonial studies.

The Afro-Pessimism movement has critiqued modernity's antiblackness most emphatically. Frank B. Wilderson III, one of the movement's most vocal theorists, underscores the transformative impact of the transatlantic slave trade on black being. The Middle Passage generated nothing short of a "new ontology": racial blackness, an ontological paradox, a kind of (non)being devoid of any relationality:

> *African*, or more precisely *Blackness*, refers to an individual who is by definition always already void of relationality.
>
> The Black has sentient capacity but no relational capacity.[13]

The ontological mutation of African lives was even more profound than the one brought about by the Shoah: "Jews went into Auschwitz and came out as Jews, Africans went into the ships and came out as Blacks. The former is a Human holocaust; the latter is a Human *and* a metaphysical holocaust."[14] Black ~~being~~ echoes Wilderson's understanding of "'Black ~~subjectivity~~' (subjectivity under erasure),"[15] an ontologically compromised subjectivity where no unity between self and being exists; a being to which "no will" can be imputed.[16] A refrain in the works of Wilderson and other Afro-Pessimists is that black slavery is "without analog":[17] "That is why it makes little sense to attempt analogy: the Jews have the Dead (the *Muselmann*) among them; the Dead have the Blacks among them."[18] In the realm of "human" comparison, he argues, blacks have strictly speaking no counterparts. Jews, Palestinians, native Americans, undocumented immigrants, refugees, queers, and so on are all extended the privileges of humanity. There is a mechanism—

however flawed—available to them to voice their wrongs, to secure the protection of the law:

> In its critique of social movements, Afro-Pessimism argues that Blacks do not function as political subjects; instead, our flesh and energies are instrumentalized for postcolonial, immigrant, feminist, LGBT, and workers' agendas. These so-called allies are never *authorized* by Black agendas predicated on Black ethical dilemmas. A Black radical agenda is terrifying to most people on the Left because it emanates from a condition of suffering for which there is no imaginable strategy for redress—no narrative of redemption.[19]

Blacks are barred from the emotional rewards of redemption. But Palestinians, for example, are not without a solution, a "strategy for redress." Their remedy is a Palestinian state, a return to a "prior plenitude," to a "spatial place that was lost";[20] for diasporic blacks, however, there is no overcoming of what Orlando Patterson calls "social death."[21] If, in the case of the Palestinians, there is a "recognition of the spatial coordinates of that demand," American blacks, for example, do not have any willing auditors capable of hearing their plight: "The collective unconscious [of the white auditors] is not ready to accept that blacks are human."[22] Why? Because to do so would trouble their "integrity as a human,"[23] precipitating a crisis in white identity. What makes racial chattel slavery without analog is the *ungeneralizability* of social death; "it is indexed to slavery and it does not travel,"[24] Jared Sexton firmly maintains.

"Slavery," as Patterson defines it, is "the permanent, violent domination of natally alienated and generally dishonored persons."[25] Racial slavery was unlike any other forms of servitude. Earlier instances of enslavement were in principle temporary, the result of a military defeat or a criminal sentence, for example. Being a slave—

doing forced labor—did not indicate that there was something intrinsically slavish about you. With chattel slavery things radically changed: "Chattel slavery, as a condition of ontology and not just as an event of experience, stuck to the African like Velcro."[26] Chattel slavery degraded Africans, liquidated their humanity, and transformed their bodies into "Black flesh"[27]—with flesh signifying "that zero degree of social conceptualization,"[28] as Hortense Spillers puts it. The Middle Passage eviscerated the slaves' gendered subjectivities; it "ungendered" them and racialized their flesh, robbing Africans of their desiring bodies:

> First of all, their New World, diasporic plight marked a *theft* of the *body*—a willful and violent (and unimaginable from this distance) severing of the captive body from its motive will, its active desire. Under these conditions, we lose at least *gender* difference *in the outcome*, and the female body and the male body become a territory of cultural and political maneuver, not at all gender-related, gender specific.[29]

Black enslavement solidified the nonbeing of blacks; their captive bodies were structurally denied humanity (a slave was "reduced to a thing, to *being* for the captor"), deprived of the human privileges of subjectivity (they lacked gender, sexuality, "a subject position" in the New World, forbidden the right to name and claim their own flesh).[30]

But how can the same modernity that gave "us" (the children of Western civilization) liberalism and human rights discourse turn a blind eye to racial chattel slavery? The answer is worse than expected. Enlightenment thinkers were not just ignorant of politics, cloistered in their ivory towers; they often rationalized the moral catastrophe of slavery, providing a conceptual justification for the mass subjugation of blacks. The logic of *subhumanizing* blacks historically revolved around the matter of rationality and their presumed incapacity to reason. As David Theo Goldberg argues, "one way for Enlightenment philosophies committed to moral notions of equality and autonomy to avoid inconsistency on the question of racialized subordination was to deny the rational capacity of blacks, to deny the very condition of their humanity."[31] Kant is a case in point. In "Observations on the Feeling of the Beautiful and Sublime," Kant clearly distinguishes whites from blacks, humans from not-quite-humans. The latter lacked reason, and the proof was unmistakably self-evident. The sheer color of their skin indexed their stupidity:

> This fellow [referring to the opinion of a "Negro carpenter"] was quite black from head to foot, a clear proof that what he said was stupid.

> So fundamental is the difference between the two races of man, and it appears to be as great in regard to mental capacities as in color.[32]

If reason is the proper of the human, blacks, perceived as deficient in rationality, are by extension excluded from humanity—aligned, in turn, with animality—and thus not subject to the protection of Kant's moral law. Conversely, the proper of the (white) human is his or her nonblackness. Being white means first and foremost *not being a slave*.

Given slavery's foundational role and immeasurable impact (its fissuring of African being and making of black being), Afro-Pessimists read racial progress—the successes of the civil rights movement in the United States—with caution and suspicion. Formal emancipation never translated into black freedom, a recuperation of their lost ontology, or unqualified access to the privileges of social life. Social death, the curse and legacy of slavery, continues to plague blacks. As Saidiya Hartman points out, slavery is an unshakable horizon for blacks:

> If slavery persists as an issue in the political life of black America, it is not because of an antiquarian obsession with bygone days or the burden of a too-long memory, but because black lives are still imperiled and devalued by a racial calculus and a political arithmetic that were entrenched centuries ago. This is the afterlife of slavery—skewed life chances, limited access to health and education, premature death, incarceration, and impoverishment.[33]

For black folks, emancipation and subjugation are not mutually exclusive. Delineating the configurations and alignments of race and freedom, Sexton explains: "Not all free persons are white (nor are they equal or equally free), but slaves are paradigmatically black. And because blackness serves as the basis of enslavement in the logic of a transnational political and legal culture, it permanently destabilizes the position of any nominally free black population."[34] Being black today entails at best a precarious ontic freedom, always qualified by the subject's blackness—read as abjection—his or her ontological marking as a would-be criminal. Sexton describes the intrinsic suffering inscribed in living black bodies, insisting that "a living death is as much a death as it is a living."[35] Slavery after emancipation is still slavery; freedom never replaced slavery, life never supplemented death. What we have are "masterless slaves"[36] and "tragic continuities"[37] in antiblackness. Racial enslavement changed its face, moving from the plantation to the prison-industrial complex and mass black incarceration in the United States: "The fact that more than half of the young black men in any large American city are currently under the control of the criminal justice system (or saddled with criminal records) is not—as many argue—just a symptom of poverty or poor choices, but rather evidence of a new racial caste system at work."[38] Wilderson dubs this socioeconomic reality "the Renaissance of slavery."[39]

While humanist liberals might point to the fact that blacks are now afforded civil rights and *formal* equality before the law, an eye for the persistence of *ontological* antiblackness, for the endless war on blackness, tells another story. Racial progress—change registered at the socio-legal level—belies the prevalent allergy to blackness. In the "afterlife of slavery," working through racial grief—making use of the humanist rhetoric to narrativize personal loss and trauma, with the affective promise of "successful" mourning—is a *human* privilege that is structurally unavailable for black folks.[40] "Black time," as Warren calls it, "is the black hole of time that resists linear narrativity."[41] To emphasize social death, the afterlife of slavery, is not to indulge in anachronism[42] but to block the humanist narrative of inclusion and empathy, which recounts that blacks were excluded in the *past*, but *now* they are included under the law and the umbrella of *human* rights. The racialized black body—the would-be convict—occupies the position of the historical slave of the plantation. Blacks are afforded formal protection from the law, but in practice their choices and activities are never really their own. What they do and desire remains more or less "the expression of the master's prerogative."[43] Even when black suffering is acknowledged, it often takes the form of a media spectacle, an obscene source of white enjoyment.[44]

This is why Wilderson pushes back against the notion of a hard distinction between police and police brutality—against the idea that police brutality is an aberration, a distortion of policing. "Our problem," he continues, "is one of complete captivity from birth to death, and coercion as the *starting point* of our interaction with the State and with ordinary white citizens."[45] The example of police brutality is dreadful but *unproductive* if it is made to stand for antiblackness. This example fails to disclose the invisible, structural, and gratuitous violence of everyday black existence—the violence that happens when nothing seems to be happening, as Žižek might put it, "when things just go on as normal."[46] In contradistinction to Arendt, it is in this "normal" state of affairs—and not in the violation of the social sphere—that antiblack violence truly resides.[47] What liberals and humanists deem racist violence—the type of antiblack violence that takes the form of media spectacle—neglects to account for the ways blackness is "always-already criminalized in the collective unconscious,"[48] that "White people are not simply 'protected' by the police, they *are* the police."[49] For white civil society, the default modality of blacks is an inhuman propensity for criminality. Blackness is both imagined and treated as a ubiquitous danger. But the sanctioned narrative of the (mis)treatment of blacks obfuscates the matter. Wilderson draws attention to the gendering of antiblack violence as a means of ideologically distorting the general violence to black bodies, so that the violence visited on black males (the would-be convicts/the essential victims) is the excess violence that must rectified:

> The violence against Black people, which we are witnessing on YouTube videos, Instagrams, and TV news, is conveniently gendered as violence against Black men. But there is a problem here, and it is twofold: we tend to lose sight of the fact that Black women, children, and LGBT people are losing their breath through the technologies of social death, just as Black heterosexual men are, albeit in less visible and less mediatized ways. We also get drawn into responding to the phobic anxieties of White and non-Black civil society, the threat of the Black man, and, as such, we offer sustenance to that juggernaut (civil society) even as we try to dismantle it.[50]

For this reason, police brutality ironically functions as a white distraction, a convenient perturbation of humanist comforts. Outraged by police brutality, liberals find an image of racism that they can live with: the perpetrators of antiblack violence are civil society's exceptions, the police's "bad apples." The problem can never be the police and civil society as such. There is a stubborn refusal to consider the policing of blacks—the *general* treatment of blacks as subhumans (the pervasiveness of antiblackness)—as a precondition for preserving and maintaining the well-being of civil society and its libidinal investment in the human.

For Afro-Pessimists, then, blackness cannot simply be redeemed within the coordinates of white civil society. It falls on the other side of the human. A black stands for criminality, always already in violation of humanity's normative ideals, the "antithesis of a Human subject."[51] "Blackness"—a term irremediably marked by/as slaveness—is the "anti-Human . . . against which Humanity establishes, maintains, and renews its coherence, its corporeal integrity."[52] The abject monstrosity of blackness defines the *white* human. In this respect, from the standpoint of blacks, white supremacy is not *the* fundamental problem of contemporary society. Rather, it is antiblackness, stemming from the modern ontology of the human, the human as defined in its basic opposition to the slave, and the alignment of nonbeing with blackness. Black humanism aspires for an ideal that is not only impossible but also devastating for black people, since it repeatedly misdiagnoses the problem, not seeing that it is grounded in the very *grammar of humanity*.[53] Aspiring for humanist goals—freedom, humanity, and equality—is not the way out of an antiblack world but a contribution to its cruel and perpetual reproduction. As Calvin Warren forcefully notes: "One cannot think the free black within an antiblack world without resorting to the fantastical and the absurd."[54] To reiterate this point: antiblackness gains its meaning in relation to the concept of the human, so recourse to liberal or humanist solutions cannot be expected to truly yield emancipatory results.

Similarly, for Saidiya Hartman, one cannot simply forget about liberalism's long investment in sovereignty, that its ideal of self-possession was predicated on a vision of "the black as will-less actant and sublime object."[55] To be sovereign meant that one was not black and that black existence itself was available for domination.[56] During Reconstruction, when blacks legally ceased to be chattel, black humanity did not simply reunite with humanity at large. How could it, considering that humanity itself was never a value-neutral category, but derived its meaning through its exclusion of blacks?[57] "Reposition the black body after Jubilee,"[58] then, is a problem rather than a given. Indeed, the human in humanist and liberal discourses still subscribes to a "racial hierarchy,"[59] functioning as a "master signifier," anchoring antiblackness, quilting the field of meaning, around which other signifiers (whiteness, blackness, animality, etc.) can crystallize. To effectively confront the challenges of antiblackness, a posthuman intervention is urgently needed. And conversely, to move beyond the human, posthumanism must reckon with the racist legacy of modernity. Being posthuman cannot bracket the question of race, conceptualizing it away as a correlationist holdover, a messy social construction that muddies the waters of ontology. A posthumanism worthy of its name must trouble the ontological difference between the human and the slave.

In the following pages of this chapter, I explore, first, what follows from this crushing assessment of black being, what ontologies of the future, what worlds, are foreclosed by antiblackness. Nihilism and pessimism are recent and thought-provoking responses to the realization that antiblack violence is constitutive of white civil society—turning black bodies into its "eternal" enemies—that ontological security or protection for blacks is structurally unavailable. Both of these responses forcefully decline the path of civil rights for remedying antiblack violence. As Hartman cogently puts it:

> Legal liberalism, as well as critical race theory, has examined issues of race, racism, and equality by focusing on the exclusion and

marginalization of those subjects and bodies marked as different and/or inferior. The disadvantage of this approach is that the proposed remedies and correctives to the problem—inclusion, protection, and greater access to opportunity—do not ultimately challenge the economy of racial production or its truth claims or interrogate the exclusion constitutive of the norm but instead seek to gain equality, liberation, and redress within its confines.[60]

Society's "economy of racial production," along with its affective and cognitive investment in the human as white, have so thoroughly barred black *being* that solutions or attempts to confront and transcend it seem doomed to fail. Warren puts the matter in stark terms: the cherished idea of agency, the heroic belief that things can get better, reflects "the humanist fantasy (or narcissism) that anything humans have created can be changed."[61]

To probe the contours of this fantasy and possible responses to it, I then turn to Boots Riley's 2018 film, *Sorry to Bother You*, which offers what we might term a "weird posthumanism" as a means of traversing the devastating existence of antiblackness. The film centers on an underemployed telemarketer, Cassius "Cash" Green, struggling to cope with the absurdity of being black in a racist society where resistance often appears futile and slavery persists under the mask of "free" contract, as workers sign themselves over to lifetime labor commitments in exchange for room and board. The film's weird posthumanism reaches its apogee when Cash discovers his employer's plan to inject its workers with a formula that transmogrifies them into more vigorous, sexually potent horse-human hybrids—*equi-sapiens* as a more lucrative source of exploitation. Though the *equi-sapiens* initially horrify Cash (consistent with a liberal-humanist response to nonhuman difference), the film foregrounds a posthuman model of solidarity across species in the revolutionary fight against racial capitalism.

Living a Nonhuman Life

Black ~~being~~ takes as its point of departure the making and reification of blackness. To be black is to appear always already as a "phobic object"[62] to white society. In a Heideggerian vein, a black is a non- or improper *Dasein*; a black ~~being~~ is "poor in world" (as in the case of animals). The black is perpetually animalized, made to stand for the other of the human (who is white, good, and virtuous). "The Negro is an animal, the Negro is bad, the Negro is wicked, the Negro is ugly," writes Frantz Fanon.[63] Originally from Martinique, Fanon recounts his "learning" experience of this phobia after moving to Lyon to complete his studies, where he is incessantly exposed to the white gaze, becoming the recipient of racist hails: "'Dirty nigger!' or simply, 'Look! a Negro!'"[64] Interpellated as some*thing*, he experienced a traumatic *negrophobia* that ruined his psychic life, hollowed out his being, and wrecked his consciousness, rendering his body an inert object in the midst of the world:

> I came into this world anxious to uncover the meaning of things, my soul desirous to be at the origin of the world, and here I am an object among other objects.
>
> My body was returned to me spread-eagled, disjointed, redone, draped in mourning on this white winter's day.[65]

Recounting the life or world of an object—a black ~~being~~ "locked in this suffocating reification [*objectivité écrasante*]"[66]—is not a mere thought experiment for racialized subjects such as Fanon, or an occasion for "alien phenomenology," to recall the title of Ian Bogost's key text from the OOO archive. In its desire to strip subjectivity of its epistemic privileges, to liberate us from the clutches of humanity, OOO turns to ontology, to "the nature of being, rather than the human philosopher's approach to it."[67] But *What It's Like to Be a Thing*, the second half of Bogost's title, takes on an ironic sense for critical race scholars for whom this formulation cannot but evoke W. E. B. Du Bois's concept of "double consciousness,"[68] the experience of living a racialized life in which you routinely see yourself from the perspective of whiteness (the putative subject), from a perspective at odds with your own (the precarious object). A racist society instills and cultivates double consciousness in its minority communities.

Confronting the reality of being a "phobic object" for white civil society hardly seems to be a regression back into the anthropocentric orbit of critique. More importantly, it exposes the limits of the critique of correlationism: the objection that correlationists restrict knowledge claims to that which is true "for us." Quentin Meillassoux laments the fetishization of the prefix "co-" from Kant to Derrida:

> The "co-" (of co-givenness, of co-relation, of the co-originary, of co-presence, etc.) is the grammatical particle that dominates modern philosophy, its veritable "chemical formula." Thus, one could say that up until Kant, one of the principal problems of philosophy was to think substance, while ever since Kant, it has consisted in trying to think the correlation.[69]

The ontological turn is indeed a corrective to "philosophers hamstrung by the 'linguistic turn.'"[70] Rather than settling for a weak epistemology, OOO affirms the existence of "that outside which [is] not relative to us . . . existing in itself regardless of whether we are thinking of it or not."[71] Yet the "us" in "for us" is never scrutinized by OOO; it is the abstract, decontextualized, and depoliticized subject position of humanity. A *world-without-me* fantasizes a world without us, the human subject, *as if* "we" all had the same access to, and the protection of, this ideological category, as if no part of the "we" (considered, no doubt, an illegitimate part in the first place) could itself be at the receiving end of epistemic violence. But blacks do not belong to this "us" in the same way white folks do. As Warren puts it, "black ~~being~~ incarnates metaphysical nothing";[72] it registers and expresses the paradoxical status of the nonsubject, the negation of a black-as-subject; black ~~being~~ gestures to a life that has been foreclosed. Blacks are (non)beings for whom Kant's categorical imperative ("act in such a way that you always treat humanity, whether in your own person or in the person of any other, never simply as a means, but always at the same time as an end"[73]) does not apply: to be black is to have one's blackness treated "simply as a means."[74] Black ~~being~~ is thus scarcely guilty of humanism's original sin—the hubris of epistemic and hermeneutic agency, the centering of the world around man. In white civil society blackness appears not as a willful subject but as a *phobic object*. "But then, why," Alessandra Raengo incisively asks, "isn't *this* object—black-as-object, the most ontologically precarious of all objects—the immediate focus of object-oriented ontology (OOO)?"[75] The posthuman desire to entertain a *world-without-me* falters precisely because it fails to consider the idea that this world is a *racist* one—and that this racism, this antiblackness, has historically played a key role in defining the proper of the human. Whiteness can accommodate humanists and posthumanists alike. A rejection of anthropocentrism does not index a departure from whiteness and antiblackness. To attend to black ~~being~~ is to reorient critical attention back to the question of race and for this reason is anything but a return to the human subject as center.

Black, Blackness, and Being Parahuman

Black ~~being~~ denotes most concretely the effects of political ontology, translating and expressing the mutilation of black ~~subjectivity~~.

A black ~~being~~ does not strictly speaking suffer from alienation, since the concept assumes too much: that there is a gap between the subject's self-image and the one imposed from the outside. But such a self-image—what humanism guarantees for the human—is precisely wanting for black folks.[76] Being human is being white, and vice versa. Ontology—access to ontology, playing the game of ontology—belongs to whites, and is a white privilege. The ~~being~~ of blacks lacks interiority, an inner life, and for this reason,

> ontology does not allow us to understand the being of the black man, since it ignores the lived experience. . . . The black man has no ontological resistance in the eyes of the white man. From one day to the next, the Blacks have had to deal with two systems of reference. Their metaphysics, or less pretentiously their customs and the agencies to which they refer, were abolished because they were in contradiction with a new civilization that imposed its own.[77]

Ontology caters exclusively to white folks since it is in the business of cultivating and preserving "the customs and resources of human beingness and not black ~~being~~."[78] Simply put, ontology belongs to civilization and/as whiteness. Black folks dwell in "a zone of nonbeing,"[79] and are left with nothing(ness), only the faint traces of their ontological evisceration.

And yet this assessment of blackness, for Fred Moten, has led too quickly to the reduction of black life to bare or frail life, to social death, and to the notion that black life is—and can only be—"overdetermined from the outside."[80] With such "critical obsession with bare life" (262n.6), blackness denotes an existential state of "absolute dereliction."[81] This is the position of Fanon, of Fanon-inspired readers, and of the Afro-Pessimists more specifically: black ~~being~~ equates blackness with objecthood.[82] Blackness is passivity and powerlessness; it is nothing but a pathology[83]—to which white civil society can generate no cure (how can it? It is the one responsible for the pathology in the first place; blackness is the disease, whiteness human health). Moten, however, moves to correct this one-sided reading of blackness ("blackness [as] associated with a certain sense of decay" [140]), decoupling it from black identity (the racist ontologization of blackness). Its adequation with mortified objecthood is hermeneutically and politically shortsighted, since it overprioritizes structural violence at the expense of lived experience, ignoring the degree to which "the history of blackness is testament to the fact that objects can and do resist."[84] Moten repeatedly troubles blackness's object status, its experience as a secured *object* of study, infusing it with a "dispossessive force,"[85] an untranslatability that derails the phenomenological pursuit of meaning (148). What blackness *is*, what it names for Moten, is quite elusive.

The ontology of blackness, if it has one, is "fugitive" (142). Moten, following Nahum Chandler, refers to this fugitivity as the "paraontological distinction" between "blackness or the thinking of blackness" and "black people."[86] In thinking paraontologically, Moten places the origins of blackness prior to ontology, thus weakening or attenuating the latter's hegemonic reach: "What emerges in the desire that constitutes a certain proximity to that thought is not (just) that blackness is ontologically prior to the logistics and regulative power that is supposed to have brought it into existence but that blackness is prior to ontology" (194). Blackness exists *alongside* ontology, working in its shadows. It calls for "an ontology of disorder, an ontology of dehiscence" (150), patiently working to undermine ontology's logic and schematization. Blackness is an anti-ontology, an improper ontology, if you will; as Chandler points out, it denotes "the general possibility of the otherwise."[87] Drawing on this insight, Moten explores the alternative life of blackness as an ontology on the run, a fleeing life that we may characterize as "being parahuman," if not altogether posthuman. Blackness as fugitivity "is a desire for and a spirit of escape and transgression of the proper and the proposed."[88] It never coincides with itself, and ontology cannot apprehend its effectively queer logic. "What is inadequate to blackness is already given ontologies," writes Moten (150). To paraphrase Luce Irigaray, this *blackness which is more than one* exceeds its designation as an absence, its relegation to the unforgiving and normative realm of nonbeing.[89] Blackness is defyingly "extraontological" (150), that is, parahuman. It is at once not to be pathologized (accepting the political ontology that determines blackness as a sign of criminality, a sickness, that assigns it to oblivion or symbolic death) but also to be seen as "pathogenic" (194) (a destabilizing, transformative, and emancipatory potential for blacks and other marginalized bodies). Unruly blackness—blackness as an irreducible becoming, defying political ontology and its (de)formation of black subjects—astonishes whiteness; it is a "dangerous supplement" (150) or threat to the powers and immunity of whiteness, a "constitutive" supplement (143) to civil society's ideological and phantasmastic attachment to the human. Moten thus infuses blackness with (im)possibility—with possible moves that can only appear as impossible from within the present ontology of the human.

While generously engaging Moten's ideas, Warren registers some concerns about the unthematizability of blackness, seeing it, through a Lacanian register, as occupying the status of the elusive *objet petit a*: "Our desire to move beyond 'ontological Blackness' . . . becomes something similar to the psychoanalytic notion of *objet (a)*. Blackness is the imaginary wholeness or origin that we are in constant pursuit of, but never can quite approach."[90] Viewing "Blackness" as akin to the cause-object of desire of (Moten's vision of) black studies seems apt. Black studies yearns for blackness, but blackness always disappoints; no movement—including Afro-Pessimism—explains, contains, or satisfies its demands. Blackness frustrates the desire for black identity/~~identity~~, where blackness and black being/~~being~~ would coincide and collapse into each other. Blackness always means more, or less, than is ontologically asserted in its name (from black humanists to Afro-Pessimists). Dissatisfaction permeates (or at least should permeate) black studies. Blackness runs the risk of losing its subversive edge, neutralizing its paraontological resistance, and becoming just another ideological fantasy that covers over the primordial gap or void. On Warren's reading, Moten's blackness is unmistakably phantasmatic, lying outside the vicissitudes of the Symbolic, embodying a pre-Lapsarian state of being: blackness before European modernity, its ontology, and the reign of the white human. Attending to blackness here sounds a lot like a romanticized mode of resistance,[91] even pointing to the mythical blackness promoted by *Négritude*. To be sure, recovering this blackness might be more tenuous; there is no ontology-free grammar capable of doing justice to blackness. Still, in its imaginary appeal to wholeness, in its desire to fill the void of being (uncorrupted by the ontology that it paradoxically aspires to corrupt), Moten's vision of blackness arguably echoes that of *Négritude*.

At the same time, I wonder whether Warren does not overstate the dangers of blackness as or like *objet petit a*, inviting us to draw the wrong parallel with *Négritude*.[92] The problem lies in Warren's understanding of *objet petit a*, which he seems to reduce to its role in fantasy: the fantasy of an originary wholeness that sustains the desire for blackness, that magically transforms the blackness of the pathologized black, black ~~being~~, "into the utopian promise of the impossible fullness of *jouissance*,"[93] the plenitude of blackness. The rejoinder to Moten is not to sacrifice the phantasmatic *objet petit a* and settle, as it were, for a more measured enjoyment of, and engagement with, blackness—but to see it as a disorienting object (as we did in Chapter 3), as an excessive and "ambiguous" object that destabilizes my world. To do so, Žižek argues, necessitates a shift from desire to drive, from the object-cause of desire to object-loss of drive:

> While, as Lacan emphasizes, the *objet a* is also the object of the drive, the relationship is here thoroughly different: although, in both cases, the link between object and loss is crucial, in the case of the *objet a* as the object-cause of *desire*, we have an object which is originally lost, which coincides with its own loss, which emerges as lost, while, in the case of the *objet a* as the object of the drive, the "object" is *directly the loss itself*—in the shift from desire to drive, we pass from the *lost object* to *loss itself as an object*.[94]

With the shift from desire to drive, blackness as *objet petit a* looks quite different; it is no longer "the 'impossible' quest for the lost object"[95]— the object of a desire that must be demythified, brought back to a post-phantasmatic reality. Blackness is antithetical to the search for impossible fullness. Its enjoyment lies in lack itself, delighting in the non-all of civil society, in the "structural inconsistency"[96] of the Symbolic. Blackness discloses a world that is non-all, where social death is *not* destiny, where blackness, in the mode of the parahuman, stubbornly and inventively remains.

Moten's account of blackness as "lawless" (141) (rather than criminal, as overdetermined by the Law), a pathogen, and a "stolen, transplanted organ, always eliciting rejection" (150), recalls as well Derrida's work on autoimmunity.[97] Making an analogy with a body's need for immune-depressants (functioning as a necessary "supplement" to the immune system) to counter its natural antibodies and render possible "the tolerance of certain organ transplants,"[98] Derrida stresses the self's more general lack of self-sufficiency and autonomy. Blackness similarly troubles humanism's body politics, its ontological values of purity and exceptionality, unraveling the "phantasmatico-theological"[99] character of the sovereign subject: "It is not some particular thing that is affected in autoimmunity but the self, the *ipse*, the *autos* that finds itself infected."[100] Being parahuman is living (with) blackness, in a state of dislocation, embracing we might say its fugitive sovereignty, a sovereignty at war with itself, with its metaphysics of self-possession (the self as a property relation):

> The paraontological distinction between blackness and blacks allows us no longer to be enthralled by the notion that blackness is a property that belongs to blacks . . . but also because ultimately it allows us to detach blackness from the question of (the meaning of) being. (205)[101]

Blackness as a pathogen is not looking for recognition or reinstatement in the fold of the immunized and immunizing human of white civil society.[102] It is decidedly not interested in reinvesting in the humanist subject. Rather, in operating alongside (*para*) the human, blackness compromises the human, de-completes its being—figures the inhuman—sickens and alters ontology, and infiltrates the culture of whiteness only to expose its fantasies of mastery and control, short-circuiting its framing, its racist machinery from within. Blackness as pathogen holds revolutionary promise: it "bears the potential to end this funeral reign with an animative breath" (194).

On this point, the advocates of black optimism, black nihilism, and Afro-Pessimism, are in agreement; the contemporary world is beyond rescue. The humanity of blacks cannot be returned. Again, black humanism—or a humanism inclusive of blacks—is not an option. If, for instance, historian and philosopher Paul Gilroy posits a redeeming "planetary humanism" that could address racial inequality and undo the "infrahumanity"[103] of blacks, the reification and denigration of blackness as less than human, Afro-

Pessimists argue that a transcendence of race—in the name of a universal humanity—is through and through a humanist fantasy, one that dangerously ignores the libidinal economy at work in white civil society, diminishing its destructive affective and psychic reach. Against prolonging the black humanist "romance with metaphysics," Warren emphasizes that the world's default ethos is that of antiblackness and as such it cannot be expected to yield any genuine remedy for black folks; quite the contrary, its humanist or liberal solutions compound "the negro problem": "There was no solution to the problem of antiblackness; it would continue without end, as long as the world exists. Furthermore, all the solutions presented rely on antiblack instruments to address antiblackness, a vicious and tortuous cycle that will only produce more pain and disappointment."[104] Wilderson vigorously repeats Fanon reiteration of Aimé Césaire's plea to his readers to bring about "the end of the world," which is the "only thing . . . worth the effort of starting."[105] But whereas for Wilderson "Blackness cannot be disimbricated from slavery,"[106] Moten can be seen as making the opposite claim— *blackness must be disimbricated from slavery.* "An agenda of total disorder"[107] is what blackness as a pathogen, as an autoimmune virus, promises and pleads for.

Ending the world entails ending the reign of the human. Black optimism, black nihilism, and Afro-Pessimism are then, to some degree, invested in a posthuman reconceptualization of the world. This is a world without antiblack violence as its dominant ethos, a posthuman world where the human is not defined by its opposition to the slave/black. How "we" bring about this seismic shift, this ontological revolution—a revolution in the ontology of world and the subject—remains both (necessarily) vague (since there is no posthuman blueprint to follow) and contested (again, who is the "we" making or calling for change)? Ontologies of an anti-racist/

posthuman future can only be teased out *via negativa*, through a discrediting of dominant models of critique.

Marxism and postcolonial theory are two models that Wilderson flatly dismisses for their complicity with antiblackness, its grammar of suffering, and its reliance on the human: "Marxist and postcolonial armed struggle," Wilderson maintains, "though radically destabilizing of the status quo, are also endeavors which, through their narrative capacity to assimilate 'universal' frameworks of liberation and redress, unwittingly work to reconstitute the paradigms they seek to destroy."[108] Wilderson isolates a tripartite structure in Marxist and postcolonial projects of emancipation:

> The arc of an emancipatory progression which ends in either equality, liberation, or redress, in other words, a narrative of liberation, is marked by the three generic moments that one finds in any narrative: a progression from equilibrium (the spatial-temporal point prior to oppression), disequilibrium (capitalist political economy or the arrival and residence taking of the settler), and equilibrium restored/reorganized/ or reimagined (the dictatorship of the proletariat or the settler's removal from one's land).[109]

For Marxism and postcolonialism, the world is restorable; its equilibrium can be set again. Their ontology of a future world is all-too-familiar. It is more of the same antiblackness: "Through their indisputably robust interventions, the world they seek to clarify and deconstruct is the world they ultimately mystify and renew."[110] That antiblackness is constitutive of the human and its symbolic order is never seriously considered. Marxists affirm a class-first worldview and treat antiblackness as an epiphenomenon of capitalism, while postcolonial theorists abstract or generalize from black suffering and antiblack violence to produce a new grammar of the oppressed.

Leftist ontologies of the future are doomed to reproduce the social death of black folks to the extent that they leave the fantasy of the human untouched. The cultural left, with its coalition-building ethos, has systematically downplayed the crushing reality of antiblackness. Marxism and postcolonialism are invested in reviving a more authentic/less alienated image of the human rather than being or becoming posthuman.[111] They project a universal subject for whom a return to plenitude is both possible and desirable, disregarding the positioning of blacks as those unworthy of metaphysical plenitude, "barred, *ab initio*, from narrative,"[112] constitutively condemned to a life of disequilibrium (another name for social death).[113] "Blackness is coterminous with slaveness: Blackness *is* social death: which is to say that there was never a prior meta-moment of plenitude, never Equilibrium: never a moment of social life."[114]

Thinking black ~~being~~ breeds a sense of critical desperation, critique "in the face of impossibility,"[115] calling for what Žižek describes as the "courage of hopelessness."[116] The available models are no solution; worse, on the one hand, society promises cures only to cruelly pacify its subjects ("it is through the promise of the cure that *the law of colonialism reaffirms itself*,"[117] as David Marriott reminds us); on the other, critical interpretive frameworks compound the problem of antiblack violence by further obfuscating black social death. Afro-Pessimism is a counter to any model of critique that seeks the reconciliation of whites and blacks without acknowledging the structural presence of antiblackness, without unsettling the human/slave divide—seeing it as the antagonism and structuring principle of civil society, uniting white and nonblacks in their claims of/to humanity. As do the Afro-Pessimists, Žižek argues that true change cannot emanate from *within* the coordinates of the existing ideological system. Žižek's own pessimism is on full display when he says that "the true courage is to admit that the light at the end of the tunnel is probably the headlight of another train approaching."[118] Afro-Pessimists arguably illustrate and enact their courage of hopelessness by denouncing humanist solutions to social injustices as literal and symbolic dead ends for blacks. The antiblack world of whites produces a pathological black ~~being~~. Fanon was perhaps the first to fully grasp this insight. "As painful as it is for us to have to say this," Fanon writes, "there is but one destiny for the black man. And it is white."[119] Ontology, put in the service of whiteness, *determines* the being of blackness as intrinsically inferior. Racist civil society produces a horizon of antiblackness for blacks, but this horizon itself is non-all (this is a point often overlooked by Afro-Pessimists). The *historical* ontology of blackness remains alterable. The courage of hopelessness consists in *first* seeing ontology as the problem, to see the problem of antiblackness *ontologically*.

The black ~~being~~ who emerges from white civil society is subsequently faced with three "options": besides simply accepting your lot—as a result of completely internalizing the white gaze—you can live with the pathology in the hope that one day your humanity will be recognized/restored; you can commit to a political program that promises to elevate your condition without thematizing the problem of black social death; or, lastly, you can acknowledge or affirm your pathology, your sickness, as quasi-proof of the rottenness of the system that has precisely produced it. In other words, you can make this psychic sickness—the fragmentation of your body—the paradoxical condition for a life-affirming and rebellious skepticism.[120] Fanon suggests this last option in the end to *Black Skin, White Masks* when he writes, "My final prayer: O my body, always make me a man who questions!"[121] To question in such a way is to place hope in negativity, to practice—now and in the future—the irreverent art of negativity, to decline the affective and cognitive lures of a symbolic order that helps lock social beings into their racial categories. Such lures can only cover up the deadlocks in the material world, the antagonisms inherent to civil society and capitalism. To question like Fanon is, then, to better confront or traverse the fantasies and pitfalls of the human ("the black man wants to be white. The white man is desperately trying to achieve *the rank of man*"[122]) and the libidinal economy that subtends it.

Coalitional Politics Otherwise

We can of course read this third option back into the second and contaminate it, so to speak. What would a political program that foregrounds skepticism look like? How would it imagine coalition-building's relation to blackness—and, by extension, the human—differently? These are key questions raised by Boots Riley's *Sorry to Bother You*, which departs in this from the tenets of Afro-Pessimism. Suspicion of cross-racial coalitions is rampant among Afro-Pessimists. For Wilderson and Sexton, solidarity movements have not fully served the interests of blacks. Their proclivity for analogies always risks "rendering equivalent slavery and other forms of oppression."[123] This runs the further risk of complicity with white civil society. An unacknowledged antiblackness would make the nonblack members of any coalition all too ready to betray the interest of their black comrades when the former's sociopolitical demands are met. The oppression of nonblacks remains an "intra-Human conflict,"[124] not a fundamental antagonism (white [human] vs. black [slave]). Take, for example, Wilderson's reluctance to endorse black-Palestinian solidarity:

> One of the things we need to deal with is the ways in which right reactionary white civil society and so-called progressive colored civil society really works to sever the black generation's

understanding of what happened in the past. So right now, pro-Palestinian people are saying, "Ferguson is an example of what is happening in Palestine, and y'all are getting what we're getting." That's just bullshit. First, there's no time period in which black police and slave domination have ever ended. Second, the Arabs and the Jews are as much a part of the black slave trade—the creation of blackness as social death—as anyone else. As I told a friend of mine, "yeah we're going to help you get rid of Israel, but the moment that you set up your shit we're going to be right there to jack you up, because anti-blackness is as important and necessary to the formation of Arab psychic life as it is to the formation of Jewish psychic life."[125]

On the human/slave divide, Palestinians, like every nonblack being, are unwilling to sacrifice their claim to sovereignty, their difference from blacks, to push back against their "negrophobogenesis"[126] (which they share with nonblacks, including their enemies—the Israelis), to let go of the affective rewards of not seeing themselves (and not being seen by the West) as slaves or subhumans. In short, the metaphysics of sovereignty necessarily breeds *negrophobia*.

Sorry to Bother You troubles the Afro-Pessimists' "absolutization of blackness"[127] and foreclosure of cross-racial coalition movements, pointing to ways black oppression and antiblack racism are not "beyond the realm of understanding"[128] and can serve as the basis for solidarity with others who are equally—but not identically—subhumanized by white civil society. Whereas Wilderson stresses the irreducibility of the plight of blacks to that of workers, insisting that "the dream of black accumulation and death" must be kept separate from "the dream of worker exploitation,"[129] *Sorry to Bother You* works to bring the two ideological dreams together.

Initially, Cassius "Cash" Green (Lakeith Stanfield) struggles to make sales. Though he follows the script given to him, his calls are systematically met with indifference or rudeness. His "luck" changes, however, when Langston (Danny Glover), his more seasoned coworker, shares with him the secret to telemarketing: one has to adopt one's "white voice." The secret obviously applies to nonwhite workers but not exclusively so. Since whites themselves have to cultivate their "white voice"—synonymous here with achieving "the rank of man," as Fanon put it—their whiteness is performed as well.[130] The inference is clear: capitalism meets racism. Cash's blackness— manifested in his "urban" voice—was getting in the way of economic success, or, more accurately, undermining his chances of meeting his basic economic needs for food and shelter (at the RegalView corporation, telemarketers get paid on commission, not salary). After repeated sales—after mastering whiteness/the white voice (dubbed by David Cross), or the ability to pass for white, a necessary condition for capitalist success—Cash is effectively deracialized[131] and receives a promotion to the prestigious position of "Power Caller." While regular telemarketers and Power Callers are both engaged in selling goods, Langston explains to Cash that they operate at radically incommensurable levels. Cash thinks he understands: "So, I guess comparing to what we doing to what they're doing is like apples to oranges." Langston corrects the analogy: "More like apples and the Holocaust." The evocation of the Holocaust is apt; it not only underscores the enormous economic disparity separating the telemarketer from the Power Caller but also associates the Holocaust with another example of moral catastrophe: the sale of slave labor (manpower from WorryFree).

Cash's rise through RegalView's ranks, however, is complicated by the efforts of his coworkers, who, spearheaded by Squeeze (Stephen Yeun), protest for better wages and threaten to unionize. Cash's activist girlfriend Detroit (Tessa Thompson) also takes part in the movement. As a Power Caller, Cash is put in charge of WorryFree's account (the corporation's motto: we sell power—manpower/ firepower). A few minutes into the film, we discover WorryFree's aggressive TV marketing campaign advertising comfort and satiety in exchange for lifetime employment. Neoliberalism's increasingly disenfranchised and destitute subjects are promised security and predictability. WorryFree is basically inculcating in its viewers— its would-be employees—a belief in voluntary servitude. This profitable company interpellates its audience as neoliberal subjects, transforming human beings into subjects ready "to turn [their life] into viable merchandise and put it up for sale."[132] Though a Senate committee has cleared WorryFree of slavery charges, the accusations persist, leading the company's CEO Steve Lift (Armie Hammer) to swiftly denounce them in an interview with Oprah: "The comparison to slavery is just ludicrous and offensive. . . . We're saving lives. It's all highlighted in my book." Voluntary servitude allegedly saves lives, like the life of Cash's uncle and landlord, who is facing repossession of his home.

Servitude is made in this campaign to represent a wise economic choice, a calculated move on the part of free, rational citizens to maximize their economic well-being. Why live with economic uncertainty, when WorryFree can guarantee food and shelter, protecting you from the vicissitudes of market forces? This is a new form of slavery—slavery 2.0—that purports to help people: Why suffer if you don't have to? Just *consent* to work indefinitely for WorryFree (bypassing the sale of the worker's labor power in traditional capitalism) for the satisfaction of your basic needs. The lure and danger of this message is highlighted in an exchange between Cash and Detroit. When Cash turns to ask Detroit what she thinks of WorryFree, her self-made earrings—reading "KILL KILL KILL/MURDER MURDER MURDER"—powerfully answer his earnest question even more than her verbal reply ("That's crazy!").

WorryFree is marketing life when it is practicing death; its business is the "dispossession of the future."[133]

To paraphrase Žižek, WorryFree is offering *slavery with a human face*. Being human and being slave are no longer mutually exclusive. This is capitalism experiencing a posthuman phase to the extent that the human as such is no longer elevated beyond all other kinds of beings. WorryFree's labor force consists of being-objects—accumulable and fungible—to be used indiscriminately and exchanged as a commodity. Within the capitalist landscape, individuals desperate for money are even willing to consent to their brutalization by going on the highly popular game show called *I Got the Shit Kicked Out of Me*, which exchanges money (and fleeting fame) for violent humiliation. In this consumerist society, human dignity is readily commodified and bought (and destroyed) for pure entertainment. Viewers enjoy the dehumanization of others: they are not only physically beaten, but also dunked in fecal matter. In *Sorry to Bother You*, the commercials for WorryFree and *I Got the Shit Kicked Out of Me* are often played back-to-back on the television, cementing their ideological affinities in the minds of the audience.

Is the political ontology decried by Afro-Pessimists, then, no longer operative? While it is tempting to see WorryFree as collapsing the humanist human/slave divide constitutive of white civil society, we must keep in mind the structural role of the white voice in their propaganda machine. Racial capitalism is undoubtedly still at work. Lift's neoliberal capitalism is one that returns to its imperialist roots. It is with good reasons that Achille Mbembe describes the effects of global capitalism as a "*Becoming Black of the world*,"[134] where only the obscenely wealthy are immune from their blackening, or exclusion from "a common humanity,"[135] from neoliberalism's labor of race and "biopolitics of disposability,"[136] that is, the voracious and intractable capitalist logic that racializes and utilizes humans as instruments, robbing them of their rights and protection—ontologically producing new slaves.

Sorry to Bother You gives this "becoming black of the world" a weird posthumanist twist when Cash discovers Lift's plan to inject his slave-workers with a formula that turns them into stronger, more vigorous, and productive horse-human hybrids: being *equi-sapiens* makes for a more lucrative source of capitalist exploitation. Still, Lift anticipates resistance from his workforce to come, fearing that they will demand more, that room and board for lifetime labor will have to be renegotiated. Lift decides to manage future acts of transgression by infiltrating the *equi-sapiens*, using Cash as a fake Martin Luther King (MLK), Jr. figure. Lift's proposal is that Cash masquerade as an MLK for *equi-sapiens* for five years, after which time he will receive a formula changing him back into a human. He will earn $100 million, and to sweeten the deal—recycling the racial stereotype of hypersexualized male black body—Lift assures him he will get to keep his "horse cock." Cash declines his offer and manages to expose WorryFree's nefarious plans by leaking a video displaying Lift's abuse of the *equi-sapiens*. The video, however, fails to produce public shame or financial damage to the corporation. Quite the contrary, WorryFree's shareholders make even more money and major media outlets dub Lift the latest tech genius.

WorryFree incarnates the changing face of capitalism. If global capitalism initially had a democratic character, enticing humans (i.e., nonblacks) with *formal* equality (which was and is always and necessarily at odds with its material expression), the neoliberal capitalism that turns WorryFree's reputation-ruining exposure into a business success story signals a new stage of capitalism, a regressive capitalism that cannibalizes blacks and whites alike. In light of neoliberalism's unfettered economic expansionism, Žižek describes the changing orientation of capitalist exploitation in the following terms:

> For Marx, capitalist exploitation has to take place in conditions of legal freedom and equality. That is to say, we all have the same rights formally and legally and we are free, but then, in effect, if you don't have money, you have to sell yourself and you are *exploited.* But now, I claim that worldwide capitalism can no longer sustain or tolerate this *global equality.* It's just too much.[137]

We might say that neoliberal capitalism is less and less inclined to discriminate between the human and the slave. WorryFree deems everyone disposable, fungible, and accumulable. The effects of this *becoming black of the world* attest to a permanent state of misery. "The spectacle of neoliberal misery," as Henry Giroux eloquently puts it, "is too great to deny anymore and the only mode of control left by corporate-controlled societies is violence, but a violence that is waged against the most disposable such as immigrant children, protesting youth, the unemployed, the new precariat and black youth."[138] Neoliberalism debilitates life and creates the misery of which WorryFree ironically purports to be the human(e) solution: slavery 2.0. But as Lift fears, proletarian resistance is coming. The *becoming black of the world* is not a cry of despair and resignation but a call aimed at reinvigorating a critique of racial thinking in the age of neoliberalism. *Sorry to Bother You* repeats Moten's claim that blackness does not equate to social death, and it insists, with Mbembe, on "the promise of liberty and universal equality."[139]

No longer committed to WorryFree, Cash fully joins the protest movement and succeeds in preventing any crossing of the picket line, leading RegalView to concede to the economic demands of the down-and-out telemarketers. A crucial factor in the success of the protests is Cash's freeing of the *equi-sapiens* from Lift's mansion. With their superior physical strength, the *equi-sapiens* neutralize the second wave of anti-riot police sent to crack down on the protests. A denouement is suggested when Cash and his fellow telemarketers prepare to return to work at RegalView. Cash has tempered his desires for material goods and now seems ready to return to his prior lifestyle, albeit with some marginal improvements: after the telemarketers at RegalView unionize, he gets paid a little more, he has a better car (he is no longer riding in a death trap), and his bedroom (the converted garage of his uncle's house) has a few additional perks (remnants of his capitalist lifestyle). But this moment of re-equilibrium is short-lived. In the final scenes of the film, we learn that Lift has tricked Cash into ingesting the formula and he is transformed before our eyes into an *equi-sapiens*.

With Cash's posthuman transmutation, *Sorry to Borrow You* declines the liberal solution of a return to a mildly improved civil society. It endorses the pessimism of the Afro-Pessimists that the world itself is the problem. RegalView, WorryFree, and the civil society that supports and is supported by them ought not to be reformed, but must be destroyed. Yet the film also deviates from the agenda of Afro-Pessimism in foregrounding cross-racial and multispecies solidarity. Antiblack violence is by no means minimized by *Sorry to Bother You*, nor is it the exclusive focus of the film. Or to put it in terms of Moten's approach, blackness works as a pathogen in the film, unsettling and challenging the control over black life, the hegemony of whiteness along with its affective attachment to the human, epitomized by the seductive force of the "white voice"—I can only invest, buy, and have confidence in a fantasized image of whiteness. The fantasy of the "white voice," in turn, teaches would-be racists to act on their implicit biases, to desire whiteness (the human like me) and fear blackness (the subhuman like them).

Whereas Wilderson works to disentangle the libidinal from the political economy (the slave is *not* the worker), *Sorry to Bother*

You keeps entangling, compelling its viewers to think about the relatedness of race and class. The film also complicates the Marxist terms of the debate. Fredric Jameson and others insist on the need to keep the struggle against domination separate from the fight against exploitation; the former is "an essentially moral or ethical [struggle] which leads to punctual revolts and acts of resistance rather than to the transformation of the mode of production as such."[140] Only a Marxist critique that exposes the naturalized violence of capitalist exploitation—a violence rendered natural, invisible, or unavoidable for the uncritical eye—can yield meaningful changes. The obvious danger here is to frame the struggle against antiblackness as a struggle exclusively against domination, rendering exploitation as such constitutively nonracial, purely economic. Detroit's solo art performance reminds us that capitalism from its inception was racial. Detroit's body stands for a fertile Africa, the site of capitalism's pillaging, its founding and ongoing violence. Life under capitalism was and is a "life shaped by exploitation" and gratuitous violence. After decrying the West's mining of coltan (a mineral used for smartphones and other lightweight electronics) in the Congo, Detroit, switching to her own "white voice" (featuring the British accent of Lily James), urges her mostly white and rich art-loving audience to throw bullet casings, cell phones, and goat blood at her almost-bare body, repeating the primal scene of racial subjugation, mimicking capitalism's exploitation-domination of black bodies and African minerals.[141]

Sorry to Bother You invites us to read WorryFree's neoliberalism through the lens of racial capitalism, staging for us how exploitation and domination were intrinsically linked from the start for blacks and are now becoming more so for nonblacks. WorryFree embodies and practices a politics of enslaveability. It brings to light capitalism's irresistible compulsion to extract and commodify: "the compulsion to put things in order as a precondition for extracting their inner value. It is the compulsion to categorize, to separate, to measure and to name, to classify and to establish equivalences between things and between things and persons, persons and animals, animals and the so-called natural, mineral, and organic world."[142] The animalization of blacks becomes a generalizable condition. If the first *equi-sapiens* were created from black beings, WorryFree's "new miracle" [143] formula is markedly available to all. The becoming *equi-sapiens* of the world reflects Lift's desire to transform his labor force from slaves into animals, epitomizing the phantasmatic desires of global capitalism: a workforce that has the endurance of animals (capable of working long hours, thus increasing profit margins) and the skills of humans (able to adapt to new environments and follow complex sets of rules).

Against this dystopian future, where the ontology of *all* humans is, in principle, reducible to a commodity (human beings are human *resources*), *Sorry to Bother You* does not yield to the humanist temptation: a depiction of abject black/animality (the much maligned and racialized other locked in its identity of victim), followed by a call for the revival or defense of the human in the age of neoliberal genetics (the Habermas-Fukuyama answer, as we saw in Chapter 1). Being human is part of the problem. It is at the origins of antiblackenss; as M. Shadee Malaklou puts it, the black other reflects anxieties about "Man's prehistorical or human-animal self."[144] But human privilege is, the film acknowledges, hard to let go. After the *equi-sapiens* rescue Cash and his fellow strikers, there is moment of solidarity, an acknowledgment of a shared commitment—"same struggle, same fight," as Squeeze puts it, that is revealed to be fleeting, as the pull of the status quo quickly reasserts itself. Cash is ready to return to RegalView and his solidarity with the *equi-sapiens* is short-lived. Yet, as already noted, *Sorry to Borrow You* refuses to end here. Reworking the classic topos of the dehumanization of human beings, the film's response to the fact of *equi-sapiens* is no humanist lamentation (humans aren't animals, and thus should not be treated as such) nor is it a plea for more humane treatment of the workers (and human rights extended to *equi-sapiens*—meaning their ethical domestication, the liberal-humanist solution). Rather, it manifests a desire to go beyond the human altogether. This traversing of the human—the affirmation of being posthuman—is synonymous with an openness to blackness and its paraontology.

Destroying the Human

What is blackness? It is the improper of ontology, a pathogen at odds with political ontology; as "the anoriginal displacement of ontology" (194), blackness is what or who remains, a reminder that the proper of the human is a phantasmatic lie. It is a commitment to *"the possibility of a non-exclusionary improvisation of the human."*[145] Or to put it more polemically, destroying a fetishized vision of the human is what blackness is after. If, as Moten argues, such paraontological unruliness is at times lost in Fanon's meditations on blackness—where blackness gets pathologized much too quickly, and its futures foreclosed[146]—one can supplement such reflections by accounting for a blackness that disidentifies with both the human (the white fantasy of completeness; the masculine figure of exception—the one who has access to full enjoyment) and black ~~being~~ (the white fantasy of nothingness; a being resigned to a life of social death), and instead claims "an irremediable homelessness common to the colonized, the enslaved, and the enclosed" (150). Blackness thrives in the mode of incompleteness, driven by a thirst for the impure, so reminiscent of that feminine logic of the non-all (142).

If whiteness is self-interestedly invested in the immunitarian demands of the human, blackness affirms and produces monsters—"insofar as blackness comes from nothing it is something after all,

the commonness of the improper."[147] The impropriety of blackness
is *not* a property of blacks. Moten boldly aligns it with society's
marginalized figures, embodying the "part of no-part," the symbolic
order's undercommons:

> What is named in the name of blackness is an undercommon
> disorder that has always been there, that is retroactively located
> there, that is embraced by the ones who stay there while living
> somewhere else. . . . Stolen life disorders positive value just as
> surely as it is not equivalent to social death or absolute dereliction.
> (150–1)

> The parontological force that is transmitted in the long chain of
> life and death performances that are the concern of black studies is
> horribly misunderstood if it is understood as exclusive. Everyone
> whom blackness claims, which is to say everyone, can claim
> blackness.[148]

In *Sorry to Bother You* blackness is represented or rather claimed in
the various figures belonging to the undercommons,[149] the commons
of the "part of no-part": Cash (a black man), Detroit (a black woman),
Squeeze (a male person of color), and the *equi-sapiens*. This lineup
clashes with Wilderson's, who prefers to maintain distance between
blacks (civil society's would-be slave) and nonblacks. And yet in
his provocative "Gramsci's Black Marx: Whither the Slave in Civil
Society?" Wilderson—while repeatedly insisting on the ruse of
analogy when it comes to blacks—does offer one analog: the cow.
Blacks are like cows in a slaughterhouse. The exploited workers in
the slaughterhouse might get some reprieve (better pay, better work
conditions), but the cows are not merely exploited. Rather, they are
being accumulated and marked for destruction/consumption. Blacks
in civil society come to a similar necropolitical end: "death of the
black body is . . . foundational to the life of American civil society."[150]

In other words, there is as much of a chance of annulling or jamming civil society's antiblackness as there is in redeeming slaughterhouse cows. Struggle for blacks is not simply futile, it is not nonexistent. Blacks do not have a seat at the table (*pace* Gramsci: civil society for blacks is not a site of struggle, for waging a "war of position"). From racial slavery to the US carceral system, the "total objectification"[151] and animality of the blacks persists: "The chief difference today, compared to several hundred years ago, is that today our bodies are desired, accumulated, and warehoused—like the cows."[152]

In his first encounter with the *equi-sapiens*, Cash sees them as fundamentally other, as faceless others, not unlike the *Muselmann* of Auschwitz or the slaves of the Middle Passage. He is repulsed by them. The extra-humanity of the *equi-sapiens* destabilizes his investment in the imago of the human: the self as not-animal. The *equi-sapiens* appear to Cash as uncanny, crisis inducing, shaking "any straightforward sense of what is inside and what is outside" of the (proper) human.[153] The *equi-sapiens* are unbearable neighbors— nonbeings with whom no relation, "no symmetrical dialogue, mediated by the symbolic Order, is possible"[154]—and are experienced in the register of the Real. They are abject beings whose altered human features affectively and cognitively overwhelm him. Cash's humanist sensibilities register a horror: Who or what did he just encounter? This reaction is understandable, for what causes him to fear the *equi-sapiens* is ingrained in the very fabric of civil society, in its humanist and racist social scripts: value the human/white, fear the subhuman/ black. Cash fears what his racist society expects him to fear. If Cash's "white voice" enables him to phantasmatically transcend, at least temporarily, his black being, becoming a disembodied figure of whiteness, after his moral conscience kicks in, after he declines WorryFree's slavery 2.0 project, Cash envisions a return to the status quo: telemarketing with a *human* face (it is uncertain whether he will continue to use his "white voice" moderately for sales, since he was abysmal at his job without it).

Cash's posthuman metamorphosis takes place in the comforts of domesticity, in his upgraded garage, throwing a wrench into his readjustment to a pre–Power Caller life and changing his plans radically. The life that awaited him before his transformation was more of the same, a somewhat pacified and compliant life that would effectively preserve the social coordinates of his social ~~being~~ (social death). In the final scene of *Sorry to Bother You*, Cash arrives at Lift's mansion, where we see his fully transformed *equi-sapiens* face on the security video monitor. He says to a puzzled Lift: "I'm Cassius Green calling on behalf of stomp-a-mudhole-in-yo-ass.com. Sorry to bother you." The video monitor shows Cash subsequently grabbing the camera with one hand, resulting in video snow. Cash has ripped the camera off and is about to breach the mansion's front door when the film cuts to black.

If the *equi-sapiens* materializes the racialized animality of blacks, Cash's metamorphosis materializes his own abyssal dimension. In being posthuman, Cash discovers himself as a neighbor,[155] acting in a way that he could not have anticipated. It is true that his revolutionary call to arms was triggered by an event not of his making, yet what actually followed from his involuntary transformation was by no means obvious or certain. There were at least two competing options: he could have reconsidered Lift's initial plan (now that he has changed, he could accept the deal—more money in exchange for retransformation along with the bonus of a "horse cock"), or he could have disappeared in shame, deciding to live in the shadows of civil society with his *semblables* (fearing for their lives, akin to the runaway slaves of old). No. He strikes back at WorryFree's CEO. Cash's mutation inspires him to act in defiance of the collective unconscious and in solidarity with the other *equi-sapiens*. Rather than identifying the *equi-sapiens* exclusively with blacks (à la Wilderson), then, Riley's *Sorry to Bother You* enacts a celebratory defetishization of the human and its grammar—meaning whiteness, along with its libidinal and economic charms—by making the *equi-sapiens'* blackness, its paraontological force, not the basis for a new ideological fantasy, but instead an engine for political disorder and social justice, aspiring for an interspecies community *à venir*. Class struggle—what Lift dreadfully feared—is knocking at the human door.[156] Exploitation and domination may not be one and the same problem—but treating anti-capitalist struggle and anti-racist struggle in isolation, keeping them analytically separated, serves a separatist agenda and can only weaken a revolutionary ethos by obfuscating their deep entanglement in today's racial-speciesist capitalism. *Animots of the world unite.*

Conclusion
Inhuman Posthumanism

The first thing to note here is how the rise of posthuman agents and the anthropocene epoch are two aspects of the same phenomenon: at exactly the time when humanity becomes the main geological factor threatening the entire balance of the life of Earth, it begins to lose its basic features and transforms itself into posthumanity. The question that underlies this problem is: how are capitalism and the prospect of posthumanity related?

SLAVOJ ŽIŽEK[1]

In the age of ontology, being posthuman takes many forms. From cyborgs to blackness, from animals to objects, what characterizes the posthuman attitude is, first, an irresistible passion for being, an insatiable hunger for exteriority, and, second, a deep mistrust of the humanist subject of philosophy. In contradistinction to transhumanism, posthumanism—understood as an ethico-political plea for thinking through the implications of the posthuman condition—leaves behind the projects of human perfection. The aforementioned avatars of the posthuman are at war with the human. And yet what the human means varies a great deal for each figure. The human is a phantasm, especially when it imagines itself as exceptional. In justifying its distinction, what it deems proper of itself, the human—as presented and propagated by humanists and Enlightenment philosophers—denigrates its others, its rejects and inferiors, the non- or subhuman. The frontal attack of the anti-humanism of 1968 philosophy proved insufficient. The human in humanism (still) stands sovereign over all of its racialized, gendered, or subjugated others.

Discrediting humanism's most cathected object—the subject—is arguably what ties together the posthuman agents studied in this book. Against this obsession with overcoming the subject, however, a psychoanalytically informed poshumanism points to an alternative deployment of subjectivity, one that in fact decouples it from the pristine and sovereign image of the human. This is Lacan's lesson, a lesson to which Žižek repeatedly returns: "[Lacan] is in search of a point at which we enter the dimension of the 'inhuman,' a point at which 'humanity' disintegrates, so that all that remains is a pure subject."[2] This inhuman subject, which throws into crisis the very idea of the proper, is clearly not the familiar Cartesian subject as a *res cogitans* nor does it conform to self-aggrandizing humanist rhetoric. But surprisingly this subject—the subject of negativity—has been ignored or simply excluded by the posthumanist champions of flat ontology. Having rooted out the subject tout court, why bother with its psychoanalytic rendition? Why insist on the inhuman subject when the posthuman is precisely supposed to be post-subject?

Well, for several reasons. First, this is not your humanist's subject, Lacan has no truck with philosophy's cognitive hubris; his subject declines to occupy humanism's authoritative position, the "subject supposed to know." The whole enterprise of psychoanalysis is to dispel this idea in the analysand and bring him or her to realize that "there is no guarantee for one's desire in the big Other."[3] Second, it complicates the (post)humanist blackmail, "either you're for or against the subject." Humanists and anti-correlationalists offer us a false choice. Psychoanalysis "answers" this blackmail with an uncompromising "Yes, Please!" Third, its political promise lies in its negative universality. This last point also allows us to better frame Žižek's question from the epigraph concerning the vexed relation of posthumanism to capitalism. The Anthropocene—an unavoidable fact of the posthuman condition—foregrounds humanity's role in the order of things while simultaneously diminishing its potential to address the crisis in the stated order. But what is capitalism's contribution to the Anthropocene? Is it a hermeneutic rival? Should we replace Anthropocene with Capitalocene?

The term "Capitalocene" corrects the Anthropocene's ideological function: "The 'Anthropocene' displaces the origins of the contemporary crisis onto the human being as species rather than as capital. It reinforces what capital wants to believe of itself: that human 'nature,' not capital, has precipitated today's planetary instability."[4] What types of posthuman agents would the Capitalocene generate? In many ways, *Being Posthuman* has been supplementing the Anthropocence with the Capitalocene, focusing from the start on the politics of the *commons*. Chapters 1 and 2 looked at the matter of inclusion: whose voice counts in the debate concerning future ontologies. We saw how an ontological crisis in the human opens up alternative ways of imagining the human: being human as non-all, incomplete. What disables enables.

The question of the animal exerts additional pressure on the human, pushing against an anthropocentric vision of the commons. Anthropocentrism is a hermeneutics, a way of interpreting the world, seeing it as something exclusively available to us. This is human privilege. Thinking humans *with* animals allows for a more generous appreciation of what constitutes a social good, a vision at odds with the predominant neoliberal ethos of privatization and commodification, extraction, and expansion. What about the object? Among the proponents of object-oriented ontology, labor almost never comes into play in the making of objects. This is not to say that the created object is determined by its creator (e.g., a novel may, and often does, exceed authorial intentions). Take as an example Harman's musings on the hammer. The point is more about the *human* involvement that brought this hammer into being—the conditions of labor for the production of such a hammer. It is because of such a lacuna that critics have rightly accused Harman of hypostatizing and fetishizing objects, arguing that his brand of ontology is complicit with the dominant capitalist logic, embodying, as it were "the metaphysics of capitalism."[5]

Jane Bennett's New Materialism seems better situated to politicize objects—the "force of things." Bennett takes up Jacques Rancière as one of her main interlocutors in *Vibrant Matter*. It is in particular Rancière's formulation, *le partage du sensible*—"the distribution/partition/sharing of the sensible"[6]—that interests her. *Le partage du sensible* is "the system of self-evident facts of sense perception that simultaneously discloses the existence of something in common and the delimitations that define the respective parts and positions within it."[7] In this distribution, partitioning, or sharing of the sensible, what is at stake are "spaces, times, and forms of activity."[8] Whereas the police order works to legitimize and reproduce the social status quo (with all its inequalities), politics for Rancière names the contestation of *le partage du sensible*; it is at its core the struggle for "a new landscape of the possible."[9] For Rancière, emancipation begins with the transformation of "the frame of our perception and the dynamism of our affects," "when we challenge the opposition between viewing and acting: when we understand that the self-evident facts that structure the relations between saying, seeing and doing themselves belong to the structure of domination and subjection."[10]

Is anthropocentric humanism, then, a regime of power, a particular kind of arrangement of *le partage du sensible*, a form of intelligibility that values human lives (some more than others—

whites over blacks) and devalues the nonhuman (again, some more than others—animates over inanimates)? If so, is posthumanism a dissensus, a struggle for a putatively *posthuman* landscape—a politicized landscape that would question what is given, the primacy of the human, the "common sense" of humanism? Bennett recounts a disappointing exchange with Rancière on this very question:

> When asked in public whether he thought that an animal or a plant or a drug or a (nonlinguistic) sound could disrupt the police order, Rancière said no: he did not want to extend the concept of the political that far; nonhumans do not qualify as participants in a demos; the disruption effect must be accompanied by the desire to engage in reasoned discourse.[11]

But Bennett reads Rancière against Rancière (as we do as well in imagining the cyborg as a candidate for the "part of no-part" and the animal as neighbor). Objects do participate; they rise up and speak (back) to humans. Nonhumans too are deemed capable of altering the human-centered "field of experience,"[12] of troubling the unjust "distribution of places and roles," and of contesting the "order of the visible and the sayable."[13] If objects in Rancière's political schema are excluded from playing a constitutive role in the *demos*, they are afforded full rights—treated as democratic agents—in Bennett's nonanthropocentric model of democracy.

Bennett's objections to Rancière's anthropocentric biases vis-à-vis the subject of politics are by no means unfounded. Rancière even confesses his generalized reluctance to take up the question of the subject in any systematic way, a question he considers "monstrous":

> Who plays the part of the subject who incarnates, represents or symbolizes work: that is the way in which, in the end, the "question of work" has presented itself for me. It is also the way in which I

have been able to address that monstrous question that has always terrorized me in the same measure as my contemporaries made it paramount: the "theory of the subject." This explains why I have only ever addressed it but from the side, through a specific aspect; namely, the relationship between subject and identity.[14]

But whereas Rancière hesitates to theorize the subject, having been terrorized by it, Bennett dispenses with the subject altogether, sidestepping its monstrosity for the more enchanting nonhuman. The pragmatic politics of Bennett's vibrant materiality is through and through inclusive; it declines to distinguish and prioritize between human/nonhuman, animate/inanimate, living/dead, and so on. It is an emphatic invitation to her readers to be "in parliament with things."[15] This is what being posthuman is about.

There is, however, something deeply depoliticizing about Bennett's posthumanist brand of politics. It is almost exclusively concerned with *domination*, with delegitimizing or jamming the anthropocentric cultural machine. A critique of exploitation and *the becoming black of the world* takes a back seat to the ethical reformation of democracy—a democracy with nonhuman faces. Is an anti-racist critique, an insistence on racial capitalism's Excluded and Included, still too indebted to an anthropocentric framework (no matter how critical it pretends to be)? A re-enchantment of things (an appreciation of the vitality of matter), a jettisoning of hegemonic modes of thought (beyond the subject/object distinction and its corollaries), and a general clamping down on modernity's compulsion to dominate (the nonhuman in all of its guises), are all that is needed in Bennett's view to transform in a significant way *le partage du sensible*. To paraphrase Jameson, it is easier to imagine an end to the humanist world than an end to capitalism; it is easier to imagine a posthuman world that shares power with things than a genuine alternative to global capitalism.

But to be clear, the shift in focus to nonhuman factors is not to be disparaged. Quite the contrary, it is itself an interpretively valuable move. As we argued in Chapter 3, the turn to objects/things rightly unsettles the primacy of the *humanist* subject and catalyzes inventive ways of seeing. Žižek, for his part, singles out Bennett's wider account of how actants relate to one another, which leads her to envisage a polluted trash site as an assemblage: "How not only humans but also the rotting trash, worms, insects, abandoned machines, chemical poisons, and so on each play their (never purely passive) role."[16] Žižek adds: "There is an authentic theoretical and ethico-political insight in such an approach."[17] Cultivating an ecological eye furthers the labor of ideology critique insofar as it is a strictly human-centered perspective that fails to discern the full impact of the Capitalocene.

Always look at the Symbolic with "inhuman eyes" is the motto of a psychoanalytic posthumanism. The critical insight that this approach yields however risks becoming eclipsed if the inhuman dimension is neutralized and if flat ontology, embarrassed by the tainted *human* subject, removes it from discussion and consideration, or simply disavows its presence. Psychoanalysis's inhuman subject—the subject released from its human coordinates—is to be affirmed but not fetishized. Being posthuman is learning to live with humanity's immanent and intrinsic inhumanity. And yet what *is*, the ontological given, is not to be programmatically endorsed, carelessly celebrated, or endlessly reproduced. An ethics of psychoanalysis addresses "the inhuman core of humanity [and] fearlessly stands up to the latent monstrosity of being human, the diabolic dimension which erupted in the phenomena broadly covered by the label 'Auschwitz,'"[18] or by what we call the Middle Passage. As argued in Chapter 4, blackness as paraontological might be another name for this inhuman lodged aside the ontological human, where humanity can only emerge against an "impenetrable ground of 'inhuman,' of something which remains opaque and resists inclusion in any narrative reconstitution of what counts as 'human.'"[19] This monstrosity—abhorred by humanists, vigilant guardians of the proper, and projected onto blackness and animality, the improper and the impure as such—is not an "absolute ill or evil" (to recall Derrida's musings on autoimmunity); it is a *pharmakon*, a disease and a cure. Without inhumanity, with absolute humanity, the neighbor, fully gentrified, would only be experienced as an extension of ourselves. We, in turn, would be "reduced to being puppets of the big Other."[20]

But the subject repeatedly fails to coincide with its symbolic rendering. Ontology without its vicissitudes remains a timeless humanist fantasy. An inhuman posthumanism takes up this abyss of impenetrability not as a curse but as a blessing.[21] This humanist scandal—the failure of humanism (and of whiteness and speciesism) to contain the human (and to exclude/immunize itself from the non-subhuman)—allows for a reconfiguration of the human, for the inclusion of the inhuman in its scope. Against humanism's attachment to sovereignty and self-transparency, an inhuman posthumanism insists on the question of the neighbor—who is my neighbor? who or what is the neighbor of the human?—on the neighbor's constitutive strangeness, a universality of strangers and strangeness that implicates us all. *What does the other want from me?* is a most pressing and enigmatic question—an inhuman question—that no posthumanism can afford to ignore or find comfort in answering definitively.

Notes

Introduction

1 Michel de Montaigne, *The Complete Essays of Montaigne*, trans. Donald Frame (Stanford: Stanford University Press, 1957), 787. From *The Complete Essays of Montaigne* by Frame, Donald M. (translator). Copyright (c) 1943 by Donald Frame. Renewed (c) 1971, 1976. (c) 1948 by the Board of Trustees of the Leland Stanford University. Renewed (c) 1957, 1958. All rights reserved. Henceforth, all references to this edition will be stated parenthetically in the text.

2 Giorgio Agamben, *The Open: Man and Animal*, trans. Kevin Attell (Stanford: Stanford University Press, 2004), 26. From *The Open: Man and Animal* by Agamben, Giorgio. Translated by Kevin Attell. Copyright (c) 2002 by Bollati Boringhieri. English translation (c) 2004 by the Board of Trustees of the Leland Stanford Junior University. All rights reserved.

3 Rosi Braidotti, *The Posthuman* (Cambridge: Polity Press, 2013), 5.

4 Richard Grusin designates as a "nonhuman turn" a motley of approaches "engaged in decentering the human in favor of a turn toward and a concern for the nonhuman, understood variously in terms of animals, affectivity, bodies, materiality, or technologies" (Richard Grusin, "Introduction," in *The Nonhuman Turn*, ed. Richard Grusin [Minneapolis: University of Minnesota Press, 2015], vii).

5 Vincent Descombes, "Apropos of the 'Critique of the Subject' and the Critique of this Critique," in *Who Comes after the Subject?* ed. Eduardo Cadava, Peter Conor, and Jean-Luc Nancy (London: Routledge, 1991), 132.

6 Pico della Mirandola, *On the Dignity of Man*, trans. Charles Glenn Wallis (Indianapolis: Hackett Publishing, 1998), 5.

7 Agamben, *The Open*, 29.

8 Agamben, *The Open*, 29.

9 Agamben, *The Open*, 15.

10 Agamben, *The Open*, 26.

11 Agamben, *The Open*, 30.

12 Agamben, *The Open*, 30.

13 Thomas Greene, "The Flexibility of the Self in Renaissance Literature," in *The Disciplines of Criticism*, ed. Peter Demetz, Thomas Greene, and Lawry Nelson Jr. (New Haven: Yale University Press, 1968), 249. Erasmus's epigram is also quoted by Greene. For Erasmus, children capture best the human potential for self-fashioning since they "possess that natural flexibility which enables them to bend in any direction, are not as yet enslaved by bad habits, and are readily inclined to imitate whatever is suggested to them" (Desiderius Erasmus, "On the Education for Children," in *Collected Works of Erasmus*, vol. 26 [Toronto: University of Toronto Press, 1985], 318).

14 Take for example Guillaume Budé for whom "To 'make' man is to achieve in him the perfection of his species, so that he holds the knowledge of things human and divine" (Guillaume Budé, *L'Etude des Lettres. Principes pour sa juste et commode institution. De studio literarum recte et commode instituendo*, ed. Marie-Madelaine de La Garanderie [Paris: Les Belles lettres, 1988], 100, my translation).

15 The Dominican friar Bartolomé de Las Casas is an exception to this dehumanizing trend, seeing in the native Americans the great possibility of spiritual transformation. Las Casas describes the indigenous population as ready-made for conversion: "They are very clean in their persons, with alert, intelligent minds, docile and open to doctrine, very apt to receive our holy Catholic faith, to be endowed with virtuous customs, and to behave in a godly fashion" (Bartolomé de Las Casas, *The Devastation of the Indies: A Brief Account*, trans. Herma Briffault [Baltimore: Johns Hopkins University Press, 1992], 28–9). To be assimilated to the Christian faith—through exposure to Spanish Catholic evangelization—is thus tantamount to an ontological upgrade. Las Cases rejected the view that the Indians were ontologically fixed in their baseness and inferiority (as many, drawing on Aristotle's ontology, felt). He considers them, on the contrary, an alter ego and thus worthy of conversion. If Las Casas upholds the fantasy of sameness (via conversion) in his rehabilitation of the Cannibals, Montaigne complicates this rhetoric of sameness by disclosing the unsettling aspects that tie Europeans and Indians together.

16 Eric Nellis, *Shaping the New World: African Slavery in the Americas, 1500–1888* (Toronto: University of Toronto Press, 2013), 9.

17 See John O'Brien, "'Le Propre de l'Homme': Reading Montaigne's 'Des Cannibales' in Context," *Forum for Modern Language Studies* 53, no. 2 (2016): 220–34.

18 Matthew Calarco, *Zoographies: The Question of the Animal from Heidegger to Derrida* (New York: Columbia University Press, 2008), 93.

19 Agamben, *The Open*, 37.

20 Agamben, *The Open*, 37. Agamben distinguishes two variants of the anthropological machine: an ancient and a modern. The former, at work in the Renaissance, produces the subhuman "by the humanization of an animal"; the latter is post-Darwinian and consists in the animalization of the human, "by isolating the non-human within the human" (Agamben, *The Open*, 37).

21 Slavoj Žižek, *The Parallax View* (Cambridge: MIT Press, 2006), 22.

22 Slavoj Žižek, *Less than Nothing: Hegel and the Shadow of Dialectical Materialism* (New York: Verso, 2012), 166.

23 Slavoj Žižek, "Neighbors and Other Monsters: A Plea for Ethical Violence," in *The Neighbor: Three Inquiries in Political Theology*, ed. Slavoj Žižek, Eric L. Santner, and Kenneth Reinhard (Chicago: University of Chicago, 2006), 160.

24 Slavoj Žižek, *In Defense of Lost Causes* (New York: Verso, 2008), 17.

25 Judith Shklar, *Ordinary Vices* (Cambridge: Harvard University Press, 1984), 8. Shklar reads Montaigne as announcing liberalism, whereas I see liberalism as gentrifying Montaigne's unsettling psychoanalytic insight of the inhuman core of humanity.

26 René Descartes, *Discourse on Method and Meditations on First Philosophy*, trans. Donald A. Cress (Indianapolis: Hackett Publishing, 1998), 35.

27 René Descartes, *Meditations, Objections, and Replies*, ed. Roger Ariew and Donald Cress (Indianapolis: Hackett Publishing, 2006), 58.

28 Julien Offray de la Mettrie, *Man Is a Machine*, trans. Richard A. Watson and Maya Rybalka (Indianapolis: Hackett Publishing, 1994), 70. In his eighteenth-century dialogue *Rameau's Nephew*, Denis Diderot's protagonist voices La Mettrie's intimate link between mood and hunger, underscoring the degree to which his intestines govern his behavior: "Who would want

to subject himself to play such a part," he says, "unless it be a poor wretch who finds in it twice or thrice a week the means to quell the tumult of his intestines?" (Denis Diderot, *Rameau's Nephew and Other Works*, trans. Jacques Barzun and Ralph H. Bowen [Indianapolis: Hackett Publishing, 2001], 41).

29 Mary Shelley, *Frankenstein: The 1818 Text, Contexts, Criticism*, ed. J. Paul Hunter (New York: Norton, 2012), 32.

30 Shelley, *Frankenstein*, 33.

31 N. Katherine Hayles, *How We Became Posthuman: Virtual Bodies in Cybernetics, Literature, and Informatics* (Chicago: University of Chicago Press, 1999), 287. Hayles is commenting on Hans Moravec's *Mind Children: The Future of Robot and Human Intelligence*, skeptically assessing his phantasmatic dream of conceivably "download[ing] human consciousness into a computer" (Hayles, *How We Became Posthuman*, 1).

32 Neil Badmington, *Alien Chic: Posthumanism and the Other Within* (New York: Routledge, 2004), 111.

33 "Being-in-itself is never either possible or impossible. It *is*. This is what consciousness expresses in anthropomorphic terms by saying that being is superfluous (*de trop*)—that is, that consciousness absolutely can not derive being from anything, either from another being, or from a possibility, or from a necessary law. Uncreated, without reason for being, without any connection with another being, being-in-itself is *de trop* for eternity" (Jean-Paul Sartre, *Being and Nothingness: An Essay on Phenomenological Ontology*, trans. Hazel E. Barnes [New York: Philosophical Library, 1956], lxvi).

34 Jean-Paul Sartre, *Existentialism Is a Humanism*, trans. Carol Macomber (New Haven: Yale University Press, 2007), 22.

35 Louis Althusser, "Ideology and Ideological State Apparatuses (Notes towards an Investigation)," in *Mapping Ideology*, ed. Slavoj Žižek (New York: Verso, 1994), 130.

36 Althusser is trying here to purify Marx of any humanist residue, evidenced in the latter's model of ideology critique as demystification of an individual's *false consciousness*. An anti-humanist ideology critique does not limit itself to the conscious beliefs of individuals; rather, it is attentive to the ways ideology operates most frequently at the level of the unconscious, soliciting and securing our libidinal investment: "the fundamental level of ideology . . . is not of an illusion masking the real state of things but that of an

(unconscious) fantasy structuring our social reality itself" (Slavoj Žižek, *The Sublime Object of Ideology* [New York: Verso, 1991], 33). Ideology secures the reproduction of the status quo, the belief in my importance as a human being (especially if economically privileged, white, male, heterosexual, able-bodied, etc.).

37 Jacques Derrida, "The Ends of Man," in *Margins of Philosophy*, trans. Alan Bass (Chicago: University of Chicago Press, 1982), 115.

38 Derrida, "The Ends of Man," 116. For Heidegger's own response to Sartre's appropriation of his philosophy, see Martin Heidegger, "Letter on Humanism," in *Basic Writings*, ed. David Farrell Krell (New York: Harper and Row, 1977), 189–242. Derrida's critique is not so easily applicable to Simone de Beauvoir's use of Corbin's translation. In her case, Beauvoir, in *The Second Sex*, critically juxtaposes "feminine reality" with "human reality," distancing herself from Sartre and his philosophy of transcendence. See Simone de Beauvoir, *The Second Sex*, trans. Constance Borde and Sheila Malovany-Chevallier (New York: Alfred Knopf, 2010), 17.

39 Anson Rabinbach, *In the Shadow of Catastrophe: German Intellectuals between Apocalypse and Enlightenment* (Berkeley: University of California Press, 1997), 122.

40 Michel Foucault, *The Order of Things: An Archaeology of the Human Sciences*, trans. Alan Sheridan (New York: Vintage, 1970), 342.

41 Jacques Derrida, "Structure, Sign, and Play in the Discourse of the Human Sciences," in *Writing and Difference* (Chicago: University of Chicago Press, 1978), 280.

42 Slavoj Žižek, *The Incontinence of the Void: Economico-Philosophical Spandrels* (Cambridge: MIT Press, 2017), 232.

43 "Mastery begins . . . through the power of naming, of imposing and legitimating appellations" (Jacques Derrida, *Monolingualism of the Other; Or, The Prosthesis of Origin*, trans. Patrick Mensah [Stanford: Stanford University Press, 1998], 39).

44 Roland Barthes, "Death of the Author," in *Image, Text, Music*, trans. Stephen Heath (New York: Hill and Wang, 1977), 142–8.

45 Michel Foucault, "What Is an Author?" in *The Foucault Reader*, ed. Paul Rabinow (New York: Pantheon Books, 1984), 118.

46 Quentin Meillassoux, *After Finitude: An Essay on the Necessity of Contingency*, trans. Ray Brassier (New York: Continuum, 2008), 7.

47 Meillassoux, *After Finitude*, 124, 119.

48 Meillassoux, *After Finitude*, 5. Meillassoux elaborates further on his concept: "Correlationism rests on an argument as simple as it is powerful, and which can be formulated in the following way: No X without givenness of X, and no theory about X without a positing of X. If you speak about something, you speak about something that is given to you, and posited by you. Consequently, the sentence: 'X is,' means: 'X is the correlate of thinking' in a Cartesian sense. That is: X is the correlate of an affection, or a perception, or a conception, or of any subjective act. To be is to be a correlate, a term of a correlation. And in particular, when you claim to think any X, you must posit this X, which cannot then be separated from this special act of positing, of conception. That is why it is impossible to conceive an absolute X, i.e., an X which would be essentially separate from a subject. We can't know what the reality of the object in itself is because we can't distinguish between properties which are supposed to belong to the object and properties belonging to the subjective access to the object" (Quentin Meillassoux, "Speculative Realism: Presentation by Quentin Meillassoux," *Collapse* 3 [2007]: 409).

49 Meillassoux distinguishes between two forms of correlationism: a weak version and a strong one. Weak correlationism rules out knowledge of the noumenal real, of the in-itself, yet without dismissing its thinkability. Strong correlationism excludes the possibility of even its thinkability: "According to Kant, we know *a priori* that the thing-in-itself is non-contradictory and that it actually exists. By way of contrast, the strong model of correlationism maintains not only that it is illegitimate to claim that we can know the in-itself, but also that it is illegitimate to claim that we can at least think it" (Meillassoux, *After Finitude*, 35).

50 Quentin Meillassoux, "Interview with Quentin Meillassoux (August 2010)," trans. Graham Harman, in Graham Harman, *Quentin Meillassoux: Philosophy in the Making* (Edinburgh: Edinburgh University Press, 2011), 166.

51 See Manuel DeLanda, *A New Philosophy of Society: Assemblage Theory and Social Complexity* (London: Continuum, 2006). A flat ontology is posthumanism's global vision of things, taking as a given the degraded status of the human, helping to further distinguish it from anti-humanism: "While posthumanism owes many debts to antihumanist thinkers such as Michel Foucault, Jacques Lacan and Louis Althusser, it tends to differ from antihumanism in one principal respect: while the antihumanists actively set out to overturn the hegemony of anthropocentrism, posthumanists begin

with the recognition that 'Man' is (always) already a falling or fallen figure. What this means is that posthumanism often tends to take humanism's waning or disappearance as something of a given" (Neil Badmington, "Posthumanism," in *The Routledge Companion to Critical Theory*, ed. Simon Malpas and Paul Wake [New York: Routledge, 2006], 240–1).

52 See Bruno Latour, *We Have Never Been Modern*, trans. Catherine Porter (Cambridge: Harvard University Press, 1993).

53 Bruno Latour, *Pandora's Hope: Essays in the Reality of Science Studies* (Cambridge: Harvard University Press, 1999), 122.

54 Jacques Lacan, *On Feminine Sexuality, The Limits of Love and Knowledge, 1972–1973: Encore, The Seminar of Jacques Lacan, Book XX*, trans. Bruce Fink (New York: Norton, 1998).

55 See Freud's example of the primal father in *Totem and Taboo* (Lacan, *On Feminine Sexuality*, 79). For Lacan, Freud's primordial father in *Totem and Taboo* "is the father from before the incest taboo, before the appearance of law, of the structures of marriage and kinship, in a word, of culture" (Jacques Lacan, "Introduction to the Names-of-the-Father Seminar," in *Television: A Challenge to the Psychoanalytic Establishment*, ed. Joan Copjec, trans. Jeffrey Mehlman [New York: Norton, 1990], 88).

56 Jacques Derrida, *Rogues: Two Essays on Reason*, trans. Pascale-Anne Brault and Michael Naas (Stanford: Stanford University Press, 2005), 152. Autoimmunity names the condition of the self, the relational self, that makes such attempts at self-enclosure impossible. The autoimmune self, for instance, is a posthuman self, a self exposed to the other, a changeable, permeable self shaped by its relations with others. In describing the self as "autoimmune," Derrida redefines the term, understanding it not as an illness or disability to lament or overcome, but rather as a condition of malleability and openness—a condition that involves vulnerability to harm but that also makes intersubjective contact and relation possible. As such, "autoimmunity" in Derrida's revaluating use of the term describes a state that has no negative or positive value in itself; it is the primordial condition of possibility for modes of relating to the self and otherness.

57 Todd McGowan, "Hegel as Marxist: Žižek's Revision of German Idealism," in *Žižek Now: Current Perspectives in Žižek Studies*, ed. Jamil Khader and Molly Anne Rothenberg (Cambridge: Polity Press, 2013).

58 Slavoj Žižek, *Tarrying with the Negative: Kant, Hegel, and the Critique of Ideology* (Durham: Duke University Press, 1993), 23.

59 Christopher Peterson, "The Posthumanism to Come," *Angelaki* 16, no. 2 (2011): 136.

60 Cary Wolfe, *What Is Posthumanism?* (Minneapolis: University of Minnesota Press, 2010), xv; qtd. in Peterson, "The Posthumanism to Come," 136.

61 Michel Foucault, "What Is Enlightenment?" in *The Foucault Reader*, ed. Paul Rabinow, trans. Catherine Porter (New York: Pantheon, 1984), 32–50.

62 Žižek, *Less than Nothing*, 741.

63 Badmington makes a similar point: "The task of posthumanism is to uncover those uncanny moments at which things start to drift, of reading humanism *in a certain way*, against itself and the grain. This clearly involves a rethinking of the meaning of the 'post-' . . . Lyotard's writings on the postmodern might be immediately relevant to the work of theorizing posthumanism along these lines" (Badmington, *Alien Chic*, 119–20).

64 Peterson, "The Posthumanism to Come," 129. The same holds for posthumanist critics who are too eager and overtly self-confident in their capacity to halt the anthropological machine: "Given how the human has historically defined itself against animal lack, we ought to remain cautious about laying claim to any power to outright jam the anthropological machine. This force risks becoming yet another self-accredited capacity thanks to which the human redraws the human/nonhuman distinction through the very movement of its alleged erasure" (Christopher Peterson, *Monkey Trouble: The Scandal of Posthumanism* [New York: Fordham University Press, 2017], 6).

Chapter 1

1 Donna Haraway, "A Cyborg Manifesto: Science, Technology, and Socialist-Feminism in the Late Twentieth Century," in *Manifestly Haraway: The Cyborg Manifesto. The Companion Species Manifesto. Companions in Conversation (with Cary Wolfe)* (Minneapolis: University of Minnesota Press, 2016), 15. From "A Cyborg Manifesto" from the volume *Manifestly Haraway* by Donna J. Haraway (University of Minnesota Press, 2016). Copyright 2016 by Donna J. Haraway. All rights reserved. Used by permission. Henceforth all references to this edition will be stated parenthetically in the text.

2 Slavoj Žižek, *Disparities* (New York: Bloomsbury, 2016), 28.

3 The term "cyborg" was coined by Manfred E. Clynes and Nathan S. Kline in 1960. See Manfred E. Clynes and Nathan S. Kline, "Cyborgs and Space," *Astronautics* (September 1960): 27–31.

4 Nick Bostrom, "In Defence of Posthuman Dignity," *Bioethics* 19, no. 3 (2005): 202–3.

5 Bostrom refers to La Mettrie's notion of "man-machine" as a precursor for his transhmanist project. So while Bostrom appreciates the Cartesian elevation of the rational mind, he is also invested in the materiality of the body (understood as "a collection of springs which wind each other up"), in our ability to control it and augment bodily performance (Nick Bostrom, "A History of Transhumanist Thought," *Journal of Evolution and Technology* 14, no. 1 [2005]: 3).

6 Slavoj Žižek, *How to Read Lacan* (New York: Norton, 2006), 100.

7 George Myerson, *Donna Haraway and GM Foods* (Cambridge: Totem Books, 2000), 24.

8 N. Katherine Hayles, "The Materiality of Informatics," *Configurations* 1, no. 1 (1993): 147.

9 Donna Haraway, "A Game of Cat's Cradle: Science Studies, Feminist Theory, Cultural Studies," *Configurations* 2, no. 1 (1994): 60.

10 While Haraway's formulation puts her at odds with psychoanalysis (against the utopia of bisexuality and the Oedipal script), her concerns really target a psychoanalysis driven by the masculine of logic of the exception, whereas, in this chapter, we are aligning the cyborg with the feminine logic of the non-all.

11 Wolfe, *What Is Posthumanism?*, 47.

12 Wolfe, *What Is Posthumanism?*, xv. Wolfe's gloss introduces an important distinction, laying the conceptual ground for a critique of transhumanism's aggressive humanism. Decoupling transhumanism and posthumanism is a precondition for thinking of an alternative form of posthumanism, a "critical" posthumanism that explores the full potential of a nonhumancentric perspective (Pramod K. Nayar, *Posthumanism* [Cambridge: Polity Press, 2013], 8–11).

13 Donna Haraway, *When Species Meet* (Minneapolis: University of Minnesota Press, 2008), 17.

14 Marianne Dekoven, "*Jouissance*, Cyborgs, and Companion Species: Feminist Experiment," *PMLA* 121, no. 5 (2006): 1694.

15 Donna Haraway, *How Like a Leaf: An Interview with Thyrza Nichols Goodeve* (New York: Routledge, 2000), 86.

16 Donna Haraway, "The Companion Species Manifesto: Dogs, People, and Significant Otherness," in *Manifestly Haraway: The Cyborg Manifesto. The Companion Species Manifesto. Companions in Conversation (with Cary Wolfe)* (Minneapolis: University of Minnesota Press, 2016), 103.

17 Haraway genders the cyborg as feminine, but she is a strikingly queer feminine subject: the cyborg "is a polychromatic girl . . . the cyborg is a bad girl, she is really not a boy. Maybe she is not so much bad as she is a shape-changer, whose dislocations are never free. She is a girl who's trying not to become Woman, but remain responsible to women of many colors and positions, and who hasn't really figured out a politics that makes the necessary articulations with the boys who are your allies. It's undone work" (Constance Penley and Andrew Ross, "Cyborgs at Large: Interview with Donna Haraway," *Social Text Social Text* 25/26 [1990]: 23).

18 Dekoven, "*Jouissance*," 1694.

19 "The cyborg has no origin story" (8). I am indebted here to Edward Said, who writes that "beginning and beginning-again are historical whereas origins are divine" (Edward Said, *Beginnings: Intention and Method* [New York: Columbia University Press, 1985], xiii).

20 Donna Haraway, *The Haraway Reader* (New York: Routledge, 2004), 3.

21 For instance, Jasbir Puar critically asks, "Why disaggregate the two when there surely must be cyborgian goddesses in our midst?" (Jasbir K. Puar, "'I would rather be a cyborg than a goddess': Becoming-Intersectional in Assemblage Theory," *philoSOPHIA* 2, no. 1 [2012]: 63).

22 Jacques Lacan, "The Signification of the Phallus," in *Écrits: The First Complete Edition in English*, trans. Bruce Fink (New York: Norton, 2006), 576.

23 Slavoj Žižek, *For They Know Not What They Do: Enjoyment as a Political Factor* (New York: Verso, 1991), 123.

24 Slavoj Žižek, "Woman Is One of the Names-of-the-Father, or How Not To Misread Lacan's Formulas of Sexuation," *Lacanian Ink* 10 (1995). Available at: http://www.lacan.com/zizwoman.htm. Accessed October 12, 2019.

25 Žižek, *For They Know Not What They Do*, xxii.

26 Žižek, *For They Know Not What They Do*, xxii.

27 Slavoj Žižek, "Holding the Place," in *Contingency, Hegemony, Universality: Contemporary Dialogues on the Left*, ed. Judith Butler, Ernesto Laclau, and Slavoj Žižek (New York: Verso, 2000), 310.

28 Slavoj Žižek, *The Metastases of Enjoyment: Six Essays on Women and Causality* (New York: Verso, 1994), 144.

29 "Cyborg unities are monstrous and illegitimate; in our present political circumstances, we could hardly hope for more potent myths for resistance and recoupling" (Haraway, "A Cyborg Manifesto," 15).

30 Agon Hamza, "Going to One's Ground," in *Slavoj Žižek and Dialectical Materialism*, ed. Agon Hamza and Frank Ruda (New York: Palgrave, 2016), 173.

31 Hamza, "Going to One's Ground," 173.

32 Francis Fukuyama, *Our Posthuman Future: Consequences of the Biotechnology Revolution* (New York: Farrar, Straus and Giroux, 2002), 10.

33 Gene technology announces the "specter of eugenics": "In the future we will likely be able to breed human beings much as we breed animals, only far more scientifically and effectively, by selecting which genes we pass on to our children" (Fukuyama, *Our Posthuman Future*, 85, 88).

34 Fukuyama, *Our Posthuman Future*, 159.

35 While Fukuyama bemoans the state of capitalism driven by an unregulated transhumanist ethos, he never problematizes capitalism as such, never scrutinizes its logic of privatization and commodification. The challenges posed by biogenetics are to be resolved exclusively by new policies.

36 Jürgen Habermas, *The Future of Human Nature* (Cambridge: Polity Press, 2003), 97.

37 Glossing Heidegger, Žižek describes the denaturing of the human under the hegemony of modern technology: "the human being reduced to an object of technological manipulation is no longer properly human, it loses the very feature of being ecstatically open to reality" (Slavoj Žižek, *Absolute Recoil: Towards a New Foundation of Dialectical Materialism* [New York: Verso, 2014], 94). See Martin Heidegger, "The Question Concerning Technology," in *Basic Writings*, ed. David Farrell Krell (New York: HarperCollins Publishers, Inc., 1993).

38 Habermas, *The Future of Human Nature*, 40.

39 Habermas, *The Future of Human Nature*, 27.

40 As with Jameson's critique of moralistic responses to postmodernism, which Haraway endorses ("Jameson also makes clear why one cannot be for or against postmodernism, an essentially moralist move" [Haraway, "A Cyborg Manifesto," 69n.5]), Fukuyama and Habermas's humanist concerns remain reactionary, keeping the posthuman at arm's length, failing to engage the posthuman world as a "cultural dominant," necessitating "radical reinvention of left politics from within" (69n.5).

41 Simon Young, *Designer Evolution: A Transhumanist Manifesto* (New York: Prometheus Books, 2006), 58.

42 As Stefan Herbrechter insightfully observes, "Both Fukuyama and Habermas are admittedly defending a 'myth,' which they see as indispensable, however, for maintaining an essential idea of human nature. In Fukuyama's case this is called 'humanity' and serves as a universal principle for human community and morality; in Habermas, it is the principle of the autonomy of 'individual freedom,' which turns human subjects into moral and social agents. The real challenge, we would propose, however, is to critically accompany the posthumanization process without having any recourse to an (ultimately, due to its inherent mystification, counterproductive) idea of human 'nature'" (Stefan Herbrechter, *Posthumanism: A Critical Analysis* [New York: Bloomsbury, 2013], 165).

43 Bostrom, "A History of Transhumanist Thought," 20.

44 Nick Bostrom, "The Transhumanist FAQ: A General Introduction," *The World Transhumanist Association* (2003). Available at: https://humanit yplus.org/philosophy/transhumanist-faq/. Accessed October 12, 2019.

45 As Andrew Edgar correctly observes, the transhumanists mischaracterize the force of the Habermasian concern: "Habermas's reservations concerning genetic technology are grounded in an analysis of the threat that genetic science and technology pose, not simply to 'subtle human values,' but to the very possibility of sustaining a meaningful human social life" (Andrew Edgar, "The Hermeneutic Challenge of Genetic Engineering: Habermas and the Transhumanists," *Medicine, Health Care and Philosophy* 12, no. 2 [2009]: 158).

46 Herbrechter, *Posthumanism*, 116.

47 Donovan Conley and Benjamin Burroughs, "*Black Mirror*, Mediated Affect and the Political," *Culture, Theory and Critique* 60, no. 2 (2019): 140.

48 Derek R. Blackwell, "All Eyes on Me: Surveillance and the Digital Archive in 'The Entire History of You,'" in *Black Mirror and Critical Media Theory*, ed. Angela M Cirucci and Barry Vacker (Lanham: Lexington Books, 2018), 58.

49 Blackwell, "All Eyes on Me," 59.

50 Slavoj Žižek, *Interrogating the Real*, ed. Rex Butler and Scott Stephens (London: Continuum, 2005), 75.

51 There is undoubtedly something odd about Liam and Ffion's sexual relation. But whereas a Habermasian reading would decry the perversion and denaturalization of the sex act, a Žižekian take would attest to society's increased hold on sexuality, to the ways posthuman fantasies about idealized sexual encounters work to deprive subjects of sexuality's real or traumatic character: "Since sexuality is the domain in which we get closest to the intimacy of another human being, totally exposing ourselves to him or her, sexual enjoyment is real for Lacan: something traumatic in its breathtaking intensity, yet impossible in the sense that we cannot ever make sense of it. This is why a sexual relation, in order to function, has to be screened through some fantasy" (Žižek, *How to Read Lacan*, 49). The grain literally screens the sexual relation for both parties.

52 Lacan, *On Feminine Sexuality*, 95.

53 Slavoj Žižek, *Looking Awry: An Introduction to Jacques Lacan through Popular Culture* (Cambridge: MIT Press, 1992), 6.

54 Slavoj Žižek, *Violence: Six Sideways Reflections* (New York: Picador, 2008), 87.

55 Jacques Lacan, *The Psychoses, 1955-1956, The Seminar of Jacques Lacan, Book III*, ed. Jacques-Alain Miller, trans. Russell Grigg (New York: Norton, 1993), 76.

56 Lacan, *The Psychoses*, 77.

57 Jonathan Derbyshire, "Interview with Slavoj Zizek," *New Statesman* (October 29, 2009). Available at https://www.newstatesman.com/ideas/2009/10/today-interview-capitalism. Accessed June 12, 2018.

58 Žižek, *For They Know Not What They Do*, 251.

59 Liam compares the enjoyment of a confirmed jealousy with the satisfaction of excising a defective part of one's self: "It's like I've had a bad tooth for years and I've just finally getting my tongue in there and I'm digging out

all the rotten shit." For Henry Jenkins, Liam's observation registers the ambivalence of the grain: "Liam compares his constant probing of his enhanced memories to a tongue seeking out a rotting tooth. For him, this metaphor describes a process of digging out rot, but it also generates more and more pain" (Henry Jenkins, "Enhanced Memory: 'The Entire History of You,'" in *Through the Black Mirror Deconstructing the Side Effects of the Digital Age*, ed. Terence McSweeney and Stuart Joy [Cham: Palgrave, 2019], 46). This, however, only tells part of the story. The pathology of jealousy—exacerbated or enhanced via the grain—yields its own surplus enjoyment (a mixture of pain *and* pleasure).

60 Žižek, *The Parallax View*, 304.

61 Slavoj Žižek, *Organs without Bodies: On Deleuze and Consequences* (New York: Routledge, 2004), 125.

62 Žižek, *Organs without Bodies*, 130.

63 Fabio Vighi, *On Zizek's Dialectics: Surplus, Subtraction, Sublimation* (New York: Continuum, 2010), 103.

64 Žižek, *Organs Without Bodies*, 124.

65 "In philosophical terms, this 'inhuman' dimension can be defined as that of a subject subtracted from all forms of human 'individuality' or 'personality'" (Žižek, *In Defense of Lost Causes*, 166).

66 Žižek, *Violence*, 87. Freud's death drive—and psychoanalysis as a whole—challenges philosophy's core ideals, such as its pursuit of knowledge, along with its phantasms of autonomy, sovereignty, and self-sufficiency. As Lacan relates, Carl Jung recalls Freud's observation upon his arrival in America in 1909 that he and Jung were "bringing them the plague"—that is, the unconscious (Jacques Lacan, "The Freudian Thing, or the Meaning of the Return to Freud in Psychoanalysis," in *Écrits: The First Complete Edition in English*, trans. Bruce Fink [New York: Norton, 2006], 336). Freud placed his discovery of the unconscious alongside Copernicus's heliocentrism and Darwin's evolutionary theory, all three leveling a "narcissistic wound" to philosophy's humanistic subject, disclosing that "*the ego is not the master in its own house*" (Sigmund Freud, "A Difficulty in the Path of Psycho-Analysis," in *The Standard Edition of the Complete Psychological Works of Sigmund Freud*, ed. James Strachey et al., vol. 17 [London: Hogwarth, 1953–1974], 141).

67 Slavoj Žižek and Glyn Daly, *Conversations with Žižek* (Cambridge: Polity Press, 2004), 94.

68 Žižek, *Disparities*, 40. While Freud himself identified the death drive with the "Nirvana principle"—a desire for self-annihilation, a yearning to return to an inorganic, peaceful state, Lacan downplayed Freud's biologism, stressing instead the death drive in relation to the symbolic order and the emergence of the subject. Žižek continues to interpret Freud's scandalous idea in this vein: "The paradox of the Freudian 'death drive' is . . . that it is Freud's name for its very opposite, for the way immortality appears within psychoanalysis, for an uncanny *excess* of life, for an 'undead' urge which persists beyond the (biological) cycle of life and death, of generation and corruption. The ultimate lesson of psychoanalysis is that human life is never 'just life': humans are not simply alive, they are possessed by the strange drive to enjoy life in excess, passionately attached to a surplus which sticks out and derails the ordinary run of things" (Žižek, *The Parallax View*, 62). The death drive, especially in its Lacanian form, is a posthuman concept insofar as it disturbs the stability of the human, foregrounding the unruly "inhuman" at the core of the subject.

69 Charlie Brooker, Annabel Jones, and Jason Arnopp, *Inside Black Mirror* (New York: Crown Archetype, 2018), 56.

70 Lee Edelman, *No Future: Queer Theory and the Death Drive* (Durham: Duke University Press, 2004), 3.

71 Edelman, *No Future*, 4.

72 Peter Sloterdijk, *You Must Change Your Life* (Cambridge: Polity Press, 2013), 9.

73 Seneca, *Epistles*, Loeb Classical Library, trans. Richard M. Gummere (Cambridge: Harvard University Press, 1996), 37.11.

74 Seneca, *Epistles*, 91.7, 91.4.

75 Michel Foucault, "Technologies of the Self," in *Technologies of the Self: A Seminar with Michel Foucault*, ed. Luther H. Martin, Huck Gutman, and Patrick H. Hutton (Amherst: University of Massachusetts Press, 1988), 18.

76 Sigmund Freud, *Beyond the Pleasure Principle*, trans. James Strachey (New York: Norton, 1961), 33.

77 Jacques Derrida, "Faith and Knowledge," in *Acts of Religion*, ed. Gil Anidjar (New York: Routledge, 2002), 80n.27.

78 Jacques Derrida, "Autoimmunity: Real and Symbolic Suicides—A Dialogue with Jacques Derrida," in *Philosophy in a Time of Terror: Dialogues with*

Jürgen Habermas and Jacques Derrida, ed. Giovanna Borradori (Chicago: University of Chicago Press, 2004), 94.

79 Derrida, *Rogues*, 34, 123.

80 "The 'human,'" Wolfe argues, "is itself a prosthetic being, who from day one is constituted *as* human by its co-evolution with and co-constitution by external archival technologies of various kinds–including, of course, language itself as the 'first' archive and prosthesis" (Cary Wolfe, "Echographies from My Life in the Bush of Ghosts," *Angelaki* 13, no. 1 [2008]: 90).

81 Jacques Derrida, "The Rhetoric of Drugs," in *Points . . . Interviews, 1974-1994*, ed. Elisabeth Weber, trans. Peggy Kamuf (Stanford: Stanford University Press, 1995), 244–5.

82 While Marie does want to protect Sara, this drive is not free from the parental pleasure of scopic control over her progeny. As George McHendry notes, "Even as the conflict in the plot intensifies and Marie is horrified while watching her daughter have sex and consume narcotics, she still derives satisfaction in the ability to look. Her horror is directed at what is seen instead of the horror of her invasion of Sara's privacy" (George F. McHendry, "'Arkangel': Postscript on Families of Control," in *Through the Black Mirror Deconstructing the Side Effects of the Digital Age*, ed. Terence McSweeney and Stuart Joy [Cham: Palgrave, 2019], 212–3).

83 Judith Butler, *Giving an Account of Oneself* (New York: Fordham, 2005), 102. "San Junipero" (Season 3, Episode 4) offers a more optimistic, if not more problematic, view of technology and the transhumanist dream of uploading human consciousnesses to computer-virtual worlds. In the episode, the lesbian protagonists Yorkie (Mackenzie Davis) and Kelly (Gugu Mbatha-Raw) find eternal happiness in the simulated world of San Junipero, overcoming vulnerability and the vicissitudes of desire. At the same time, the episode's optimism is somewhat qualified by the existence of the nightclub Quagmire in San Junipero, which serves as an anti-Tucker (the nightclub of your dreams). Quagmire is a place where dissatisfaction reigns, where desire for more persists. Why does such a dystopian space exist in utopia? Is this an indication that the vicissitudes of desire can never really disappear even in the sanctioned afterlife of San Junipero?

84 Slavoj Žižek, *The Courage of Hopelessness: Chronicles of a Year of Acting Dangerously* (New York: Allen Lane, 2017), 5.

85 Žižek, *The Courage of Hopelessness*, xix.

86 Chela Sandoval, *Methodology of the Oppressed* (Minneapolis: University of Minnesota Press, 2000), 170.1. See also Malini Johar Schueller, *Locating Race: Global Sites of Post-Colonial Citizenship* (Albany: State University of New York Press, 2009): 60–2.

87 Qtd. in Sandoval, *Methodology of the Oppressed*, 171.2.

88 Aligning the cyborg with the global struggle for the commons sustains Haraway's paradoxical formulations for a feminism to come: "One is too few, but two are too many" (60) and "one is too few, and two is only one possibility" (65). A feminism worthy of its name dismantles and moves beyond the stale logic of self versus other. Women are not monads, nor are they locked in the slot of the eternal feminine (the Woman). Solidarity—the call for cyborg commons—should and must depart from the predictable logic of us versus them that informs much of the cultural Left's mode of resistance. To put it differently, the "one" ought to be read along the lines of the feminine formula of sexuation: the one is not an instance of self-unity, the male fantasy of self-possession; rather, the one is "non-all."

89 A more moderate reading of "we are all cyborgs" simply stresses our shared ontology—that the artificial is constitutive of human biology: "It is meaningless to imagine a human being as a biological entity without the complex network of his or her tools—such a notion is the same as, say, the goose without her feathers" (Žižek, *Organs without Bodies*, 19).

90 Slavoj Žižek, *Demanding the Impossible*, ed. Yong-June Park (Cambridge: Polity Press, 2013), 31–2.

91 Slavoj Žižek, "How to Begin from the Beginning," *New Left Review* 57 (2009): 53.

92 Slavoj Žižek, *Against the Double Blackmail: Refugees, Terror and Other Troubles with the Neighbors* (London: Penguin Random House, 2016), 105.

93 The "part of no-part" is a notion that Žižek freely borrows from Jacques Rancière. See Jacques Rancière, *Disagreement: Politics and Philosophy*, trans. J. Rose (Minneapolis: University of Minnesota Press, 1999), 11.

94 Žižek, *Disparities*, 27.

95 Slavoj Žižek, *First As Tragedy, Then As Farce* (New York: Verso, 2009), 4.

96 Slavoj Žižek, "A Leftist Plea for 'Eurocentrism,'" *Critical Inquiry* 24, no. 4 (1998): 997.

97 Slavoj Žižek, *Trouble in Paradise: From the End of History to the End of Capitalism* (Brooklyn: Melville House, 2014), 244.

98 Ricki Harris, "Elon Musk: Humanity Is a Kind of 'Biological Boot Loader' for AI," *wired.com* (September 1, 2019). Available at https://www.wired.com/story/elon-musk-humanity-biological-boot-loader-ai/. Accessed June 7, 2020.

99 Harris, "Elon Musk."

100 Harris, "Elon Musk."

101 Harris, "Elon Musk."

102 https://www.neuralink.com/

103 Jonathan Jacobson, "Slavoj Zizek's 'Brutal, Dark' Formula for Saving the World," *Haaretz* (April 06, 2020). Available at https://www.haaretz.com/world-news/.premium.MAGAZINE-slavoj-zizek-s-brutal-dark-formula-to-save-the-world-1.8898051?v=1591571554964. Accessed June 7, 2020. See also Žižek, *Hegel in A Wired Brain* (New York: Bloomsbury, 2020).

104 Slavoj Žižek, *Like a Thief in Broad Daylight* (New York: Allen Lane, 2018), 39, 40.

105 Žižek, *Like a Thief*, 40.

Chapter 2

1 Emmanuel Levinas, "The Paradox of Morality: An Interview with Emmanuel Levinas," in *The Provocation of Levinas: Rethinking the Other*, ed. Robert Bernasconi and David Wood (New York: Routledge, 1988), 172.

2 Jacques Derrida, *The Animal that Therefore I Am*, trans. David Willis (New York: Fordham University Press, 2008), 9.

3 Cary Wolfe, *Animal Rites: American Culture, the Discourse of Species, and Posthumanist Theory* (Chicago: Chicago University Press, 2003), 161. See also Kelly Oliver, *Animal Lessons: How They Teach Us to Be Human* (New York: Columbia University Press, 2009), 25–48.

4 See, for example, Martha C. Nussbaum, "Beyond 'Compassion and Humanity': Justice for Nonhuman Animals," in *Animal Rights: Current Debates and New Directions*, ed. Cass R. Sunstein and Martha C. Nussbaum (Oxford: Oxford University Press, 2004), 299–320.

5 Wolfe, *Animal Rites*, 53.

6 Giles Deleuze and Félix Guattari, *A Thousand Plateaus: Capitalism and Schizophrenia*, trans. Brian Massumi (Minneapolis: University of Minnesota Press, 1987), 238.

7 Gerald L. Bruns, "Becoming-Animal (Some Simple Ways)," *New Literary History* 38, no. 4 (2007): 703–4.

8 Deleuze and Guattari, *A Thousand Plateaus*, 239.

9 Wolfe, *Animal Rites*, 161.

10 Deleuze and Guattari, *A Thousand Plateaus*, 242.

11 Deleuze and Guattari, *A Thousand Plateaus*, 240.

12 Derrida, "Some Statements and Truisms about Neologisms, Newisms, Postisms, Parasitisms, and Other Small Seismisms," in *The States of "Theory,"* ed. David Carroll (New York: Columbia University Press, 1989), 80.

13 Derrida, "Passages—from Traumatism to Promise," in *Points . . .: Interviews, 1974–1994*, ed. Elisabeth Weber, trans. Peggy Kamuf (Stanford: Stanford University Press, 1992), 386.

14 Haraway, *When Species Meet*, 28. Christopher L. Miller condemns the project of becoming-animal as "a form of exoticism": "Becoming woman, becoming animal, becoming minoritarian and 'third world' is a masquerade invented expressly for white male majoritarian humans to play" (Christopher L. Miller, *Nationalists and Nomads: Essays on Francophone African Literature and Culture* [Chicago: University of Chicago Press, 1998], 23).

15 Derrida, *The Animal*, 6.

16 Derrida, *The Animal*, 9.

17 Montaigne, *The Complete Essays*, 330, 331. Derrida, *The Animal*, 6.

18 Derrida, *The Animal*, 163n8.

19 Derrida, *The Animal*, 137. Lacan may acknowledge the animality of the human but only to quickly mark its difference from other animals to the extent that a human being is "an animal at the mercy of language" (Lacan, "The Direction of the Treatment and the Principles of Its Power," in *Écrits: The First Complete Edition in English*, trans. Bruce Fink [New York: Norton, 2006], 525); qtd. in Derrida, *The Animal*, 120.

20 Rosi Braidotti, "Posthuman, All Too Human Towards a New Process Ontology," *Theory, Culture & Society* 23, nos. 7–8 (2006): 200.

21 Cynthia Willett, *Interspecies Ethics* (New York: Columbia University Press, 2014), 72.

22 Braidotti, *The Posthuman*, 79.

23 Haraway, "The Companion Species Manifesto," 145.

24 Haraway, *When Species Meet*, 20.

25 Haraway, *When Species Meet*, 17.

26 Jacques Derrida and Élisabeth Roudinesco, *For What Tomorrow . . .: A Dialogue*, trans. Jeff Fort (Stanford: Stanford University Press, 2004), 62–3.

27 Jacques Derrida, "'Eating Well,' or the Calculation of the Subject," in *Who Comes after the Subject?*, ed. Eduardo Cadava, Peter Connor, and Jean-Luc Nancy (New York: Routledge, 1991), 96.

28 Derrida, "'Eating Well,'" 118.

29 Levinas, at one point, entertains the possibility that the animal may have a face but it is clearly not attributed the full privileges of a human face. The animal face, if it exists, is derivative—extended to animals without any significant questioning of the ethical priority of the human face, preserving the absolute singularity of the face for humans (Levinas, "The Paradox of Morality," 168); indeed, Levinas puts his anthropocentrism on full display by insisting that the "human face is completely different and only afterwards do we discover the face of an animal" (Levinas, "The Paradox of Morality," 172).

30 Hélène Cixous, *Stigmata: Escaping Texts* (London: Routledge, 1989), 123.

31 Cixous, *Stigmata*, 123.

32 J. M. Coetzee, *The Lives of Animals* (Princeton: Princeton University Press, 1999), 43. Henceforth, all references to this edition will be stated parenthetically in the text.

33 Isaac Bashevis Singer, "The Letter Writer," in *The Séance and Other Stories* (New York: Farrar, Strauss and Giroux, 1968), 270, emphasis added.

34 "Agriculture is now a mechanized food industry in essence the same as the production of corpses in the gas chambers and extermination camps, the same as the blockading and starving of countries, the same as the production of hydrogen bombs" (Heidegger, *Einblick in das was ist*, in

Bremer und Freiburger Vorträge, Gesamtausgabe 79 [Frankfurt am Main: Klostermann, 1994], 27).

35 Derrida, *The Animal*, 101.

36 "There are . . . animal genocides: the number of species endangered because of man takes one's breath away" (Derrida, *The Animal*, 26).

37 Derrida, "'Eating Well,'" 118.

38 "If I do not subject my discourse to reason, whatever that is, what is left for me but to gibber and emote and knock over my water-glass and generally make a monkey of myself?" (Coetzee, *The Lives of Animals*, 23).

39 Derrida, *The Animal*, 5.

40 Amy Gutmann, "Introduction," in J. M. Coetzee, *The Lives of Animals* (Princeton: Princeton University Press, 1999), 5.

41 "To be a living bat is to be full of being; being fully a bat is like being fully human, which is also to be full of being. Bat-being in the first case, human-being in the second, maybe; but those are secondary considerations. To be full of being is to live as a body-soul. One name for the experience of full being is joy" (Coetzee, *The Lives of Animals*, 33).

42 Gutmann, "Introduction," 4.

43 In one of her lectures, Costello brings up bullfighting, first condemning it before couching the sport in more favorable terms: "We can call [bullfighting] primitivism. It is an attitude that is easy to criticize, to mock. It is deeply masculine, masculinist. Its ramifications into politics are to be mistrusted. But when all is said and done, there remains something attractive about it at an ethical level" (Coetzee, *The Lives of Animals*, 52). What exactly would make bullfighting ethical? Is it the heroism of killing with your own hands as opposed to the impersonality of the slaughterhouse? Is it the risk to human life involved in the contest?

44 Derrida, "Autoimmunity," 128–9.

45 Jacques Derrida, *Of Hospitality: Anne Dufourmantelle Invites Jacques Derrida to Respond* (Stanford: Stanford University Press, 2000), 77.

46 Roberto Esposito, *Terms of the Political: Community, Immunity, Biopolitics* (New York: Fordham University Press, 2006).

47 Theodor W. Adorno also aligns animals with Jews in his critical discussion of the anthropocentric violence inherent to idealism, questioning its

arrogant elevation of human dignity above all animals: "Nothing is more abhorrent to the Kantian than a reminder of the resemblance of human beings to animals. . . . Animals play for the idealist system virtually the same role as the Jews for fascism. To revile human animality—that is genuine idealism. To deny the possibility of salvation for animals absolutely and at any price is the inviolable boundary of its metaphysics" (Theodor W. Adorno, *Beethoven: The Philosophy of Music*, ed. Rolf Tiedemann, trans. Edmund Jephcott [Cambridge: Polity Press, 1998], 80).

48 Stanley Cavell, "Companionable Thinking," in *Philosophy and Animal Life*, ed. Stanley Cavell, Cora Diamond, John McDowell, Ian Hacking, and Cary Wolfe (New York: Columbia University Press, 2009), 112.

49 Haraway, *When Species Meet*, 336n23.

50 Haraway, *When Species Meet*, 336n23.

51 David Wood, *The Step Back: Ethics and Politics after Deconstruction* (Albany: State University of New York Press, 2005), 49.

52 The flipside must also be kept in mind. There is a predisposition to align genocides with the past, to categorize them as things of a less glorious time gone by. We can talk about previous traumatic events *but only* as long as they are comfortably located in a prior moment—only, that is, if doing so does not require any radical changes or immediate intervention in the current humanist order of things. In *Dead Meat*, Susan Coe expresses this moral exasperation: "The Holocaust keeps coming into my mind, which annoys the hell out of me. I see this reference in so many animal rights magazines. Is this the comforting measuring rod by which all horrors are evaluated? My annoyance is exacerbated by the fact that the suffering I am witnessing now cannot exist on its own, it has to fall into the hierarchy of a 'lesser animal suffering.' . . . Twenty million murdered humans deserve to be more than a reference point. I am annoyed that I don't have more power in communicating what I've seen apart from stuttering: 'It's like the Holocaust'" (Susan Coe, *Dead Meat* [New York: Four Walls Eight Windows, 1996], 72).

53 Wood, *The Step Back*, 49. In another exchange with Nancy, Derrida confronted a similar attitude. Nancy states that Derrida's investment in animals is excessive ("isn't this just a bit much?"), fearing that Derrida substitutes animals for humans, before being *reassured* by Derrida that he cares about human animals as well. Nancy responds half-jokingly: "Then I already feel better. I was afraid you were going to institute a law that allowed you to be cruel to me but not to your cat." To which Derrida replies that this is yet another worn-out humanist objection (Jacques Derrida and Jean-Luc Nancy, "Responsibility—Of the Sense to Come," in *For Strasbourg: Conversations of Friendship and Philosophy*, trans. and ed. Pascal-Anne Brault and Michael Naas [New York: Fordham University Press, 2014], 85).

54 As Cathy Caruth observes, Freud had already "compar[ed] the history of the Jews with the structure of a trauma" (Cathy Caruth, "Trauma and Experience: Introduction," in *Trauma: Explorations in Memory*, ed. Cathy Caruth [Baltimore: John Hopkins University Press, 1995], 7).

55 Cécile Winter, "The Master-Signifier of the New Aryans," in *Polemics*, trans. Steve Corcoran (New York: Verso, 2006), 223.

56 Aimé Césaire, *Discourse on Colonialism*, trans. Joan Pinkham (New York: Monthly Review Press, 2000), 36.

57 David Wood also draws attention to the historical connection between the death camps and the Chicago stockyards, underscoring where the charge of obscenity truly lies: "It has been argued that the architecture and logistical organization of the death camps was not, in fact, invented specially by the Nazis. It was stolen, or borrowed from the successful designs of the Chicago stockyards, also fed directly by the railway system. If the industrialization of killing was first perfected on cattle, and then applied to humans, we have not an obscene analogy, but an obscene piece of history" (Wood, *The Step Back*, 49).

58 Derrida, *The Animal*, 136.

59 Žižek, *Violence*, 53.

60 Simon Hajdini, "Dialectic at Its Impurest: Žižek's Materialism of Less Than Nothing," in *Žižek and Dialectical Materialism*, ed. Agon Hamza and Frank Ruda (New York: Palgrave, 2016), 91.

61 Hajdini, "Dialectic at Its Impurest," 91.

62 Todd McGowan, "Two Forms of Fetishism: From Commodity to Revolution in 'US,'" *Galactica Media* 1 (2019): 68.

63 Slavoj Žižek, *Living in the End Times* (New York: Verso, 2010), 440.

64 Žižek, *In Defense of Lost Causes*, 15–16.

65 Jacques Derrida, *The Beast and the Sovereign, Volume I*, ed. Michel Lisse, Marie-Louise Mallet, and Ginette Michaud, trans. Geoffrey Bennington (Chicago: University of Chicago Press, 2009), 346. See Martin Heidegger,

The Fundamental Concepts of Metaphysics, trans. William Mcneill and
Nicholas Walker (Bloomington: Indiana University Press, 1995), 197–226.

66 Žižek, *Less than Nothing*, 408–9.

67 Derrida, *The Animal*, 48.

68 Derrida, *The Animal*, 41.

69 Žižek, *Less than Nothing*, 409.

70 Derrida, *The Animal*, 14.

71 Derrida credits Bentham's prioritization of the question whether animals
    can suffer for highlighting that what humans and animals share is a
    negative state of "*passivity*," of "not-being-able" (Derrida, *The Animal*, 27).

72 Žižek, *Less than Nothing*, 409.

73 Stanley Rosen, *G. W. F. Hegel: An Introduction to the Science of Wisdom*
    (New Haven: Yale University Press 1974), 118. Qtd. in David Gray Carlson,
    A Commentary to Hegel's Science of Logic (New York: Palgrave Macmillan,
    2007), 22n.42.

74 Žižek, *Less than Nothing*, 410.

75 Žižek underscores the singularity of the human subject: "when one
    submits a human subject to a traumatic intrusion, the outcome is the
    empty form of the 'living-dead' subject, but when one does the same to
    an animal, the result is simply total devastation: what remains after the
    violent traumatic intrusion onto a human subject which erases all its
    substantial content is the pure form of subjectivity, the form which already
    must have been there" (Žižek, *Disparities*, 339). For Žižek, it is the death
    drive that marks most clearly how humans break with the animal kingdom
    (Žižek, *Less than Nothing*, 824). As with Derrida (see note 77 below), this
    difference is not intended to be fetishized but philosophically analyzed:
    What kind of subject is the human?

76 Derrida and Roudinesco, *For What Tomorrow*, 72.

77 Derrida, *The Animal*, 29. Matthew Calarco faults Derrida for remaining
    committed to the human-animal distinction despite his deconstructive
    challenge to philosophical dualism: "*We could simply let the human-animal
    distinction go* or, at the very least, not insist on maintaining it. Even if one
    agrees with Derrida that the task for thought is to attend to differences that
    have been overlooked and hidden by philosophical discourse, this does
    not mean that every difference and distinction that guides common sense

and philosophy should be maintained and refined" (Calarco, *Zoographies*, 149; see also Calarco, *Thinking through Animals: Identity, Difference, Indistinction* [Stanford: Stanford University Press, 2015], 47). I agree with Calarco that not all distinctions ought to be protected; to do so would risk fetishizing the concept of difference. Sometimes what is needed is an ideology critique of difference (e.g., racial difference or nationalist difference). Such is the case with the human-animal distinction (human difference/exceptionalism). Derrida offers a sustained deconstruction of its humanist ideology. The distinction after Derrida clearly does not mean the same as it did before. It is a distinction without hierarchy and repression, a distinction without its humanist reasoning and metaphysical certainties. It is not, however, a distinction without violence. There is always a degree of violence when talking about "animots," but this violence is neither legitimized nor rendered invisible as it is in humanist discourses.

78 Gerard Bruns, "Derrida's Cat (Who Am I?)," *Research in Phenomenology* 38 (2008): 415.

79 Oxana Timofeeva, "The Two Cats: Žižek, Derrida, and Other Animals," in *Repeating Žižek*, ed. Agon Hamza (Durham: Duke University Press, 2015), 104.

80 Žižek, *In Defense of Lost Causes*, 16.

81 I am of course adapting here Rimbaud's famous formulation, "Je est un autre [*I is an other*]" (Arthur Rimbaud, *Œuvres complètes*, ed. Rolland de Renéville and Jules Mouquet [Paris: Gallimard, 1963], 268).

82 Žižek, *Less than Nothing*, 411. Alain Badiou is the latest philosopher who retains the term "human animal" to designate a condition to transcend and overcome. The subject of the event breaks with its human-animal form (Žižek, *Less than Nothing*, 411). Moreover, Badiou aligns human victims with their animality. Only human beings are capable of what he calls immortality. Badiou concedes that "man is *the being who is capable of recognizing himself as a victim*" (Alain Badiou, *Ethics: An Essay on the Understanding of Evil*, trans. Peter Hallward [New York: Verso, 2002], 10). But he quickly moves to underscore the irreducibility of this status. "Man" is more than "his animal substructure" (Badiou, *Ethics*, 11). His identity is not exhausted by his designation as a victim. We are unlike other animals to the extent that we are capable of transcendence: "we are dealing with an animal whose resistance, unlike that of a horse, lies not in his fragile body but in his stubborn determination to remain what he is—that is to say, precisely something other than a victim, other than a being-for-death,

and thus: *something other than a mortal being*" (Badiou, *Ethics*, 11–12). What makes every human being "*capable* of being this immortal" is an openness to the truth-event (Badiou, *Ethics*, 12), to a truth that "traverses and transcends" all differences or particularities (Alain Badiou, *Saint Paul: The Foundation of Universalism*, trans. Ray Brassier [Stanford: Stanford University Press, 2003], 106).

83 Žižek, *In Defense of Lost Causes*, 16.

84 Following G. K. Chesterton, Žižek reverses the roles of the human and animals, entertaining an appreciation of trauma from the standpoint of the latter: "instead of asking what animals are for humans, for our experience, we should ask what man is for animals. . . . Chesterton conducts a wonderful mental experiment along these lines, imagining the monster that man might have seemed at first to the merely natural animals around him" (Žižek, *Less than Nothing*, 414).

85 Žižek, *Less than Nothing*, 411.

86 Žižek, "Neighbors and Other Monsters," 161.

87 Žižek, "Neighbors and Other Monsters," 140–1.

88 Qtd. in Slavoj Žižek, Eric L. Santner, and Kenneth Reinhard, "Introduction," in *The Neighbor: Three Inquiries in Political Theology*, ed. Slavoj Žižek, Eric L. Santner, and Kenneth Reinhard (Chicago: University of Chicago Press, 2006), 4.

89 Žižek, "Neighbors and Other Monsters," 162.

90 Žižek, "Neighbors and Other Monsters," 140.

91 Žižek, "Neighbors and Other Monsters," 162.

92 Žižek, "Neighbors and Other Monsters," 162.

93 Žižek and Daly, *Conversations with Žižek*, 71.

94 Žižek, *Less than Nothing*, 414.

95 Hélène Cixous, "Castration or Decapitation?" trans. Annette Kuhn, *Signs* 7, no. 1 (1981): 45.

96 See also Julia Kristeva, *Strangers to Ourselves*, trans. Leon S. Roudiez (New York: Columbia University Press, 1991).

97 For an alternative reading of Lacan's registers in relation to Derrida's cat, see Timofeeva, "The Two Cats," 107–9.

98 Not unlike Levinas and Maurice Blanchot, Derrida deploys the formulation of "relation without relation," or its multiple variations such as "community without community," "sovereign without sovereignty," "messianity without messianism," for its unsettling logic.

99 Derrida, "'Eating Well,'" 115.

100 See Carol Adams, *The Sexual Politics of Meat: A Feminist-Vegetarian Critical Theory* (New York: Continuum, 1990).

101 Kelly Oliver, "Derrida and Eating," in *Encyclopedia of Food and Agricultural Ethics*, ed. Paul B. Thompson and David M. Kaplan (Heidelberg: Springer Netherlands, 2014), 460.

102 Derrida, "'Eating Well,'" 113.

103 Oliver points out with good reason that "challenging the man/animal binary from the side of the animal can help explode the man/woman binary" (Oliver, *Animal Lessons*, 139–40).

104 Derrida, "'Eating Well,'" 112.

105 Jacques Derrida, Daniel Birnbaum, and Anders Olsson, "An Interview with Jacques Derrida on the Limits of Digestion," trans. Brian Manning Delaney, *e-flux* 2 (2009): 2.

106 Derrida, "'Eating Well,'" 113.

107 Derrida, "'Eating Well,'" 112.

108 Decision for Derrida is always shot through with uncertainty, marked even by a certain "madness": "If the decision is simply the final moment of a knowing process, it is not a decision. So the decision first of all has to go through *a terrible process of undecidability*, otherwise it would not be a decision, and it has to be heterogeneous to the space of knowledge. If there is a decision it has to go through undecidability and make a leap beyond the field of theoretical knowledge. So when I say 'I don't know what to do,' this is not the negative condition of decision. It is rather the possibility of a decision" (Jacques Derrida, "Hospitality, Justice and Responsibility," in *Questioning Ethics: Contemporary Debates in Philosophy*, ed. Richard Kearney and Mark Dooley [London: Routledge, 1999], 66, emphasis added). To see meat eating as a series of decisions that one takes counterbalances the dominant social view of carnivorous practices as mechanical, the result of either biology or sedimented cultural norms.

109 Derrida, "'Eating Well,'" 112.

110 Derrida and Roudinesco, *For What Tomorrow*, 71.

111 Derrida and Roudinesco, *For What Tomorrow*, 72.

112 Qtd. in David Wood, "*Comment ne pas manger*: Derrida and Humanism,"
     in *Thinking after Heidegger* (Cambridge: Polity Press, 2002), 140.

113 Derrida, "'Eating Well,'" 112.

114 Derrida, "'Eating Well,'" 114–15. Disappointed by Derrida's assimilation
     of real and symbolic sacrifice, and the making of carno-phallogocentrism
     a quasi-ontological feature of the social order of things, which
     renders resistance to its regime futile, David Wood argues that carno-
     phallogocentrism is not destiny, but "a mutually reinforcing network of
     powers, schemata of domination and investments that has to reproduce
     itself to stay in existence." Deconstruction must contest this power
     rather than fetishize its pervasiveness. Deconstruction as vegetarianism
     performs such a critique: "It can . . . spearhead a powerful, practical,
     multidimensional transformation of our broader political engagement"
     (Wood, "*Comment ne pas manger*," 150). Yet, as Matthew Calarco shows
     in his response to Wood's argument, Derrida is not assimilating but
     complicating the two forms of sacrifice. This is not mere hermeneutic
     hairsplitting. Wood's reliance on the fact that we can decouple real from
     symbolic sacrifice is a move ironically unsupported by deconstruction.
     Derrida's point is not vegetarians like carnivores display the same
     violence toward humans and animals alike, since they are both guilty of
     participating in their culture's carno-phallogocentrism. Calarco stresses the
     importance of Derrida's qualifier that vegetarians practice a "*different form
     of denegation*," which requires a deconstructive pursuit of its specificity
     (Matthew Calarco, "Deconstruction is Not Vegetarianism: Humanism,
     Subjectivity, and Animal Ethics," *Continental Philosophy Review* 37, 2
     [2004]: 193–4).

115 Oliver, "Derrida and Eating," 460.

116 Derrida and Roudinesco, *For What Tomorrow*, 70.

117 Indigenous critics have also objected to the politics of veganism and
     vegetarianism. As Billy-Ray Belcourt maintains, "neither the abolition of
     speciesism nor the production of more ethical human-animal relationalities
     can occur in at least the North American context without the end of settler
     colonialism" (Billy-Ray Belcourt, "An Indigenous critique of Critical Animal
     Studies," in *Colonialism and Animality: Anti-Colonial Perspectives in Critical
     Animal Studies*, ed. Kelly Struthers Montford and Chloë Taylor [New York:

Routledge, 2020], 20). Unless it confronts the specific legacy of settler colonialism (the elimination of natives and the theft of their lands), a project animated by an anti-speciesist ethos will always fall short of its emancipatory potential. Worse, while arguing against animal oppression and for animal liberation might be a liberal dream, it is currently experienced as an indigenous nightmare: "If settler colonialism is to remain both 'territorially acquisitive in perpetuity' and about the production of an unhuman suffering, then animals are colonial subjects par excellence, at once the means to genocidal ends (clearing of the plains of Indigenous peoples) and made to take on an impoverished non-existence that results in premature death" (21). Another line of indigenous inquiry stresses what is disavowed or left out of a discussion framed by the choice "to eat or not eat meat." Kim TallBear challenges veganism's putative rhetoric of purity. "Shopp[ing] at Whole Foods," for instance, gives the "typical vegan" the illusion of moral superiority, of *personally* doing something about the problem of animal suffering. But this vegan is not immune from complicity with the food system: "he buys fruits and vegetables that are being shipped using fossil fuels, and his soy is being produced in the Amazon and that's displacing humans and nonhumans" (Kim TallBear, "Being in Relation," in *Messy Eating: Conversations on Animals as Food*, ed. Samantha King [New York: Fordham University Press, 2019], 60).

118 Derrida, Birnbaum, and Olsson, "An Interview with Jacques Derrida," 3.

119 "And insofar as vegetarianism holds itself up as the moral mode of eating, it risks stalling the question of eating well and collapsing into a self-assured form of good conscience (a tendency that is evident in a number of contemporary discourses on vegetarianism)" (Calarco, "Deconstruction," 195).

120 Derrida, *The Animal*, 26.

121 Oliver, *Animal Lessons*, 104.

122 As the just judge—whose legal judgment does not simply consist of "applying the law" like "a calculating machine," but requires that each decision be the result of an *invention*—the subject who eats well ingests and interprets without any assurance (Derrida, "Force of Law: The 'Mystical Foundation of Authority,'" in *Acts of Religion*, ed. Gil Anidjar [New York: Routledge, 2002], 252).

123 Erica Fudge, *Animal* (London: Reaktion, 2002), 33.

124 Cixous, "A Refugee," in *The Animal Question in Deconstruction*, ed. Lynn Turner (Edinburgh: Edinburgh University Press, 2013), 9–12, 11.

125 Derrida and Roudinesco, *For What Tomorrow*, 64.

126 Derrida, "Hostipitality," in *Acts of Religion*, ed. Gil Anidjar (New York: Routledge, 2002), 361.

127 I am indebted to Slavoj Žižek's following formulation: "In a well-known Marx Brothers joke Groucho answers the standard question 'Tea or coffee?' with 'Yes, please!'—a refusal of choice . . . [O]ne should answer in the same way the false alternative today's critical theory seems to impose on us: either 'class struggle' (the outdated problematic of class antagonism, commodity production, etc.) or 'postmodernism' (the new world of dispersed multiple identities, of radical contingency, of an irreducible ludic plurality of struggles). Here, at least, we can have our cake and eat it" (Slavoj Žižek, "Class Struggle or Postmodernism? Yes, Please!" in *Contingency, Hegemony, Universality: Contemporary Dialogues on the Left*, ed. Judith Butler, Ernesto Laclau, and Slavoj Žižek [New York: Verso, 2000], 90).

128 Derrida and Roudinesco, *For What Tomorrow*, 66.

Chapter 3

1 Timothy Morton, "Here Comes Everything: The Promise of Object-Oriented Ontology," *Qui Parle* 19, no. 2 (2011): 165. Copyright, 2011, Editorial Board, *Qui Parle*. All rights reserved. Republished by permission of the copyright holder, and the present publisher, Duke University Press. www.dukeupress.edu.

2 Jean-Paul Sartre, *Nausea*, trans. Lloyd Alexander (New York: New Directions, 1964), 10. Henceforth all references to this edition will be stated parenthetically in the text. From *La Nausée* by Jean-Paul Sartre © Editions Gallimard, 1938. (English translation by Lloyd Alexander © New Directions, 1964). Reprinted by permission of New Directions Publishing Corp.

3 Alenka Zupančič, *What Is Sex?* (Cambridge: MIT Press, 2017), 119.

4 DeLanda, *A New Philosophy of Society*, 16.

5 Jacques Derrida, *Of Grammatology*, trans. Gayatri Chakravorty Spivak (Baltimore: John Hopkins University Press, 1976), 158.

6 Glyn Daly, *Speculation: Politics, Ideology, Event* (Evanston: Northwestern University Press, 2019), 17.

7 Graham Harman, "The Well-Wrought Broken Hammer: Object-Oriented Literary Criticism," *New Literary History* 43 (2012): 185.

8 Bruno Latour, *Reassembling the Social: An Introduction to Actor-Network-Theory* (Oxford: Oxford University Press, 2005), 71.

9 Bruno Latour, *Politics of Nature: How to Bring the Sciences into Democracy*, trans. Catherine Porter (Cambridge: Harvard University Press, 2004), 69.

10 Latour, *We Have Never Been Modern*, 144–5. See also Levi R. Bryant, *The Democracy of Objects* (Ann Arbor: Open Humanities Press, 2011).

11 Latour, *Politics of Nature*, 69.

12 Latour, *Reassembling the Social*, 245.

13 Bruno Latour, "Why Has Critique Run Out of Steam? From Matters of Fact to Matters of Concern," *Critical Inquiry* 30 (2004): 239.

14 Latour, "Why Has Critique Run Out of Steam?" 240.

15 Latour, "Why Has Critique Run Out of Steam?" 232.

16 Jane Bennett, *Vibrant Matter: A Political Ecology of Things* (Durham: Duke University Press, 2010), 3.

17 Bennett, *Vibrant Matter*, 18.

18 Bennett, *Vibrant Matter*, 14, ix. Bennett also adds: "Another way to cultivate this new discernment might be to elide the question of the human. Postpone for a while the topics of subjectivity or the nature of human interiority, or the question of what really distinguishes the human from the animal, plant, and thing. Sooner or later, these topics will lead down the anthropocentric garden path, will insinuate a hierarchy of subjects over objects, and obstruct freethinking about what agency really entails" (Bennett, *Vibrant Matter*, 2).

19 Bennett, *Vibrant Matter*, 2.

20 On the one hand, according "agency" to nonhumans signals an anti-anthropocentric gesture; on the other, as Puar observes, "agency as it has historically been deployed refers to the capacities of the liberal humanist subject, an anthropocentric conceptualization of movement" (Puar, "I would rather be a cyborg than a goddess," 65n.10). This awareness qualifies, if not undermines, Bennett's posthuman framework.

21 "I will emphasize, even overemphasize, the agentic contributions of nonhuman forces . . . in an attempt to counter the narcissistic reflex of human language and thought" (Bennett, *Vibrant Matter*, xvi).

22 Bennett, *Vibrant Matter*, xiv.

23 Graham Harman, *Tool-Being: Heidegger and the Metaphysics of Objects* (Chicago: Open Court, 2002), 2. And again: "However interesting we humans may be to ourselves, we are apparently in no way central to the cosmic drama, marooned as we are on an average-sized planet near a mediocre sun and confined to a tiny portion of the history of the universe" (Graham Harman, *The Quadruple Object* [Winchester: Zero Books, 2011], 63).

24 Harman, *Tool-Being*, 232.

25 Graham Harman, *Immaterialism: Objects and Social Theory* (Cambridge: Polity Press, 2016), 1.

26 Harman, *Immaterialism*, 98.

27 Graham Harman, *Prince of Networks: Bruno Latour and Metaphysics* (Melbourne, re.press, 2009), 180–1.

28 Harman, *Immaterialism*, 2.

29 Harman, *Immaterialism*, 106.

30 Ian Bogost, *Alien Phenomenology, or What It's Like to Be a Thing* (Minneapolis: University of Minnesota Press, 2012), 7.

31 "We shall call those entities which we encounter in concern *'equipment.'* In our dealings we come across equipment for writing, sewing, working, transportation, measurement" (Martin Heidegger, *Being and Time*, trans. John Macquarrie and Edward Robinson [New York: Harper & Row, 1962], 97).

32 Graham Harman, "Zero-Person and the Psyche," in *Mind that Abides: Panpsychism in the New Millennium*, ed. David Skrbina (Philadelphia: John Benjamins Publishing Company, 2009), 258.

33 Harman, *The Quadruple Object*, 42.

34 Harman, *Tool-Being*, 134.

35 Harman, *The Quadruple Object*, 112, 80.

36 Graham Harman, *Guerrilla Metaphysics: Phenomenology and the Carpentry of Things* (Chicago: Open Court, 2005), 171.

37 "While there may be an infinity of objects in the cosmos, they come in only two kinds: the real object that withdraws from all experience, and

the sensual object that exists only in experience" (Harman, *The Quadruple Object*, 49).

38 "The real is something that cannot be known, only loved" (Graham Harman, *Third Table/Der dritte Tisch* [Ostfildern: Hatje Cantz, 2012], 15).

39 Harman, *Third Table*, 12.

40 Harman, *Guerrilla Metaphysics*, 192.

41 Harman, "The Well-Wrought Broken Hammer," 187. A philosophy that does justice to objects cannot be "a philosophy of access to the world" (Harman, *The Quadruple Object*, 136).

42 Morton, "Here Comes Everything," 165.

43 Jane Bennett, "Systems and Things: On Vital Materialism and Object-Oriented Philosophy," in *The Nonhuman Turn*, ed. Richard Grusin (Minneapolis: University of Minnesota Press, 2015), 233.

44 Bennett, *Vibrant Matter*, 23–4.

45 Bennett, *Vibrant Matter*, 34.

46 Puar, "I would rather be a cyborg than a goddess," 57.

47 Jacques Derrida, *Archive Fever: A Freudian Impression*, trans. Eric Prenowitz (Chicago: University of Chicago Press, 1998), 91.

48 Carolyn Steedman, *Dust: The Archive and Cultural History* (New Brunswick: Rutgers University Press, 2002), 77.

49 Wendy Kozol, *Distant Wars Visible: The Ambivalence of Witnessing* (Minneapolis: University of Minnesota Press, 2014), 137.

50 Derrida, *Archive Fever*, 68. "The archivist produces more archive, and that is why the archive is never closed" (Derrida, *Archive Fever*, 68).

51 Žižek, *Less than Nothing*, 697.

52 For Felski, posthumanism is not immune to the lure of critique. As she observes, "the animal studies scholar Cary Wolfe opens his discussion of a recent novel by Michael Crichton by observing that it seems to 'radically question the discourse of speciesism.' Any nascent hopes we might have, however, are quickly dashed, as Wolfe serves up the bad news: in spite of its apparent progressiveness, Crichton's novel 'leaves intact the category of the human and its privileged forms of accomplishment and representation in the novel: technoscience and neocolonialism'" (Rita Felski, *The Limits of*

Critique [Chicago: University of Chicago Press, 2015], 128). Wolfe's actual reading of the Crichton's novel betrays its posthumanist promise, a would-be Latourian embrace of nonhuman actants, returning instead to critique as its primary mode.

53 Latour, "Why Has Critique Run Out of Steam?" 231.

54 Bruno Latour, "The Politics of Explanation: An Alternative," in *Knowledge and Reflexivity: New Frontiers in the Sociology of Knowledge*, ed. Steve Woolgar (London: Sage, 1988), 173.

55 Latour, "The Politics of Explanation," 173.

56 Bruno Latour, "An Attempt at a 'Compositionist Manifesto,'" *New Literary History* 41 (2010): 476.

57 Eve Kosofsky Sedgwick, "Paranoid Reading and Reparative Reading, Or, You're So Paranoid, You Probably Think This Essay Is about You," in *Novel Gazing: Queer Readings in Fiction*, ed. Eve Kosofsky Sedgwick (Durham: Duke University Press, 1997), 9–10.

58 Sedgwick, "Paranoid Reading and Reparative Reading," 24.

59 Raz Yosef, "War Fantasies: Memory, Trauma and Ethics in Ari Folman's *Waltz with Bashir*," *Journal of Modern Jewish Studies* 9, no. 3 (2010): 323–4.

60 Rupert Read, *A Film-Philosophy of Ecology and Enlightenment* (New York: Routledge, 2019), 25.

61 Felski wants to reassure other literary critics that Latour still allows them to be politically engaged in their criticism: "Actor-network theory does not exclude the political—it is deeply interested in conflicts, asymmetries, struggles—but its antipathy to reductionism means that political discourse cannot serve as a metalanguage into which everything can be translated" (Rita Felski, "Latour and Literary Studies," *PMLA* 130 [2015]: 740). But I question the effectiveness of a politics that willfully evacuates ideology from its interpretive toolbox. Is there not a place in ANT for a model of ideology critique that is not reductive and totalizing?

62 Esther Alloun, "'That's the beauty of it, it's very simple!' Animal Rights and Settler Colonialism in Palestine–Israel," *Settler Colonial Studies* 8, no. 4 (2018): 559–74.

63 Latour, "Why Has Critique Run Out of Steam?" 225.

64 Postcritique enthusiasts do not typically frame their position as one of anti-critique. In *Generous Thinking*, for example, Kathleen Fitzpatrick

tries to reassure her theory-friendly readers that she does not believe that "critique per se is the problem" (Kathleen Fitzpatrick, *Generous Thinking: A Radical Approach to Saving the University* [Baltimore: Johns Hopkins University Press, 2019], 128). What is needed rather is a paradigmatic shift from ungenerous critique to "generous listening" which, we are told, is "the heart of generosity" (76), laying "the necessary ground for generous thinking" (77). But here the irony is striking; while professing the virtues of generosity, Fitzpatrick never practices anything like a generous hermeneutics when it comes to the theorists of critique (Derrida, Butler, Žižek, to name a few). Indeed, the labor of critical theory is ignored or simply seen as a symptom of the problem rather than a fruitful counter to the neoliberalization of the university. What we get instead is an endorsement of Felski's postcritical approach (38), which has already done the ideological and ungenerous work of simplifying the choice of beyond critique (read as against critique) for a new generation of readers who are encouraged to reinvest in the "public good," in community as "a form of solidarity, of coalition-building" (11).

65 Jonathan Freedland, "Lest We Forget," *The Guardian* (October 25, 2008). Available at http://www.theguardian.com/film/2008/oct/25/waltz-with-bashir-ari-folman. Accessed July 17, 2015.

66 Livia Alexander also credits the dogs for setting into motion Folman's retracing of his involvement in the drama of Sabra and Shatila: "The dogs, as a reference to Palestinians, function as a catalyst that triggers the suppressed memory for the traumatized Israeli soldier" (Livia Alexander, "Confessing without Regret: An Israeli Film Genre," in *Screening Torture: Media Representations of State Terror and Political Domination*, ed. Michael Flynn and Fabiola F. Salek [New York: Columbia University Press, 2012], 206).

67 Read, *A Film-Philosophy*, 24.

68 Žižek, "Neighbors and Other Monsters," 162.

69 Slavoj Žižek, *Welcome to the Desert of the Real! Five Essays on September 11 and Related Dates* (New York: Verso, 2002), 116.

70 Žižek, "Neighbors and Other Monsters," 160.

71 Žižek, *In Defense of Lost Causes*, 16.

72 Bénédicte Boisseron, *Afro-Dog: Blackness and the Animal Question* (New York: Columbia University Press, 2018), xx.

73 Žižek, *Living in the End Times*, 120.

74 Meillassoux, *After Finitude*, 5.

75 Harman, "Object-Oriented Ontology," in *The Palgrave Handbook of Posthumanism in Film and Television*, ed. Michael Hauskeller, Curtis D. Carbonell, and Thomas D. Philbeck (Basingstoke: Palgrave Macmillan, 2015), 405.

76 OOO enthusiasts refer to the listing of objects as "Latour litanies" (Bogost, *Alien Phenomenology*, 38).

77 Žižek, *How to Read Lacan*, 72.

78 Bennett, *The Enchantment of Modern Life: Attachments, Crossings, and Ethics* (Princeton: Princeton University Press, 2001), 4.

79 Halfway through the diary, an anguished Roquentin trusts that his words will elucidate the nature of things, that his phenomenological *epoché*— his bracketing of presuppositions about the objective world will prove successful in curing him from his nausea: "As long as I could stare at things nothing would happen: I looked at them as much as I could, pavement, houses, gaslights; my eyes went rapidly from one to another, to catch them unaware, stop them in the midst of their metamorphosis. They did not look natural, but *I told myself forcibly*: this is a gaslight, this is a drinking fountain, and I tried to reduce them to their everyday aspect by the power of *my gaze*" (Sartre, *Nausea*, 78, emphasis added). Roquentin assumes here the position of an authoritative meaning-giving subject, situating his perception (and tacitly his logos) as something outside of the realm of discursivity. However, to maintain such a *human* privileged, Roquentin must master the world of things and adopt the cherished anthropocentric position of a metaphysical Adam. But Roquentin's logos fails to rise to the task. A seemingly innocuous tramway seat subverts his semiotic universe. After losing its social (instrumental and utilitarian) function (its ready-to-handness), the seat is unable to be subdued by Roquentin's gaze and speech. By resisting Roquentin's nominalization, the seat in question breaks free from linguistic domestication and instrumentality. Roquentin murmurs: "'It's a seat,' a little like an exorcism" (Sartre, *Nausea*, 125). But the word stays on his lips, no longer corresponding to its "natural" extralinguistic entity: "It refuses to go and put itself on the thing. It stays what it is, with its red plush, thousands of red little red paws in the air, all still, little dead paws. This enormous belly turned upward, bleeding, inflated—bloated with all its dead paws, this belly floating in this car, in this grey sky, is not a seat. It could just as well be a dead donkey tossed

about in the water, floating with the current, belly in the air in a great grey river, a river of floods; and I could be sitting on the donkey's belly, my feet dangling in the clear water" (Sartre, *Nausea*, 125, emphasis added). Stupefied to see that the meaning that he tries to impute orally has failed miserably—and this right after his unconventional metaphorization of the seat: a tramway seat *is like* the belly of a dead donkey floating in a river of blood—Roquentin, in the midst of this linguistic flux, is forced to conclude that his words (figurative and otherwise) are ultimately inadequate, that things are in fact unnamable: "*Things are divorced from their name. They are there*, grotesque, headstrong, gigantic and *it* seems ridiculous to call them seats or say anything at all about them: I am in the midst of things, *nameless things*" (Sartre, *Nausea*, 125, emphasis added).

80 Sartre, *Being and Nothingness*, 83.

81 The event of the epiphany undergoes even further displacement when Roquentin's confesses his inability to determine whether his epiphany was lived or imagined: "Had I dreamed of this enormous presence?" (Sartre, *Nausea*, 134).

82 Alain Robbe-Grillet, *For a New Novel: Essays on Fiction*, trans. Richard Howard (New York: Grove Press, 1966), 53.

83 Robbe-Grillet, *For a New Novel*, 62.

84 Jean-Paul Sartre, *The Words: The Autobiography of Jean-Paul Sartre*, trans. Bernard Frechtman (New York: George Braziller, 1964), 32.

85 Graham Harman, "On Vicarious Causation," *Collapse* 2 (2007): 171–208.

86 Harman, *Immaterialism*, 7.

87 Harman, *Guerrilla Metaphysics*, 106. To be fair, Harman does privilege the horror fiction of H.P. Lovecraft for its metaphorical powers to disclose a reality that is itself "incommensurate with any attempt to represent or measure it" (Graham Harman, *Weird Realism: Lovecraft and Philosophy* [Winchester: Zero Books, 2012], 51). Lovecraft's weird realism is said to afford us "*indirect* access" to the things-in-themselves, making its author something of a "Kantian writer of 'noumenal' horror" (Harman, *Weird Realism*, 17, 27). At the same time, it is unclear *how* and *why* Lovecraft's art enables such indirect contact with real objects. As Benjamin Boysen points out, "Lovecraft's horror fiction and his literary creation of the monster Cthulhu are no weirder than more traditional and classic animalistic cults (real or fictitious) devoted to malevolent deities or spirits (and the monster is also worshipped as such by 'primitive' people in Lovecraft's fiction)"

(Benjamin Boysen, "The Embarrassment of Being Human: A Critique of New Materialism and Object-Oriented Ontology," *Orbis Litterarum* 73, no. 3 [2018]: 234).

88 Žižek, *How to Read Lacan*, 72.

89 Benjamin Noys, "Žižek's Reading Machine," in *Repeating Žižek*, ed. Agon Hamza (Durham: Duke University Press, 2015), 76.

90 Slavoj Žižek, "Afterword: Objects, Objects Everywhere," in *Slavoj Žižek and Dialectical Materialism*, ed. Agon Hamza and Frank Ruda (New York: Palgrave Macmillan, 2016), 185.

91 "It is not even remotely Kantian. I make that quite clear. If there is a notion of the real, it is extremely complex and in that sense it is not graspable, not graspable in a way that would constitute a whole" (Jacques Lacan, "The Triumph of Religion," in *The Triumph of Religion, Preceded by Discourse to Catholics*, trans. Bruce Fink [Cambridge: Polity Press, 2013], 80).

92 Zupančič, *What Is Sex?* 121.

93 Žižek, "Afterword: Objects, Objects Everywhere," 187. Elsewhere, Žižek also avers: "for Freud and Lacan, external shocks, unexpected brutal encounters or intrusions owe their properly traumatic impact to the way they touch on a pre-existing traumatic 'psychic reality'" (Žižek, *Living in the End Times*, 292).

94 Slavoj Žižek, *The Fright of Real Tears: Krzystof Kieslowski between Theory and Post-Theory* (London: British Film Institute, 2001), 204n.54).

95 Roquentin got his facts wrong about the song. The singer Sophie Tucker was Jewish and the composer Shelton Brooks was black.

96 Žižek, "Afterword: Objects, Objects Everywhere," 188. "In late Lacan," Žižek points out, "the focus shifts to the object that the subject itself 'is,' to the *agalma, secret* treasure, which guarantees a minimum of phantasmic consistency to the subject's being. That is to say: *objet petit a,* as the object of fantasy, is that 'something in me more than myself' on account of which I perceive myself as 'worthy of the Other's desire'" (Slavoj Žižek, *The Plague of Fantasies* [New York: Verso, 1997], 9).

97 Žižek, *The Plague of Fantasies*, 81.

98 Slavoj Žižek, *Tarrying with the Negative*, 37.

99 Jacques Lacan, *The Ethics of Psychoanalysis, 1959-1960, The Seminar of Jacques Lacan, Book VII*, ed. Jacques-Alain Miller, trans. Dennis Porter (New York: Norton, 1992), 53.

100 Zupančič, *What Is Sex?* 24. As Russell Sbriglia further points out, "the subject stands for the radical negativity, the radical out-of-jointness, of reality (in) itself, the hole in reality that renders being unwhole, disoriented—or, even better, like the topological figures Lacan was so fond of invoking (the torus, Möbius strip, crosscap, Klein bottle, etc.), non-orientable" (Russell Sbriglia, "Object-Disoriented Ontology; Or, the Subject of *What Is Sex?*" *Continental Thought and Theory* 2, no. 2 [2018]: 40).

101 Žižek, "Afterword: Objects, Objects Everywhere," 190.

102 Lacan, *The Ethics of Psychoanalysis*, 71. See also Molly Anne Rothenberg, "Twisting 'Flat Ontology': Harman's 'Allure' and Lacan's Extimate Cause," in *Subject Lessons: Hegel, Lacan, and the Future of Materialism*, ed. Russell Sbriglia and Slavoj Žižek (Evanston: Northwestern University Press, 2020), 190–208.

103 Yosef, "War Fantasies," 312.

104 Žižek, "Afterword: Objects, Objects Everywhere," 187.

105 Žižek, *How to Read Lacan*, 71.

106 Slavoj Žižek, "Marx Reads Object-Oriented Ontology," in *Reading Marx*, ed. Slavoj Žižek, Frank Ruda, and Agon Hamza (Cambridge: Polity Press, 2018), 57.

107 Žižek, "Afterword: Objects, Objects Everywhere," 190.

108 Žižek, "Afterword: Objects, Objects Everywhere," 176.

109 Žižek, "Marx Reads Object-Oriented Ontology," 57.

Chapter 4

1 Zakiyyah Iman Jackson, "Outer Worlds: The Persistence of Race in Movement 'Beyond the Human,'" *GLQ* 21, nos. 2–3 (2015): 216. Copyright, 2015, Duke University Press. All rights reserved. Republished by permission of the copyright holder, Duke University Press. www.dukeupress.edu.

 2 Frank B. Wilderson III, "'We're Trying to Destroy the World': Anti-Blackness and Police Violence after Ferguson Pages," in *Shifting Corporealities in Contemporary Performance Danger, Im/mobility and Politics*, ed. Marina Gržinić and Aneta Stojnić (New York: Palgrave, 2018), 50.

3 Alexander Weheliye, *Habeas Viscus: Racializing Assemblages, Biopolitics, and Black Feminist Theories of the Human* (Durham: Duke University Press, 2014), 6.

4 Wolfe, *Animal Rites*, 7. Qtd. Weheliye, *Habeas Viscus*, 10.

5 Likewise, Charles "Chip" P. Linscott's typical anti-racist claim bemoaning "the exclusion of black people from the category of the human" would solicit a posthumanist rejoinder: the problem with exclusion must be supplemented with the problem with the human (Charles "Chip" P. Linscott, "All Lives (Don't Matter): The Internet Meets Afro-Pessimism," *Black Camera* 8, no. 2 (2017): 105.

6 Gary Francione, "Animals—Property or Persons?" in *Animal Rights: Current Debates and New Directions*, ed. Cass R. Sunstein and Martha C. Nussbaum (Oxford: Oxford University Press, 2004), 131.

7 Weheliye, *Habeas Viscus*, 10–11.

8 Calvin L. Warren, *Ontological Terror: Blackness, Nihilism, and Emancipation* (Durham: Duke University Press, 2018), 28.

9 Zakiyyah Iman Jackson, *Becoming Human: Matter and Meaning in an Antiblack World* (New York: Fordham University Press, 2020), 4.

10 Giorgio Agamben, *Means without End*, trans. Vincenzo Binetti and Cesare Casarino (Minneapolis: University of Minnesota Press, 2000), 38.

11 Achille Mbembe, "Necropolitics," *Public Culture* 15, no. 1 (2003): 12. See also Fred Moten, *Black and Blur* (Durham: Duke University Press, 2017), 198.

12 Weheliye, *Habeas Viscus*, 6.

13 Frank B. Wilderson III, *Red, White & Black: Cinema and the Structure of U.S. Antagonisms* (Durham: Duke University Press, 2010), 18, 56.

14 Wilderson, *Red, White & Black*, 38. Bryan Wagner also underscores the historical making of blackness as opposed to its African givenness: "Blackness does not come from Africa. Rather, Africa and its diaspora become black at a particular stage in their history. It sounds a little strange to put it this way, but the truth of this description is widely acknowledged. Blackness is an adjunct to racial slavery" (Bryan Wagner, *Disturbing the Peace: Black Culture and the Police Power after Slavery* [Cambridge: Harvard University Press, 2009], 1–2).

15 Wilderson, *Red, White & Black*, xi.

16 Patricia J. Williams, *The Alchemy of Race and Rights: Diary of a Law Professor* (Cambridge: Harvard University Press, 1991), 219.

17 Wilderson, *Red, White & Black*, 38.

18 Wilderson, *Red, White & Black*, 38. Wilderson takes his inspiration from Frantz Fanon, who qualifies the rhetoric of Shoah unprecedentedness. Unlike the Shoah, racial slavery marked an ontological division in the human as such: "[Jews] have been hunted, exterminated, and cremated, but these are just minor episodes in the family history. The Jew is not liked as soon as he has been detected. But with me things take on a *new* face" (Frantz Fanon, *Black Skin, White Masks*, trans. Richard Philcox [New York: Grove Press, 2008], 95).

19 Frank B. Wilderson III, "Afro-Pessimism and the End of Redemption," *Humanities Futures. Franklin Humanities Institute: Duke University* [October 20, 2015]). Available at https://humanitiesfutures.org/papers/afr o-pessimism-end-redemption/. Accessed September 23, 2019.

20 Wilderson, "We're Trying to Destroy the World," 58.

21 "Slavery . . . is a highly symbolized domain of human experience. While all aspects of the relationship are symbolized, there is an overwhelming concentration of the profound natal alienation of the slave. The reason for this is not hard to discern: it was the slave's isolation, his strangeness that made him most valuable to the master, but it was his very strangeness that most threatened the community . . . On the cognitive and mythic level, one dominant theme emerges, which lends an unusually loaded meaning to the act of natal alienation: this is the social death of the slave" (Orlando Patterson, *Slavery and Social Death: A Comparative Study* [Cambridge: Harvard University Press, 1982], 38).

22 Wilderson, "We're Trying to Destroy the World," 58.

23 Wilderson, "We're Trying to Destroy the World," 58.

24 Jared Sexton, "The Social Life of Social Death: On Afro-Pessimism and Black Optimism," *InTensions* 5 (2011): 21.

25 Patterson, *Slavery and Social Death*, 13.

26 Wilderson, *Red, White & Black*, 18. See also Stephanie Smallwood, *Saltwater Slavery: A Middle Passage from Africa to American Diaspora* (Cambridge: Harvard University Press, 2007).

27 Wilderson, *Red, White & Black*, 18.

28 Hortense J. Spillers, "Mama's Baby, Papa's Maybe: An American Grammar Book," in *Black, White, and in Color: Essays on American Literature and Culture* (Chicago: University of Chicago Press, 2003), 206.

29 Spillers, "Mama's Baby, Papa's Maybe," 206. Gendered relations arguably reemerge on the Plantation. Slaves form bonds and kinship, albeit precarious ones. Toni Morrison's *Beloved* recounts the doing and undoing of relationality under conditions of racial slavery. Morrison is particularly attentive to the gendering of pain. After Sethe's violation—the rape and theft of her milk—Paul D, a fellow slave, can only register her physical abuse, unable to comprehend or identify with her pain as a mother:

> "After I left you, those boys came in there and took my milk. That's what they came in there for. Held me down and took it. I told Mrs. Garner on em. [. . .] Them boys found out I told on em. Schoolteacher made one open up my back, and when it closed it made a tree. It grows there still."
> "They used cowhide on you?"
> "And they took my milk."
> "They beat you and you was pregnant."
> "And they took my milk!" (Toni Morrison, *Beloved* [New York: Knopf, 1987], 16–17)

Paul D's masculinity is humiliated, if not systematically denied, to the point that he starts to envy the sovereignty of Mister (the deformed rooster of Sweet Home): "Mister, he looked so . . . free. Better than me. Stronger, tougher. Son a bitch couldn't even get out of the shell by hisself but he was still king and I was . . ." (Morrison, *Beloved*, 72).

30 Spillers, "Mama's Baby, Papa's Maybe," 206. Spillers urges black men in the United States to decline their gendered interpellation into the patriarchal and racist symbolic order. They must disidentify with the phantasmatic image of the male subject (the Human) proffered by white civil society by affirming the feminine within them: "The African-American male must regain as an aspect of his own personhood—the power of 'yes' to the 'female' within" (Spillers, "Mama's Baby, Papa's Maybe," 228). Living without a symbolic father (without "the father's name, the father's law"), black males were psychically sustained by their mothers who fulfilled that paternal role in slavery and continue to occupy that position in the era of the school-to-prison pipeline.

31 David Theo Goldberg, "Modernity, Race, and Morality," *Cultural Critique* 24 (1993): 214. Calvin Warren deepens and exerts further pressure on the relationship between racism and philosophy: "If philosophy follows paths created by sociopolitical realities, then we must talk about antiblackness not just as a violent political formation but also as a *philosophical orientation*" (Warren, *Ontological Terror*, 12).

32 Immanuel Kant, *Observations on the Feeling of the Beautiful and the Sublime*, trans. John T. Goldthwait (Berkeley: University of California Press, 1960), 113, 111. Goldberg anticipates a defense of Kant that might excuse his racist statements as shortcomings of his precritical thinking, and thus not illustrative of his more mature ethical works: "Some may object that this is an early, pre-Critical, and so immature work, and that this sort of reasoning does not appear in the Critical and, especially, moral writings with which it is inconsistent. To respond, it need only be noted that Kant expresses similar sentiments in his 1775 essay on race and repeats them in his physical anthropology of 1791. The latter are hardly products of an immature mind" (Goldberg, "Modernity, Race, and Morality," 225n.13).

33 Saidiya V. Hartman, *Lose Your Mother: A Journey along the Atlantic Slave Route* (New York: Farrar, Straus and Giroux, 2007), 6. Hortense Spillers makes a similar point: "Even though the captive flesh/body has been 'liberated,' and no one need pretend that even the quotation marks do not *matter*, dominant symbolic activity, the ruling episteme that releases the dynamics of naming and valuation, remains grounded in the originating metaphors of captivity and mutilation so that it is as if neither time nor history, nor historiography and its topics, shows movement, as the human subject is 'murdered' over and over again by the passions of a bloodless and anonymous archaism, showing itself in endless disguise" (Spillers, "Mama's Baby, Papa's Maybe," 208).

34 Jared Sexton, "People-of-Color-Blindness: Notes on the Afterlife of Slavery," *Social Text* 28, no. 2 103 (2010): 6.

35 Sexton, "The Social Life of Social Death," 28.

36 Warren, *Ontological Terror*, 18.

37 Hartman, *Scenes of Subjection: Terror, Slavery, and Self-Making in Nineteenth-Century America* (Oxford: Oxford University Press, 1997), 7.

38 Michelle Alexander, *The New Jim Crow: Mass Incarceration in the Age of Colorblindness* (New York: The New Press, 2010), 16. America's criminal justice institutions structurally disadvantage blacks, crippling, if not foreclosing, their possibilities for social and economic mobility: "What is completely missed in the rare public debates today about the plight of African Americans is that a huge percentage of them are not free to move

up at all. It is not just that they lack opportunity, attend poor schools, or are plagued by poverty. They are barred by law from doing so. . . . To put the matter starkly: The current system of control permanently locks a huge percentage of the African American community out of the mainstream society and economy. The system operates through our criminal justice institutions, but it functions more like a caste system than a system of crime control. . . . Although this new system of racialized social control purports to be colorblind, it creates and maintains racial hierarchy much as earlier systems of control did. Like Jim Crow (and slavery), mass incarceration operates as a tightly networked system of laws, policies, customs, and institutions that operate collectively to ensure the subordinate status of a group defined largely by race" (Alexander, *The New Jim Crow*, 13). See also Loïc Wacquant, "From Slavery to Mass Incarceration: Rethinking the 'Race Question in the US," *New Left Review* 13 (2002): 41–60; Angela Davis, *Are Prisons Obsolete?* (New York: Seven Stories Press, 2003); Douglas Blackmon, *Slavery by Another Name: The Re-Enslavement of Black Americans from the Civil War to World War II* (New York: Anchor Books, 2008).

39 Frank B. Wilderson III, "Gramsci's Black Marx: Whither the Slave in Civil Society?" *Social Identities* 9, no. 2 (2003): 230.

40 Saidiya V. Hartman, "The Time of Slavery," *South Atlantic Quarterly* 100, no 4 (2002): 757–77. See also Christina Sharpe, *In the Wake: On Blackness and Being* (Durham: Duke University Press, 2016).

41 Calvin L. Warren, "Black Time: Slavery, Metaphysics, and the Logic of Wellness," in *The Psychic Hold of Slavery: Legacies in American Expressive Culture*, ed. Soyica Diggs Colbert, Robert J. Patterson, and Aida Levy-Hussen (New Brunswick: Rutgers University Press, 2016), 65.

42 Claire Maria Chambers, *Performance Studies and Negative Epistemology: Performance Apophatics* (New York: Palgrave, 2017), 189.

43 Saidiya Hartman and Frank B. Wilderson III, "The Position of the Unthought," *Qui Parle* 13, 2 (2003): 188.

44 See Hartman, *Scenes of Subjection*.

45 Wilderson, "We're Trying to Destroy the World," 46.

46 Žižek, "Against the Grain: 'What if violence is needed to keep things as they are?'" *The Independent* (January 24, 2008). Available at https://www.independent.co.uk/news/education/higher/against-the-grain-what-if-violence-is-needed-to-keep-things-as-they-are-772960.html. Accessed September 4, 2019.

47 See Hannah Arendt, "Reflections on Little Rock," *Dissent* 6, no. 1 (1959): 45–56. Moten rejects Arendt's objections to equality sought through educational desegregation during the Jim Crow era. Whereas Arendt condemns the violence of desegregation (since it violates whites' social right of free association), Moten foregrounds the naturalized violence of the status quo—Arendt's white privilege renders her unable to see that "separation's constant and violent assault on equality is always most emphatically an assault on black social life." Segregation in the public sphere is precisely how that assault takes place (Fred Moten, *The Universal Machine* [Durham: Duke University Press, 2018], 100). Henceforth all references to this edition will be stated parenthetically in the text. See also, Katherine T. Gines, *Hannah Arendt and the Negro Question* (Bloomington: Indiana University Press, 2014), 5.

48 Wilderson, "We're Trying to Destroy the World," 47.

49 Wilderson, *Red, White & Black*, 82.

50 Wilderson, "Afro-Pessimism and the End of Redemption."

51 Wilderson, *Red, White & Black*, 9.

52 Wilderson, *Red, White & Black*, 11.

53 See Spillers, "Mama's Baby, Papa's Maybe."

54 Warren, *Ontological Terror*, 51.

55 Hartman, *Scenes of Subjection*, 63.

56 "Black existence is . . . a fungible object, infinitely malleable in its content due to the abstraction of its quality and open for use for anyone who can claim subjecthood" (R. L. "Wanderings of the Slave: Black Life and Social Death," *Mute* [June 5, 2013]). Available at http://www.metamute.org/e ditorial/articles/wanderings-slave-black-life-and-social-death. Accessed September 22, 2019.

57 Likewise, to be a bourgeois subject meant that one was not black: "The slave is the object or the ground that makes possible the existence of the bourgeois subject and, by negation or contradistinction, defines liberty, citizenship, and the enclosures of the social body" (Hartman, *Scenes of Subjection*, 62). A similar logic applied to the white worker as well. If the worker could sell his or her labor power as a commodity (and, in turn, enjoy the pleasures of agency from his or her paid labor and capacity to purchase things), the slave's ~~being~~-object is used and exchanged as a commodity. In stark opposition to the worker, then, the slave is

ontologically incapable of creating or realizing himself or herself in labor. For the worker, alienation indexes the failure to self-actualize under capitalism, signaling a frustration at not being (fully) human; for the slave, alienation remains an unavoidable feature of black being, of the black's inhumanity. There is no slave subjectivity to emancipate since the slave is first and foremost a "human tool," a mere object, or animal-like, for the white captor (Patterson, *Slavery and Social Death*, 7).

58 Hartman and Wilderson, "The Position of the Unthought," 183.

59 Hartman, *Scenes of Subjection*, 5.

60 Hartman, *Scenes of Subjection*, 234n.8.

61 Warren, *Ontological Terror*, 24.

62 Wilderson, "We're Trying to Destroy the World," 50.

63 Fanon, *Black Skin*, 93.

64 Fanon, *Black Skin*, 89.

65 Fanon, *Black Skin*, 89, 93.

66 Fanon, *Black Skin*, 89.

67 Bogost, *Alien Phenomenology*, 31.

68 "It is a peculiar sensation, this double-consciousness, this sense of always looking at one's self through the eyes of others, of measuring one's soul by the tape of a world that looks on in amused contempt and pity. One ever feels his two-ness,—an American, a Negro; two souls, two thoughts, two unreconciled strivings; two warring ideals in one dark body, whose dogged strength alone keeps it from being torn asunder" (W. E. B. Du Bois, *The Souls of Black Folk*, ed. Henry Louis Gates, Jr., and Terri Hulme Oliver [New York: Norton, 1999], 11).

69 Meillassoux, *After Finitude*, 5–6.

70 Morton, "Here Comes Everything," 169.

71 Meillassoux, *After Finitude*, 7.

72 Warren, *Ontological Terror*, 5.

73 Immanuel Kant, *Groundwork of the Metaphysic of Morals*, trans. H. J. Paton (New York: Harper & Row, 1964), 96.

74 Calvin L. Warren, "Black Mysticism: Fred Moten's Phenomenology of (Black) Spirit," *Zeitschrift für Anglistik und Amerikanistik* 65, no. 2 (2017): 223.

75 Alessandra Raengo, "Black Matters," *Discourse* 38, no. 2 (2016): 248.
Zoe Todd is critical of the neglect of race and racism among the major
proponents of the ontological turn—along with a general neglect of
indigenous thinkers whose work resonates with the preoccupations of
OOO, NM, and ANT—leading her to characterize "ontology [as] just
another word for colonialism" (Zoe Todd, "An Indigenous Feminist's
Take on the Ontological Turn: 'Ontology' Is Just Another Word for
Colonialism," *Journal of Historical Sociology* 29 [2016]: 4–22). Warren
also decries OOO for "project[ing] humanism onto objects" while tacitly
denying it to black objects (Warren, *Ontological Terror*, 13). Harman does
say something about Edward Said and the racist discourse of Orientalism.
In "Objects and Orientalism," Harman undertakes a preemptive defense
of OOO against potential postcolonial objectors. If the exotic Orient is
the quintessential trope of Orientalism, and Harman has a propensity to
describe objects as exotic, then OOO might be seen as ripe for the charge
of Orientalism. Harman's overall message, however, is—don't be fooled
by the appearances. OOO is in fact good for the Orient. It is even better
than Said's own critique of Orientalism because, unlike Said's critique,
OOO does not settle for anti-realism (what Said inherits from Foucault):
"For if we disdain all notion of realities concealed from view, and see
the world instead as an immanent surface where everything is merely
staged or performed without any secret back rooms . . . , then entities
will hold nothing in reserve that can ever surprise us. . . . Any doctrine
of post-colonial *resistance* requires some element outside the current
grid-work of things that is *able* to resist, and such a dark fibre is woven
into the very fabric of OOO" (Harman, "Objects and Orientalism," in *The
Agon of Interpretations: Towards a Critical Intercultural Hermeneutics*, ed.
Ming Xie [Toronto: University of Toronto Press, 2014], 137). Or to be
clearer, Harman maintains a distinction between epistemological realism
and ontological realism. OOO acknowledges the violence of the former
but defends the emancipatory politics of the latter. Cognitive mastery
of its object is precisely what OOO declines. Its emphasis on the exotic
is meant to counter the epistemic will to dominate. And here Harman
assures us that there is nothing uniquely exotic about the Orient. A strip
mall in Indianapolis is equally exotic: *all* objects withdraw; all objects
are intrinsically mysterious and resistant to symbolic digestion. So again,
why is OOO good for the non-European? It is the ontological reserve
that all beings possess by virtue of their existence. Being posthuman for
Harman means championing all essences as being always more than
their representations. He suspends human exceptionalism. The humanist
script that we are distinct subjects, surrounded by objects is nothing

more than an ideological fantasy. In fact, there are no subjects—only objects. But there is something deeply unsatisfying with this reading of the other/Oriental. OOO's flat ontology gives you a flat hermeneutics, a hermeneutics unable to register the subtleties of power. I don't see how Harman's generalizing exoticism, making it *a fact of ontology*, resolves anything. If every object is exotic, nothing is exotic. Orientalism is a challenge to racist ontology. If "race is the child of racism, not the father," as Ta-Nehisi Coates puts it, then we might critically reassert that *the Orient is the child of Orientalism, not the father* (Ta-Nehisi Coates, *Between the World and Me* [New York: Spiegel and Grau, 2015], 7). Harman's ontologization of the Orient positions it as a paternal source. Moreover, there is nothing in OOO or NM to account for the working of ideological fantasies—those fantasies that construct the non-European as exotic, the source of fascination and repulsion.

76 David Marriott, *Whither Fanon? Studies in the Blackness of Being* (Stanford: Stanford University Press, 2018), 48–9. "Natal alienation" does a better job of addressing the specificity of black alienation, referring to the radical and traumatic unplugging of black people (Africans) from their organic communities (Patterson, *Slavery and Social Death*, 5).

77 Fanon, *Black Skin*, 90.

78 Warren, *Ontological Terror*, 42.

79 Fanon, *Black Skin*, xii.

80 Fanon, *Black Skin*, 95.

81 Wilderson, "The Prison Slave as Hegemony's (Silent) Scandal," *Social Justice* 30, no. 2 (2003): 25.

82 "The Afro-pessimists are theorists of Black positionality who share Fanon's insistence that, though Blacks are indeed sentient beings, the structure of the entire world's semantic field . . . is sutured by anti-Black solidarity" (Wilderson, *Red, White & Black*, 58).

83 "[Blacks] more than symbolize or signify various social pathologies—they become them. In our anti-black world, blacks are pathology" (Lewis R. Gordon, *Existentia Africana: Understanding Africana Existential Thought* [New York: Routledge, 2000], 87).

84 Fred Moten, *In the Break: The Aesthetics of the Black Radical Tradition* (Minneapolis: University of Minnesota Press, 2003), 1.

85 Moten, *In the Break*, 1.

86 Moten, "Black Optimism/Black Operation," unpublished paper on file with the author. (2007) https://lucian.uchicago.edu/blogs/politicalfeeling/file s/2007/12/moten-black-optimism.doc. Accessed August 22, 2019.

87 Nahum Chandler, "Of Exorbitance: The Problem of the Negro as a Problem for Thought," *Criticism* 50, no. 3 (2008): 351.

88 Fred Moten, *Stolen Life* (Durham: Duke University Press, 2018), 131.

89 Sexton also adapts Irigaray's formulation, referring to the black subject as a "subject-that-is-not-one" in his contribution to a roundtable organized by Noura Erakat on the question of black-Palestinian solidarity. See "Roundtable on Anti-Blackness and Black-Palestinian Solidarity" (June 3, 2015). Available at www.jadaliyya.com/pages/index/21764/roundtable-on-anti-blackness- and-black-palestinian. Accessed December 3, 2019.

90 Warren, "Black Mysticism," 228.

91 Sexton, "People-of-Color-Blindness," 35.

92 Warren also seems to problematically Kantianize blackness, compromising its critical force by treating it as a "noumenon" (Warren, "Black Mysticism," 224).

93 Žižek, *In Defense of Lost Causes*, 327.

94 Žižek, *In Defense of Lost Causes*, 328.

95 Žižek, *In Defense of Lost Causes*, 328.

96 Žižek, "Holding the Place," 310.

97 Incidentally, Moten considers Derrida "the most radical—which might, in this case, be taken to mean the blackest—of philosophers" (Moten, *In the Break*, 77).

98 Derrida, "Faith and Knowledge," 80n.27.

99 Jacques Derrida, *The Death Penalty*, vol. 1, trans. Peggy Kamuf (Chicago: University of Chicago Press, 2013), 5.

100 Derrida, *Rogues*, 109.

101 See also: "Blackness . . . is a strain that pressures the assumption of the equivalence of personhood and subjectivity" (Moten, *In the Break*, 1).

102 Sexton qualifies and counterbalances Moten's celebratory use of blackness as pathogen: "blackness is not the pathogen in Afropessimism, the world is. Not the earth, but the world, and maybe even the whole possibility

of and desire for a world" (Sexton, The Social Life of Social Death, 31). Against Moten's allegedly promiscuous use of the term, Sexton aligns the pathogen exclusively with the destructive forces of antiblackness, with white civil society's libidinal economy. But to do so is to remove the *pharmacotic* fact of blackness, its paraontological force. Blackness is not only on the receiving end of the world's pathologizing ways, it is an agent of disorder as well, stealing life from or smuggling it back into murderous ontology.

103 See Paul Gilroy, *Against Race: Imagining Political Culture beyond the Color Line* (Cambridge: Harvard University Press, 2000).

104 Warren, *Ontological Terror*, 4, 7.

105 Wilderson, *Red, White & Black*, 28.

106 Frank B. Wilderson III, "The Black Liberation Army and the Paradox of Political Engagement," in *Postcoloniality-Decoloniality-Black Critique: Joints and Fissures*, ed. Sabine Broeck and Carsten Junker (Frankfurt: Campus Verlag, 2014), 203.

107 Frantz Fanon, *The Wretched of the Earth*, trans. Richard Philcox (New York: Grove Press, 2004), 2.

108 Wilderson, "The Black Liberation Army," 177.

109 Wilderson, "The Black Liberation Army," 178.

110 Wilderson, *Red, White & Black*, 338.

111 Against the anti-humanism of Althusser, David Harvey revives the idea of a Marxist "revolutionary humanism" (David Harvey, *Seventeen Contradictions and the End of Capitalism* [Oxford: Oxford University Press, 2014], 287).

112 Wilderson, "Afro-Pessimism and the End of Redemption."

113 See Patrice Douglass and Frank B. Wilderson III, "The Violence of Presence: Metaphysics in a Blackened World," *The Black Scholar* 3, no. 4 (2013): 117–23.

114 Frank B. Wilderson III, "Social Death and Narrative Aporia in 12 Years a Slave," *Black Camera* 7, no. 1 (2015): 139.

115 Jared Sexton, "Afro-Pessimism: The Unclear Word," *Rhizomes* 29 (2016). Available at https://doi.org/10.20415/rhiz/029.e02. Accessed September 23, 2019.

116 Žižek borrows the formulation from Agamben. See Agamben, "Thought is the Courage of Hopelessness: An Interview with Philosopher Giorgio

Agamben," Interview by Jordan Skinner. Verso Books (June 17, 2014). Available at https://www.versobooks.com/blogs/1612-thought-is-the-co urage-of-hopelessness-an-interview-with-philosopher-giorgio-agamben. Accessed August 29, 2019.

117 Marriott, *Whither Fanon*, 220.

118 Žižek, *The Courage of Hopelessness*, xi–xii.

119 Fanon, *Black Skin*, xiv.

120 I agree with David Marriot that for Fanon "the need to affirm affirmation through negation" does not take the form of "a moral imperative"—akin to a Sartrean vision of authenticity—but, I would add, it is also more than a "psychopolitical necessity" (David Marriott, *Haunted Life: Visual Culture and Black Modernity* [New Brunswick: Rutgers University Press, 2007], 273n.9). If Fanon declines the Sartrean temptation to moralize his plight, his prayer for a perpetual mode of questioning locates an *ethics* of skepticism, a skeptical ethos, a life-affirming form of hermeneutic negativity, at the heart of his anti-colonial project.

121 Fanon, *Black Skin*, 206.

122 Fanon, *Black Skin*, xiii, emphasis added.

123 Jared Sexton, *Amalgamation Schemes: Antiblackness and the Critique of Multiracialism* (Minneapolis: University of Minnesota Press, 2008), 293n.9.

124 Wilderson, *Red, White & Black,* 126.

125 Wilderson, "We're Trying to Destroy the World," 52.

126 Wilderson, "Afro-Pessimism and the End of Redemption."

127 Mbembe, "Conversation: Achille Mbembe and David Theo Goldberg on *Critique of Black Reason*," *Theory, Culture, and Society* (July 3, 2018). Available at https://www.theoryculturesociety.org/conversation-achille-mb embe-and-david-theo-goldberg-on-critique-of-black-reason/. Accessed September 6, 2019.

128 Keeanga-Yamahtta Taylor, *From #BlackLivesMatter to Black Liberation* (Chicago: Haymarket Books, 2016), 187.

129 Wilderson, "Gramsci's Black Marx," 233.

130 As Riley notes, "white voice doesn't really exist. White people don't even have it. They use it, and it's a performance. There's a performance of whiteness that is all about saying that everything is OK, you've got your bills paid, and that—and, you know, this kind of smooth and easy thing"

(Amy Goodman and Juan González, "Boots Riley's Dystopian Satire 'Sorry to Bother You' Is an Anti-Capitalist Rallying Cry for Workers," *Democracy Now!* (July 17, 2018). Available at https://www.democracynow.org/2018/7/17/sorry_to_bother_you_boots_rileys. Accessed September 1, 2019. In psychoanalytic terms, the "white voice" refers to the "ideal ego," standing for the idealized self-image of whiteness: the privileged white person I would like to be and, more importantly, that I would like others to see me as (Žižek, *How to Read Lacan*, 80).

131 "In the antiblack world there is but one race, and that race is black. Thus, to be racialized is to be pushed 'down' toward blackness, and to be deracialized is to be pushed 'up' toward whiteness" (Lewis R. Gordon, *Her Majesty's Other Children: Sketches of Racism from a Neocolonial Age* (Lanham: Rowman & Littlefield, 1997), 76.

132 Mbembe, *Critique of Black Reason*, trans. Laurent Dubois (Durham: Duke University Press, 2017), 4.

133 Mbembe, *Critique of Black Reason*, 5.

134 Mbembe, *Critique of Black Reason*, 6.

135 Mbembe, *Critique of Black Reason*, 54.

136 See Henry A. Giroux, *Stormy Weather: Katrina and the Politics of Disposability* (Boulder: Paradigm Publishers, 2006).

137 Žižek, *Demanding the Impossible*, 58.

138 Henry A. Giroux, *Dangerous Thinking in the Age of the New Authoritarianism* (New York: Routledge, 2016), 53.

139 Mbembe, *Critique of Black Reason*, 7.

140 Fredric Jameson, *Representing Capital: A Reading of Volume One* (New York: Verso, 2011), 150. While recognizing the "infectious" factor that race or gender plays in the reproduction of capital, Harvey does not consider them central to the inner logic of capital, "specific to the form of circulation and accumulation that constitutes the economic engine of capitalism" (Harvey, *Seventeen Contradictions and the End of Capitalism*, 7–8). In other words, an anti-racist struggle (against domination) does not *necessarily* bring about an anti-capitalist one (against exploitation).

141 Detroit's own art performance does not escape the logic of commodification, the white voyeurism, and enjoyment of black goods. Still, the reflexivity of the scene solicits a further distancing between

Detroit's audience and Riley's. What *Sorry to Bother to You* is after is the destruction of the world—not an indulgence in sentimentality or an evening of entertainment.

142 Mbembe, "Conversation."

143 "In a world where slavery is in effect legal, the scientific establishment has no ethical quandary about fusing humans and horses. This is not a vision of a dystopian future; it is a commentary on five hundred years of human history" (Robin D. G. Kelley, "Sorry, Not Sorry," *Boston Review* (September 13, 2018). Available at http://bostonreview.net/race-literature-culture/ robin-d-g-kelley-sorry-not-sorry#.XMdwpNHrLCE.email. Accessed September 24, 2019.

144 M. Shadee Malaklou, "'Dilemmas' of Coalition and the Chronopolitics of Man: Towards an Insurgent Black Feminine Otherwise," *Theory & Event* 21, no. 1 (2018): 216.

145 Fred Moten, "Bridge and One: Improvisations of the Public Sphere," in *Performing Hybridity*, ed. May Joseph and Jennifer Natalya Fink (Minneapolis: University of Minnesota Press, 1999), 234.

146 "The zone of nonbeing is experimental, is a kind of experiment, this double edge of the experiment, this theater of like and unlike in which friendship's sociality overflows its political regulation" (Moten, *The Universal Machine*, 224).

147 Moten, *Stolen Life*, 26.

148 Moten, *Stolen Life*, 159.

149 See Stefano Harney and Fred Moten, *The Undercommons: Fugitive Planning and Black Study* (New York: Autonomedia, 2013).

150 Wilderson, "Gramsci's Black Marx," 233.

151 Wilderson, "Gramsci's Black Marx," 237.

152 Wilderson, "Gramsci's Black Marx," 238.

153 Nicholas Royle, *The Uncanny* (Manchester: Manchester University Press, 2003), 2.

154 Žižek, "Neighbors and Other Monsters," 143.

155 Žižek, *Living in the End Times*, 120.

156 Goodman and González, "Boots Riley's Dystopian Satire." Riley's rap group, The Coup, enacts this anti-capitalist sensibility in many of its songs,

perhaps none more forcefully and violently than "The Guillotine," with its refrain, "We got the guillotine you better run." The "you" here is the capitalists, with or without a human face, that Steve Lift embodies in the film.

Conclusion

1 Žižek, *Like a Thief*, 46. From *Like A Thief In Broad Daylight* by copyright © Slavoj Žižek 2018 published by Allen Lane 2018, Penguin Books 2019. Reproduced by permission of Penguin Books Ltd. ©.

2 Žižek, *The Parallax View*, 42.

3 Žižek, *How to Read Lacan*, 39.

4 Justin McBrien, "Accumulating Extinction: Planetary Catastrophism in the Necrocene," in *Anthropocene or Capitalocene? Nature, History, and the Crisis of Capitalism*, ed. Jason W. Moore (Oakland: PM Press, 2016), 119. See also Andreas Malm, "The Anthropocene Myth," *Jacobin* (March 30, 2015). Available at https://www.jacobinmag.com/2015/03/anthropocene-ca pitalism-climate-change/. Acccessed July 24, 2020.

5 Andrew Cole, "Those Obscure Objects of Desire," *Artforum* 53, no. 10 (2015): 323. See also Alexander R. Galloway, "The Poverty of Philosophy: Realism and Post-Fordism," *Critical Inquiry* 39, 2 (2013): 347–66. For Harman's less-than-convincing rejoinder to his critics from the Left, see Harman, "Object-Oriented Ontology and Commodity Fetishism: Kant, Marx, Heidegger, and Things," *Eidos* 2 (2017): 28–36.

6 Jacques Rancière, *The Politics of Aesthetics: Distribution of the Sensible*, trans. G. Rockhill (New York, Continuum, 2004).

7 Rancière, *The Politics of Aesthetics*, 12.

8 Rancière, *The Politics of Aesthetics*, 12.

9 Jacques Rancière, *The Emancipated Spectator*, trans. G. Elliott (New York, Verso, 2009), 103.

10 Rancière, *Emancipated Spectator*, 82, 13.

11 Bennett, *Vibrant Matter*, 106.

12 Rancière, *Disagreement*, 35.

13 Rancière, *Disagreement*, 28–9.

14 Rancière, "Work, Identity, Subject," in *Jacques Rancière and the Contemporary Scene: The Philosophy of Radical Equality*, ed. Jean-Philippe Deranty and Alison Ross (New York: Continuum, 2012), 205–16, 206.

15 Jane Bennett, "In Parliament with Things," in *Radical Democracy: Politics between Abundance and Lack*, ed. Lars Tønder and Lasse Thomassen (Manchester: Manchester University Press, 2006), 133–48.

16 Slavoj Žižek, *Sex and the Failed Absolute* (New York: Bloomsbury, 2020), 361.

17 Žižek, *Sex and the Failed Absolute*, 361.

18 Žižek, *How to Read Lacan*, 46.

19 Žižek, *The Parallax View*, 111.

20 Žižek, *Absolute Recoil*, 330.

21 This is not to emphasize the content of the experience, to assume a commonality to the experience of the subject's ontological void/gap (as if differentiated subjects did not exist). Positionality matters. Just as Fanon pointedly reminded Sartre, that he "forgets that the black man suffers in his body quite differently from the white man" (Fanon, *Black Skin*, 117), we must not forget that the "inhuman" within is experienced/suffered by those deemed and treated as inhuman quite differently. The irreducibility of difference is not an oversight of inhuman posthumanism but a precondition of its mode of analysis.

Bibliography

Adams, Carol. *The Sexual Politics of Meat: A Feminist-Vegetarian Critical Theory*. New York: Continuum, 1990.

Adorno, Theodor W. *Beethoven: The Philosophy of Music*. Ed. Rolf Tiedemann. Trans. Edmund Jephcott. Cambridge: Polity Press, 1998.

Agamben, Giorgio. *Means without End*. Trans. Vincenzo Binetti and Cesare Casarino. Minneapolis: University of Minnesota Press, 2000.

Agamben, Giorgio. *The Open: Man and Animal*. Trans. Kevin Attell. Stanford: Stanford University Press, 2004.

Agamben, Giorgio. "Thought Is the Courage of Hopelessness: An Interview with Philosopher Giorgio Agamben." Interview by Jordan Skinner. Verso Books (June 17, 2014). https://www.versobooks.com/blogs/1612-thought -is-the-courage-of-hopelessness-an-interview-with-philosopher-giorgio- agamben.

Alexander, Livia. "Confessing without Regret: An Israeli Film Genre." In *Screening Torture: Media Representations of State Terror and Political Domination*. Ed. Michael Flynn and Fabiola F. Salek. New York: Columbia University Press, 2012. 191–216.

Alexander, Michelle. *The New Jim Crow: Mass Incarceration in the Age of Colorblindness*. New York: The New Press, 2010.

Alloun, Esther. "'That's the beauty of it, it's very simple!' Animal Rights and Settler Colonialism in Palestine–Israel." *Settler Colonial Studies* 8, no. 4 (2018): 559–74.

Althusser, Louis. "Ideology and Ideological State Apparatuses (Notes towards an Investigation)." In *Mapping Ideology*. Ed. Slavoj Žižek. New York: Verso, 1994. 100–40.

Arendt, Hannah. "Reflections on Little Rock." *Dissent* 6, no. 1 (1959): 45–56.

Badiou, Alain. *Ethics: An Essay on the Understanding of Evil*. Trans. Peter Hallward. New York: Verso, 2002.

Badiou, Alain. *Saint Paul: The Foundation of Universalism*. Trans. Ray Brassier. Stanford: Stanford University Press, 2003.

Badmington, Neil. *Alien Chic: Posthumanism and the Other Within*. New York: Routledge, 2004.

Badmington, Neil. "Posthumanism." In *The Routledge Companion to Critical Theory*. Ed. Simon Malpas and Paul Wake. New York: Routledge, 2006. 240–1.

Barthes, Roland. "Death of the Author." In *Image, Text, Music*. Trans. Stephen Heath. New York: Hill and Wang, 1977. 142–8.

Beauvoir, Simone de. *The Second Sex*. Trans. Constance Borde and Sheila Malovany-Chevallier. New York: Alfred Knopf, 2010.

Belcourt, Billy-Ray. "An Indigenous Critique of Critical Animal Studies." In *Colonialism and Animality: Anti-Colonial Perspectives in Critical Animal Studies*. Ed. Kelly Struthers Montford and Chloë Taylor. New York: Routledge, 2020. 19–28.

Bennett, Jane. *The Enchantment of Modern Life: Attachments, Crossings, and Ethics*. Princeton: Princeton University Press, 2001.

Bennett, Jane. "In Parliament with Things." In *Radical Democracy: Politics between Abundance and Lack*. Ed. Lars Tønder and Lasse Thomassen. Manchester: Manchester University Press, 2006. 133–48.

Bennett, Jane. "Systems and Things: On Vital Materialism and Object-Oriented Philosophy." In *The Nonhuman Turn*. Ed. Richard Grusin. Minneapolis: University of Minnesota Press, 2015. 223–39.

Bennett, Jane. *Vibrant Matter: A Political Ecology of Things*. Durham: Duke University Press, 2010.

Blackmon, Douglas. *Slavery By Another Name: The Re-Enslavement of Black Americans from the Civil War to World War II*. New York: Anchor Books, 2008.

Blackwell, Derek R. "All Eyes on Me: Surveillance and the Digital Archive in 'The Entire History of You.'" In *Black Mirror and Critical Media Theory*. Ed. Angela M. Cirucci and Barry Vacker. Lanham: Lexington Books, 2018. 55–67.

Bogost, Ian. *Alien Phenomenology, or What It's Like to Be a Thing*. Minneapolis: University of Minnesota Press, 2012.

Boisseron, Bénédicte. *Afro-Dog: Blackness and the Animal Question*. New York: Columbia University Press, 2018.

Bostrom, Nick. "In Defence of Posthuman Dignity." *Bioethics* 19, no. 3 (2005): 202–14.

Bostrom, Nick. "A History of Transhumanist Thought." *Journal of Evolution and Technology* 14, no. 1 (2005): 1–25.

Bostrom, Nick. "The Transhumanist FAQ: A General Introduction." *The World Transhumanist Association* (2003). https://humanityplus.org/philosophy/transhumanist-faq/.

Boysen, Benjamin. "The Embarrassment of Being Human: A Critique of New Materialism and Object-Oriented Ontology." *Orbis Litterarum* 73, no. 3 (2018): 222–42.

Braidotti, Rosi. *The Posthuman*. Cambridge: Polity Press, 2013.

Braidotti, Rosi. "Posthuman, All Too Human Towards a New Process Ontology." *Theory, Culture & Society* 23, nos. 7–8 (2006): 197–208.

Brooker, Charlie, Annabel Jones, and Jason Arnopp. *Inside Black Mirror*. New York: Crown Archetype, 2018.

Bruns, Gerald L. "Becoming-Animal (Some Simple Ways)." *New Literary History* 38, no. 4 (2007): 703–20.

Bruns, Gerald L. "Derrida's Cat (Who Am I?)." *Research in Phenomenology* 38 (2008): 404–23.

Bryant, Levi R. *The Democracy of Objects*. Ann Arbor: Open Humanities Press, 2011.

Budé, Guillaume. *L'Etude des Lettres. Principes pour sa juste et commode institution. De studio literarum recte et commode instituendo*. Ed. Marie-Madelaine de La Garanderie. Paris: Les Belles lettres, 1988.

Butler, Judith. *Giving an Account of Oneself*. New York: Fordham, 2005.

Calarco, Matthew. "Deconstruction Is Not Vegetarianism: Humanism, Subjectivity, and Animal Ethics. *Continental Philosophy Review* 37, no. 2 (2004): 175–201.

Calarco, Matthew. *Thinking Through Animals: Identity, Difference, Indistinction*. Stanford: Stanford University Press, 2015.

Calarco, Matthew. *Zoographies: The Question of the Animal from Heidegger to Derrida*. New York: Columbia University Press, 2008.

Carlson, David Gray. *A Commentary to Hegel's Science of Logic*. New York: Palgrave Macmillan, 2007.

Caruth, Cathy. "Trauma and Experience: Introduction." In *Trauma: Explorations in Memory*. Ed. Cathy Caruth. Baltimore: John Hopkins University Press, 1995. 3–12.

Cavell, Stanley. "Companionable Thinking." In *Philosophy and Animal Life*. Ed. Stanley Cavell, Cora Diamond, John McDowell, Ian Hacking, and Cary Wolfe. New York: Columbia University Press, 2009. 91–126.

Césaire, Aimé. *Discourse on Colonialism*. Trans. Joan Pinkham. New York: Monthly Review Press, 2000.

Chambers, Claire Maria. *Performance Studies and Negative Epistemology: Performance Apophatics*. New York: Palgrave, 2017.

Chandler, Nahum. "Of Exorbitance: The Problem of the Negro as a Problem for Thought." *Criticism* 50, no. 3 (2008): 345–410.

Cixous, Hélène. "Castration or Decapitation?" Trans. Annette Kuhn. *Signs* 7, no. 1 (1981): 41–55.

Cixous, Hélène. "A Refugee." In *The Animal Question in Deconstruction*. Ed. Lynn Turner. Edinburgh: Edinburgh University Press, 2013. 9–12.

Cixous, Hélène. *Stigmata: Escaping Texts*. London: Routledge, 1989.

Clynes, Manfred E. and Nathan S. Kline. "Cyborgs and Space." *Astronautics* (September 1960): 27–31.

Coates, Ta-Nehisi. *Between the World and Me*. New York: Spiegel and Grau, 2015.

Coe, Susan. *Dead Meat*. New York: Four Walls Eight Windows, 1996.

Coetzee, J.M. *The Lives of Animals*. Princeton: Princeton University Press, 1999.

Cole, Andrew. "Those Obscure Objects of Desire." *Artforum* 53, no. 10 (2015): 318–23.

Conley, Donovan and Benjamin Burroughs. "*Black Mirror*, Mediated Affect and the Political." *Culture, Theory and Critique* 60, no. 2 (2019): 139–53.

Daly, Glyn. *Speculation: Politics, Ideology, Event*. Evanston: Northwestern University Press, 2019.

Davis, Angela. *Are Prisons Obsolete?* New York: Seven Stories Press, 2003.

Dekoven, Marianne. "*Jouissance*, Cyborgs, and Companion Species: Feminist Experiment." *PMLA* 121, no. 5 (2006): 1690–6.

DeLanda, Manuel. *A New Philosophy of Society: Assemblage Theory and Social Complexity*. London: Continuum, 2006.

Deleuze, Giles and Felix Guattari, *A Thousand Plateaus: Capitalism and Schizophrenia*. Trans. Brian Massumi. Minneapolis: University of Minnesota Press, 1987.

Derbyshire, Jonathan. "Interview with Slavoj Zizek." *New Statesman* (October 29, 2009). https://www.newstatesman.com/ideas/2009/10/today-interview-c apitalism.

Derrida, Jacques. *The Animal that Therefore I Am*. Trans. David Willis. New York: Fordham University Press, 2008.

Derrida, Jacques. *Archive Fever: A Freudian Impression*. Trans. Eric Prenowitz. Chicago: University of Chicago Press, 1998.

Derrida, Jacques. "Autoimmunity: Real and Symbolic Suicides—A Dialogue with Jacques Derrida." In *Philosophy in a Time of Terror: Dialogues with Jürgen Habermas and Jacques Derrida*. Ed. Giovanna Borradori. Chicago: University of Chicago Press, 2004. 85–136.

Derrida, Jacques. *The Beast and the Sovereign, Volume I*. Ed. Michel Lisse, Marie-Louise Mallet, and Ginette Michaud. Trans. Geoffrey Bennington. Chicago: University of Chicago Press, 2009.

Derrida, Jacques. *The Death Penalty. Vol. 1*. Trans. Peggy Kamuf. Chicago: University of Chicago Press, 2013.

Derrida, Jacques. "'Eating Well,' or the Calculation of the Subject." In *Who Comes after the Subject?* Ed. Eduardo Cadava, Peter Connor, and Jean-Luc Nancy. New York: Routledge, 1991. 96–119.

Derrida, Jacques. "The Ends of Man." In *Margins of Philosophy*. Trans. Alan
    Bass. Chicago: University of Chicago Press, 1982. 109–36.
Derrida, Jacques. "Faith and Knowledge." In *Acts of Religion*. Ed. Gil Anidjar.
    New York: Routledge, 2002. 40–101.
Derrida, Jacques. "Force of Law: The 'Mystical Foundation of Authority.'"
    In *Acts of Religion*. Ed. Gil Anidjar. New York: Routledge, 2002.
    228–98.
Derrida, Jacques. "Hospitality, Justice and Responsibility." In *Questioning Ethics:
    Contemporary Debates in Philosophy*. Ed. Richard Kearney and Mark Dooley.
    London: Routledge, 1999. 65–83.
Derrida, Jacques. "Hostipitality." In *Acts of Religion*. Ed. Gil Anidjar. New York:
    Routledge, 2002. 356–420.
Derrida, Jacques. *Monolingualism of the Other; Or, The Prosthesis of Origin*.
    Trans. Patrick Mensah. Stanford: Stanford University Press, 1998.
Derrida, Jacques. *Of Grammatology*. Trans. Gayatri Chakravorty Spivak.
    Baltimore: John Hopkins University Press, 1976.
Derrida, Jacques. *Of Hospitality: Anne Dufourmantelle Invites Jacques Derrida to
    Respond*. Stanford: Stanford University Press, 2000.
Derrida, Jacques. "Passages—from Traumatism to Promise." In *Points…:
    Interviews, 1974–1994*. Ed. Elisabeth Weber. Trans. Peggy Kamuf. Stanford:
    Stanford University Press, 1992. 372–95.
Derrida, Jacques. "The Rhetoric of Drugs." In *Points . . . Interviews, 1974–1994*.
    Ed. Elisabeth Weber. Trans. Peggy Kamuf. Stanford: Stanford University
    Press, 1995. 228–54.
Derrida, Jacques. *Rogues: Two Essays on Reason*. Trans. Pascale-Anne Brault
    and Michael Naas. Stanford: Stanford University Press, 2005.
Derrida, Jacques. "Some Statements and Truisms about Neologisms, Newisms,
    Postisms, Parasitisms, and other small Seismisms." In *The States of "Theory."*
    Ed. David Carroll. New York: Columbia University Press, 1989. 63–94.
Derrida, Jacques. "Structure, Sign, and Play in the Discourse of the Human
    Sciences." In *Writing and Difference*. Chicago: University of Chicago Press,
    1978. 278–93.
Derrida, Jacques, Daniel Birnbaum, and Anders Olsson. "An Interview with
    Jacques Derrida on the Limits of Digestion." Trans. Brian Manning Delaney.
    e-flux 2 (2009): 1–5.
Derrida, Jacques and Jean-Luc Nancy, "Responsibility—Of the Sense to Come."
    In *For Strasbourg: Conversations of Friendship and Philosophy*. Trans. and ed.
    Pascal-Anne Brault and Michael Naas. New York: Fordham University Press,
    2014. 56–86.
Derrida, Jacques and Elisabeth Roudinesco. *For What Tomorrow…: A Dialogue*.
    Trans. Jeff Fort. Stanford: Stanford University Press, 2004.

Descartes, René. *Discourse on Method and Meditations on First Philosophy.* Trans. Donald A. Cress. Indianapolis: Hackett Publishing, 1998.

Descartes, René. *Meditations, Objections, and Replies.* Ed. Roger Ariew and Donald Cress. Indianapolis: Hackett Publishing, 2006.

Descombes, Vincent. "Apropos of the 'Critique of the Subject' and the Critique of this Critique." In *Who Comes after the Subject?* Ed. Eduardo Cadava, Peter Conor, and Jean-Luc Nancy. London: Routledge, 1991. 120–34.

Diderot, Denis. *Rameau's Nephew and Other Works.* Trans. Jacques Barzun and Ralph H. Bowen. Indianapolis: Hackett Publishing, 2001.

Douglass, Patrice and Frank B. Wilderson III. "The Violence of Presence: Metaphysics in a Blackened World." *The Black Scholar* 3, no. 4 (2013): 117–23.

Du Bois, W. E. B. *The Souls of Black Folk.* Ed. Henry Louis Gates, Jr. and Terri Hulme Oliver. New York: Norton, 1999.

Edelman, Lee. *No Future: Queer Theory and the Death Drive.* Durham: Duke University Press, 2004.

Edgar, Andrew. "The Hermeneutic Challenge of Genetic Engineering: Habermas and the Transhumanists." *Medicine, Health Care and Philosophy* 12, no. 2 (2009): 157–67.

Erasmus, Desiderius. "On the Education for Children." In *Collected Works of Erasmus.* Vol. 26. Toronto: University of Toronto Press, 1985.

Esposito, Roberto. *Terms of the Political: Community, Immunity, Biopolitics.* New York: Fordham University Press, 2006.

Fanon, Frantz. *Black Skin, White Masks.* Trans. Richard Philcox. New York: Grove Press, 2008.

Fanon, Frantz. *The Wretched of the Earth.* Trans. Richard Philcox. New York: Grove Press, 2004.

Felski, Rita. "Latour and Literary Studies." *PMLA* 130 (2015): 737–42.

Felski, Rita. *The Limits of Critique.* Chicago: University of Chicago Press, 2015.

Fitzpatrick, Kathleen. *Generous Thinking: A Radical Approach to Saving the University.* Baltimore: Johns Hopkins University Press, 2019.

Foucault, Michel. *The Order of Things: An Archaeology of the Human Sciences.* Trans. Alan Sheridan. New York: Vintage, 1970.

Foucault, Michel. "Technologies of the Self." In *Technologies of the Self: A Seminar with Michel Foucault.* Ed. Luther H. Martin, Huck Gutman, and Patrick H. Hutton. Amherst: University of Massachusetts Press, 1988. 16–49.

Foucault, Michel. "What Is an Author?" In *The Foucault Reader.* Ed. Paul Rabinow. New York: Pantheon Books, 1984. 101–20.

Foucault, Michel. "What Is Enlightenment?" In *The Foucault Reader.* Ed. Paul Rabinow. Trans. Catherine Porter. New York: Pantheon, 1984. 32–50.

Francione, Gary. "Animals—Property or Persons?" In *Animal Rights: Current Debates and New Directions*. Ed. Cass R. Sunstein and Martha C. Nussbaum. Oxford: Oxford University Press, 2004. 108–42.

Freedland, Jonathan. "Lest We Forget." *The Guardian* (October 25, 2008). http://www.theguardian.com/film/2008/oct/25/waltz-with-bashir-ari-folman.

Freud, Sigmund. *Beyond the Pleasure Principle*. Trans. James Strachey. New York: Norton, 1961.

Freud, Sigmund. "A Difficulty in the Path of Psycho-Analysis." In *The Standard Edition of the Complete Psychological Works of Sigmund Freud*. Ed. James Strachey et al. Vol. 17. London: Hogwarth, 1953–1974. 135–44.

Fudge, Erica. *Animal*. London: Reaktion, 2002.

Fukuyama, Francis. *Our Posthuman Future: Consequences of the Biotechnology Revolution*. New York: Farrar, Straus and Giroux, 2002.

Galloway, Alexander R. "The Poverty of Philosophy: Realism and Post-Fordism." *Critical Inquiry* 39, no. 2 (2013): 347–66.

Gilroy, Paul. *Against Race: Imagining Political Culture beyond the Color Line*. Cambridge: Harvard University Press, 2000.

Gines, Katherine T. *Hannah Arendt and the Negro Question*. Bloomington: Indiana University Press, 2014.

Giroux, Henry A. *Dangerous Thinking in the Age of the New Authoritarianism*. New York: Routledge, 2016.

Giroux, Henry A. *Stormy Weather: Katrina and the Politics of Disposability*. Boulder: Paradigm Publishers, 2006.

Goldberg, David Theo. "Modernity, Race, and Morality." *Cultural Critique* 24 (1993): 193–27.

Goodman, Amy and Juan González, "Boots Riley's Dystopian Satire 'Sorry to Bother You' Is an Anti-Capitalist Rallying Cry for Workers." *Democracy Now!* (July 17, 2018). https://www.democracynow.org/2018/7/17/sorry_to_bother_you_boots_rileys.

Gordon, Lewis R. *Existentia Africana: Understanding Africana Existential Thought*. New York: Routledge, 2000.

Gordon, Lewis R. *Her Majesty's Other Children: Sketches of Racism from a Neocolonial Age*. Lanham: Rowman & Littlefield, 1997.

Greene, Thomas. "The Flexibility of the Self in Renaissance Literature." In *The Disciplines of Criticism*. Ed. Peter Demetz, Thomas Greene, and Lawry Nelson Jr. New Haven: Yale University Press, 1968. 241–64.

Grusin, Richard. "Introduction." In *The Nonhuman Turn*. Ed. Richard Grusin. Minneapolis: University of Minnesota Press, 2015. vii–xxix.

Gutmann, Amy. "Introduction." In J. M. Coetzee, *The Lives of Animals*. Princeton: Princeton University Press, 1999. 3–14.

Habermas, Jürgen. *The Future of Human Nature*. Cambridge: Polity Press, 2003.

Hajdini, Simon. "Dialectic at Its Impurest: Žižek's Materialism of Less Than Nothing." In *Žižek and Dialectical Materialism*. Ed. Agon Hamza and Frank Ruda. New York: Palgrave, 2016. 85–99.

Hamza, Agon. "Going to One's Ground." In *Slavoj Žižek and Dialectical Materialism*. Ed. Agon Hamza and Frank Ruda. New York: Palgrave, 2016. 163–75.

Haraway, Donna. "The Companion Species Manifesto: Dogs, People, and Significant Otherness." In *Manifestly Haraway: The Cyborg Manifesto. The Companion Species Manifesto. Companions in Conversation (with Cary Wolfe)*. Minneapolis: University of Minnesota Press, 2016. 91–198.

Haraway, Donna. "A Cyborg Manifesto: Science, Technology, and Socialist-Feminism in the Late Twentieth Century." In *Manifestly Haraway: The Cyborg Manifesto. The Companion Species Manifesto. Companions in Conversation (with Cary Wolfe)*. Minneapolis: University of Minnesota Press, 2016. 3–90.

Haraway, Donna. "A Game of Cat's Cradle: Science Studies, Feminist Theory, Cultural Studies." *Configurations* 2, no. 1 (1994): 59–71.

Haraway, Donna. *The Haraway Reader*. New York: Routledge, 2004.

Haraway, Donna. *How Like a Leaf: An Interview with Thyrza Nichols Goodeve*. New York: Routledge, 2000.

Haraway, Donna. *When Species Meet*. Minneapolis: University of Minnesota Press, 2008.

Harman, Graham. *Guerrilla Metaphysics: Phenomenology and the Carpentry of Things*. Chicago: Open Court, 2005.

Harman, Graham. *Immaterialism: Objects and Social Theory*. Cambridge: Polity Press, 2016.

Harman, Graham. "Object-Oriented Ontology." In *The Palgrave Handbook of Posthumanism in Film and Television*. Ed. Michael Hauskeller, Curtis D. Carbonell, and Thomas D. Philbeck. Basingstoke: Palgrave Macmillan, 2015. 401–9.

Harman, Graham. "Object-Oriented Ontology and Commodity Fetishism: Kant, Marx, Heidegger, and Things." *Eidos* 2 (2017): 28–36.

Harman, Graham. "Objects and Orientalism." In *The Agon of Interpretations: Towards a Critical Intercultural Hermeneutics*. Ed. Ming Xie. Toronto: University of Toronto Press, 2014. 123–39.

Harman, Graham. *Prince of Networks: Bruno Latour and Metaphysics*. Melbourne: re.press, 2009.

Harman, Graham. *The Quadruple Object*. Winchester: Zero Books, 2011.

Harman, Graham. *Third Table/Der dritte Tisch*. Ostfildern: Hatje Cantz, 2012.

Harman, Graham. *Tool-Being: Heidegger and the Metaphysics of Objects*. Chicago: Open Court, 2002.

Harman, Graham. "On Vicarious Causation." *Collapse* 2 (2007): 171–208.

Harman, Graham. *Weird Realism: Lovecraft and Philosophy*. Winchester: Zero Books, 2012.

Harman, Graham. "The Well-Wrought Broken Hammer: Object-Oriented Literary Criticism." *New Literary History* 43 (2012): 183–203.

Harman, Graham. "Zero-Person and the Psyche." In *Mind That Abides: Panpsychism in the New Millennium*. Ed. David Skrbina. Philadelphia: John Benjamins Publishing Company, 2009. 253–82.

Harney, Stefano and Fred Moten. *The Undercommons: Fugitive Planning and Black Study*. New York: Autonomedia, 2013.

Harris, Ricki. "Elon Musk: Humanity Is a Kind of 'Biological Boot Loader' for AI." *wired.com* (September 1, 2019). https://www.wired.com/story/elon-mu sk-humanity-biological-boot-loader-ai/.

Hartman, Saidiya V. *Lose Your Mother: A Journey along the Atlantic Slave Route*. New York: Farrar, Straus and Giroux, 2007.

Hartman, Saidiya V. *Scenes of Subjection: Terror, Slavery, and Self-Making in Nineteenth-Century America*. Oxford: Oxford University Press, 1997.

Hartman, Saidiya V. "The Time of Slavery." *South Atlantic Quarterly* 100, no. 4 (2002): 757–77.

Hartman, Saidiya and Frank B. Wilderson III. "The Position of the Unthought." *Qui Parle* 13, no. 2 (2003): 183–201.

Harvey, David. *Seventeen Contradictions and the End of Capitalism*. Oxford: Oxford University Press, 2014.

Hayles, N. Katherine. *How We Became Posthuman: Virtual Bodies in Cybernetics, Literature, and Informatics*. Chicago: University of Chicago Press, 1999.

Hayles, N. Katherine. "The Materiality of Informatics." *Configurations* 1, no. 1 (1993): 147–70.

Heidegger, Martin. *Being and Time*. Trans. John Macquarrie and Edward Robinson. New York: Harper & Row, 1962.

Heidegger, Martin. "Einblick in das was ist." In *Bremer und Freiburger Vorträge*. Gesamtausgabe 79. Frankfurt am Main: Klostermann, 1994. 1–77.

Heidegger, Martin. *The Fundamental Concepts of Metaphysics*. Trans. William Mcneill and Nicholas Walker. Bloomington: Indiana University Press, 1995.

Heidegger, Martin. "Letter on Humanism." In *Basic Writings*. Ed. David Farrell Krell. New York: Harper and Row, 1977. 189–242.

Heidegger, Martin. "The Question Concerning Technology." In *Basic Writings*. Ed. David Farrell Krell. New York: HarperCollins Publishers, Inc., 1993. 307–41.

Herbrechter, Stefan. *Posthumanism: A Critical Analysis*. New York: Bloomsbury, 2013.

Jackson, Zakiyyah Iman. *Becoming Human: Matter and Meaning in an Antiblack World*. New York: Fordham University Press, 2020.

Jackson, Zakiyyah Iman. "Outer Worlds: The Persistence of Race in Movement 'Beyond the Human.'" *GLQ* 21, nos. 2–3 (2015): 215–18.

Jacobson, Jonathan. "Slavoj Zizek's 'Brutal, Dark' Formula for Saving the World." *Haaretz* (April 6, 2020). https://www.haaretz.com/world-news/.premium.M AGAZINE-slavoj-zizek-s-brutal-dark-formula-to-save-the-world-1.8898051 ?v=1591571554964.

Jameson, Fredric. *Representing Capital: A Reading of Volume One*. New York: Verso, 2011.

Jenkins, Henry. "Enhanced Memory: 'The Entire History of You.'" In *Through the Black Mirror Deconstructing the Side Effects of the Digital Age*. Ed. Terence McSweeney and Stuart Joy. Cham: Palgrave, 2019. 43–54.

Kant, Immanuel. *Groundwork of the Metaphysic of Morals*. Trans. H. J. Paton. New York: Harper & Row, 1964.

Kant, Immanuel. *Observations on the Feeling of the Beautiful and the Sublime*. Trans. John T. Goldthwait. Berkeley: University of California Press, 1960.

Kelley, Robin D. G. "Sorry, Not Sorry." *Boston Review* (September 13, 2018). http://bostonreview.net/race-literature-culture/robin-d-g-kelley-sorry-not-sorry#.XMdwpNHrLCE.email.

Kozol, Wendy. *Distant Wars Visible: The Ambivalence of Witnessing*. Minneapolis: University of Minnesota Press, 2014.

Kristeva, Julia. *Strangers to Ourselves*. Trans. Leon S. Roudiez. New York: Columbia University Press, 1991.

Lacan, Jacques. "The Direction of the Treatment and the Principles of Its Power." In *Écrits: The First Complete Edition in English*. Trans. Bruce Fink. New York: Norton, 2006. 489–542.

Lacan, Jacques. *The Ethics of Psychoanalysis, 1959–1960, The Seminar of Jacques Lacan*, Book VII. Ed. Jacques-Alain Miller. Trans. Dennis Porter. New York: Norton, 1992.

Lacan, Jacques. *On Feminine Sexuality, The Limits of Love and Knowledge, 1972–1973: Encore, The Seminar of Jacques Lacan*, Book XX. Trans. Bruce Fink. New York: Norton, 1998.

Lacan, Jacques. "The Freudian Thing, or the Meaning of the Return to Freud in Psychoanalysis." In *Écrits: The First Complete Edition in English*. Trans. Bruce Fink. New York: Norton, 2006. 334–66.

Lacan, Jacques. "Introduction to the Names-of-the-Father Seminar." In *Television: A Challenge to the Psychoanalytic Establishment*. Ed. Joan Copjec. Trans. Jeffrey Mehlman. New York: Norton, 1990. 81–95.

Lacan, Jacques. *The Psychoses, 1955–1956, The Seminar of Jacques Lacan*, Book III. Ed. Jacques-Alain Miller. Trans. Russell Grigg. New York: Norton, 1993.

Lacan, Jacques. "The Signification of the Phallus." In *Écrits: The First Complete Edition in English*. Trans. Bruce Fink. New York: Norton, 2006. 575–84.

Lacan, Jacques. "The Triumph of Religion." In *The Triumph of Religion, Preceded by Discourse to Catholics*. Trans. Bruce Fink. Cambridge: Polity Press, 2013. 53–85.

La Mettrie, Julien Offray de. *Man a Machine*. Trans. Richard A. Watson and Maya Rybalka. Indianapolis: Hackett Publishing, 1994.

Las Casas, Bartolomé de. *The Devastation of the Indies: A Brief Account*. Trans. Herma Briffault. Baltimore: Johns Hopkins University Press, 1992.

Latour, Bruno. "An Attempt at a 'Compositionist Manifesto.'" *New Literary History* 41 (2010): 471–90.

Latour, Bruno. *Pandora's Hope: Essays in the Reality of Science Studies*. Cambridge: Harvard University Press, 1999.

Latour, Bruno. "The Politics of Explanation: An Alternative." In *Knowledge and Reflexivity: New Frontiers in the Sociology of Knowledge*. Ed. Steve Woolgar. London: Sage, 1988. 155–76.

Latour, Bruno. *Politics of Nature: How to Bring the Sciences into Democracy*. Trans. Catherine Porter. Cambridge: Harvard University Press, 2004.

Latour, Bruno. *Reassembling the Social: An Introduction to Actor-Network-Theory*. Oxford: Oxford University Press, 2005.

Latour, Bruno. *We Have Never Been Modern*. Trans. Catherine Porter. Cambridge: Harvard University Press, 1993.

Latour, Bruno. "Why Has Critique Run Out of Steam? From Matters of Fact to Matters of Concern." *Critical Inquiry* 30 (2004): 225–48.

Levinas, Emmanuel. "The Paradox of Morality: An Interview with Emmanuel Levinas." In *The Provocation of Levinas: Rethinking the Other*. Ed. Robert Bernasconi and David Wood. New York: Routledge, 1988. 168–80.

Linscott, Charles "Chip" P. "All Lives (Don't Matter): The Internet Meets Afro-Pessimism." *Black Camera* 8, no. 2 (2017): 104–19.

Malaklou, M. Shadee. "Dilemmas' of Coalition and the Chronopolitics of Man: Towards an Insurgent Black Feminine Otherwise." *Theory & Event* 21, no. 1 (2018): 215–58.

Malm, Andreas. "The Anthropocene Myth." *Jacobin* (March 30, 2015). https://www.jacobinmag.com/2015/03/anthropocene-capitalism-climate-change/.

Marriott, David. *Haunted Life: Visual Culture and Black Modernity*. New Brunswick: Rutgers University Press, 2007.

Marriott, David. *Whither Fanon? Studies in the Blackness of Being*. Stanford: Stanford University Press, 2018.

Mbembe, Achille. "Conversation: Achille Mbembe and David Theo Goldberg on *Critique of Black Reason*." *Theory, Culture, and Society* (July 3, 2018).

https://www.theoryculturesociety.org/conversation-achille-mbembe-and-d
avid-theo-goldberg-on-critique-of-black-reason/.

Mbembe, Achille. *Critique of Black Reason*. Trans. Laurent Dubois. Durham:
Duke University Press, 2017.

Mbembe, Achille. "Necropolitics." *Public Culture* 15, no. 1 (2003): 11–40.

McBrien, Justin. "Accumulating Extinction: Planetary Catastrophism in the
Necrocene." In *Anthropocene or Capitalocene? Nature, History, and the Crisis
of Capitalism*. Ed. Jason W. Moore. Oakland: PM Press, 2016. 116–37.

McGowan, Todd. "Hegel as Marxist: Žižek's Revision of German Idealism." In
Žižek Now: Current Perspectives in Žižek Studies. Ed. Jamil Khader and Molly
Anne Rothenberg. Cambridge: Polity Press, 2013. 31–54.

McGowan, Todd. "Two Forms of Fetishism: From Commodity to Revolution in
'US.'" *Galactica Media* 1 (2019): 63–85.

McHendry, George F. "'Arkangel': Postscript on Families of Control." In *Through
the Black Mirror Deconstructing the Side Effects of the Digital Age*. Ed.
Terence McSweeney and Stuart Joy. Cham: Palgrave, 2019. 205–16.

Meillassoux, Quentin. *After Finitude: An Essay on the Necessity of Contingency*.
Trans. Ray Brassier. New York: Continuum, 2008.

Meillassoux, Quentin. "Interview with Quentin Meillassoux (August 2010)."
Trans. Graham Harman. In Graham Harman, *Quentin Meillassoux: Philosophy
in the Making*. Edinburgh: Edinburgh University Press, 2011. 159–74.

Meillassoux, Quentin. "Speculative Realism: Presentation by Quentin
Meillassoux." *Collapse* 3 (2007): 408–49.

Miller, Christopher L. *Nationalists and Nomads: Essays on Francophone African
Literature and Culture*. Chicago: University of Chicago Press, 1998.

Mirandola, Pico della. *On the Dignity of Man*. Trans. Charles Glenn Wallis.
Indianapolis: Hackett Publishing, 1998.

Montaigne, Michel de. *The Complete Essays of Montaigne*. Trans. Donald Frame.
Stanford: Stanford University Press, 1957.

Morrison, Toni. *Beloved*. New York: Knopf, 1987.

Morton, Timothy. "Here Comes Everything: The Promise of Object-Oriented
Ontology." *Qui Parle* 19, no. 2 (2011): 163–90.

Moten, Fred. *Black and Blur*. Durham: Duke University Press, 2017.

Moten, Fred. "Black Optimism/Black Operation." Unpublished paper on file
with the author. (2007). https://lucian.uchicago.edu/blogs/politicalfeeling/
files/2007/12/moten-black-optimism.doc.

Moten, Fred. "Bridge and One: Improvisations of the Public Sphere."
In *Performing Hybridity*. Ed. May Joseph and Jennifer Natalya Fink.
Minneapolis: University of Minnesota Press, 1999. 229–46.

Moten, Fred. *In the Break: The Aesthetics of the Black Radical Tradition*.
Minneapolis: University of Minnesota Press, 2003.

Moten, Fred. *Stolen Life*. Durham: Duke University Press, 2018.

Moten, Fred. *The Universal Machine*. Durham: Duke University Press, 2018.

Myerson, George. *Donna Haraway and GM Foods*. Cambridge: Totem Books, 2000.

Nayar, Pramod K. *Posthumanism*. Cambridge: Polity Press, 2013.

Nellis, Eric. *Shaping the New World: African Slavery in the Americas, 1500–1888*. Toronto: University of Toronto Press, 2013.

Noys, Benjamin. "Žižek's Reading Machine." In *Repeating Žižek*. Ed. Agon Hamza. Durham: Duke University Press, 2015. 72–83.

Nussbaum, Martha C. "Beyond 'Compassion and Humanity': Justice for Nonhuman Animals." In *Animal Rights: Current Debates and New Directions*. Ed. Cass R. Sunstein and Martha C. Nussbaum. Oxford: Oxford University Press, 2004. 299–320.

O'Brien, John. "'Le Propre de l'Homme': Reading Montaigne's 'Des Cannibales' in Context." *Forum for Modern Language Studies* 53, no. 2 (2016): 220–34.

Oliver, Kelly. *Animal Lessons: How They Teach Us to Be Human*. New York: Columbia University Press, 2009. 25–48.

Oliver, Kelly. "Derrida and Eating." In *Encyclopedia of Food and Agricultural Ethics*. Ed. Paul B. Thompson and David M. Kaplan. Heidelberg: Springer Netherlands, 2014. 459–65.

Patterson, Orlando. *Slavery and Social Death: A Comparative Study*. Cambridge: Harvard University Press, 1982.

Penley, Constance and Andrew Ross, "Cyborgs at Large: Interview with Donna Haraway." *Social Text Social Text* 25/26 (1990): 8–23.

Peterson, Christopher. *Monkey Trouble: The Scandal of Posthumanism*. New York: Fordham University Press, 2017.

Peterson, Christopher. "The Posthumanism to Come." *Angelaki* 16, no. 2 (2011): 127–41.

Puar, Jasbir K. "'I would rather be a cyborg than a goddess': Becoming-Intersectional in Assemblage Theory." *philoSOPHIA* 2, no. 1 (2012): 49–66.

Rabinbach, Anson. *In the Shadow of Catastrophe: German Intellectuals between Apocalypse and Enlightenment*. Berkeley: University of California Press, 1997.

Raengo, Alessandra. "Black Matters." *Discourse* 38, no. 2 (2016): 246–64.

Rancière, Jacques. *Disagreement: Politics and Philosophy*. Trans. J. Rose. Minneapolis: University of Minnesota Press, 1999.

Rancière, Jacques. *The Emancipated Spectator*. Trans. G. Elliott. New York, Verso, 2009.

Rancière, Jacques. *The Politics of Aesthetics: Distribution of the Sensible*. Trans. G. Rockhill. New York, Continuum, 2004.

Rancière, Jacques. "Work, Identity, Subject." In *Jacques Rancière and the Contemporary Scene: The Philosophy of Radical Equality*. Ed. Jean-Philippe Deranty and Alison Ross. New York: Continuum, 2012. 205–16.

Read, Rupert. *A Film-Philosophy of Ecology and Enlightenment*. New York: Routledge, 2019.

Rimbaud, Arthur. *Œuvres complètes*. Ed. Rolland de Renéville and Jules Mouquet. Paris: Gallimard, 1963.

R. L. "Wanderings of the Slave: Black Life and Social Death." *Mute* (June 5, 2013). http://www.metamute.org/editorial/articles/wanderings-slave-black-life-and-social-death.

Robbe-Grillet, Alain. *For a New Novel: Essays on Fiction*. Trans. Richard Howard. New York: Grove Press, 1966.

Rosen, Stanley. *G. W. F. Hegel: An Introduction to the Science of Wisdom*. New Haven: Yale University Press, 1974.

Rothenberg, Molly Anne. "Twisting 'Flat Ontology': Harman's 'Allure' and Lacan's Extimate Cause." In *Subject Lessons: Hegel, Lacan, and the Future of Materialism*. Ed. Russell Sbriglia and Slavoj Žižek. Evanston: Northwestern University Press, 2020. 190–208.

Royle, Nicholas. *The Uncanny*. Manchester: Manchester University Press, 2003.

Said, Edward. *Beginnings: Intention and Method*. New York: Columbia University Press, 1985.

Sandoval, Chela. *Methodology of the Oppressed*. Minneapolis: University of Minnesota Press, 2000.

Sartre, Jean-Paul. *Being and Nothingness: An Essay on Phenomenological Ontology*. Trans. Hazel E. Barnes. New York: Philosophical Library, 1956.

Sartre, Jean-Paul. *Existentialism Is a Humanism*. Trans. Carol Macomber. New Haven: Yale University Press, 2007.

Sartre, Jean-Paul. *Nausea*. Trans. Lloyd Alexander. New York: New Directions, 1964.

Sartre, Jean-Paul. *The Words: The Autobiography of Jean-Paul Sartre*. Trans. Bernard Frechtman. New York: George Braziller, 1964.

Sbriglia, Russell. "Object-Disoriented Ontology; Or, the Subject of What Is *Sex*?" *Continental Thought and Theory* 2, no. 2 (2018): 35–57.

Schueller, Malini Johar. *Locating Race: Global Sites of Post-Colonial Citizenship*. Albany: State University of New York Press, 2009.

Sedgwick, Eve Kosofsky. "Paranoid Reading and Reparative Reading, or, You're So Paranoid, You Probably Think This Essay Is about You." In *Novel Gazing: Queer Readings in Fiction*. Ed. Eve Kosofsky Sedgwick. Durham: Duke University Press, 1997. 1–37.

Seneca, *Epistles*. Loeb Classical Library. Trans. Richard M. Gummere. Cambridge: Harvard University Press, 1996.

Sexton, Jared. "Afro-Pessimism: The Unclear Word." *Rhizomes* 29 (2016). https://doi.org/10.20415/rhiz/029.e02.

Sexton, Jared. *Amalgamation Schemes: Antiblackness and the Critique of Multiracialism*. Minneapolis: University of Minnesota Press, 2008.

Sexton, Jared. "People-of-Color-Blindness: Notes on the Afterlife of Slavery." *Social Text* 28, no. 2 103 (2010): 31–56.

Sexton, Jared. "The Social Life of Social Death: On Afro-Pessimism and Black Optimism." *InTensions* 5 (2011): 1–47.

Sharpe, Christina. *In the Wake: On Blackness and Being*. Durham: Duke University Press, 2016.

Shelley, Mary. *Frankenstein: The 1818 Text, Contexts, Criticism*. Ed. J. Paul Hunter. New York: Norton, 2012.

Shklar, Judith. *Ordinary Vices*. Cambridge: Harvard University Press, 1984.

Singer, Isaac Bashevis. "The Letter Writer." In *The Séance and Other Stories*. New York: Farrar, Strauss and Giroux, 1968. 239–75.

Sloterdijk, Peter. *You Must Change Your Life*. Cambridge: Polity Press, 2013.

Smallwood, Stephanie. *Saltwater Slavery: A Middle Passage from Africa to American Diaspora*. Cambridge: Harvard University Press, 2007.

Spillers, Hortense J. "Mama's Baby, Papa's Maybe: An American Grammar Book." In *Black, White, and in Color: Essays on American Literature and Culture*. Chicago: University of Chicago Press, 2003. 203–29.

Steedman, Carolyn. *Dust: The Archive and Cultural History*. New Brunswick: Rutgers University Press, 2002.

TallBear, Kim. "Being in Relation." In *Messy Eating: Conversations on Animals as Food*. Ed. Samantha King. New York: Fordham University Press, 2019. 54–67.

Taylor, Keeanga-Yamahtta. *From #BlackLivesMatter to Black Liberation*. Chicago: Haymarket Books, 2016.

Timofeeva, Oxana. "The Two Cats: Žižek, Derrida, and Other Animals." In *Repeating Žižek*. Ed. Agon Hamza. Durham: Duke University Press, 2015. 100–9.

Todd, Zoe. "An Indigenous Feminist's Take on the Ontological Turn: 'Ontology' Is Just Another Word for Colonialism." *Journal of Historical Sociology* 29 (2016): 4–22.

Vighi, Fabio. *On Zizek's Dialectics: Surplus, Subtraction, Sublimation*. New York, Continuum, 2010.

Wacquant, Loïc. "From Slavery to Mass Incarceration: Rethinking the 'Race Question in the US." *New Left Review* 13 (2002): 41–60.

Wagner, Bryan. *Disturbing the Peace: Black Culture and the Police Power after Slavery*. Cambridge: Harvard University Press, 2009.

Warren, Calvin L. "Black Mysticism: Fred Moten's Phenomenology of (Black) Spirit." *Zeitschrift für Anglistik und Amerikanistik* 65, no. 2 (2017): 219–29.

Warren, Calvin L. "Black Time: Slavery, Metaphysics, and the Logic of Wellness." In *The Psychic Hold of Slavery: Legacies in American Expressive Culture.* Ed. Soyica Diggs Colbert, Robert J. Patterson, and Aida Levy-Hussen. New Brunswick: Rutgers University Press, 2016. 55–68.

Warren, Calvin L. *Ontological Terror: Blackness, Nihilism, and Emancipation.* Durham: Duke University Press, 2018.

Weheliye, Alexander. *Habeas Viscus: Racializing Assemblages, Biopolitics, and Black Feminist Theories of the Human.* Durham: Duke University Press, 2014.

Wilderson III, Frank B. "Afro-Pessimism and the End of Redemption." *Humanities Futures. Franklin Humanities Institute: Duke University* (October 20, 2015). https://humanitiesfutures.org/papers/afro-pessimism-end-rede mption/.

Wilderson III, Frank B. "The Black Liberation Army and the Paradox of Political Engagement." In *Postcoloniality-Decoloniality-Black Critique: Joints and Fissures.* Ed. Sabine Broeck and Carsten Junker. Frankfurt: Campus Verlag, 2014. 175–210.

Wilderson III, Frank B. "Gramsci's Black Marx: Whither the Slave in Civil Society?" *Social Identities* 9, no. 2 (2003): 225–40.

Wilderson III, Frank B. "The Prison Slave as Hegemony's (Silent) Scandal." *Social Justice* 30, no. 2 (2003): 18–27.

Wilderson III, Frank B. *Red, White & Black: Cinema and the Structure of U.S. Antagonisms.* Durham: Duke University Press, 2010.

Wilderson III, Frank B. "Social Death and Narrative Aporia in 12 Years a Slave." *Black Camera* 7, no. 1 (2015): 134–49.

Wilderson III, Frank B. "'We're Trying to Destroy the World': Anti-Blackness and Police Violence after Ferguson Pages." In *Shifting Corporealities in Contemporary Performance Danger, Im/mobility and Politics.* Ed. Marina Gržinić and Aneta Stojnić. New York: Palgrave, 2018. 45–59.

Willett, Cynthia. *Interspecies Ethics.* New York: Columbia University Press, 2014.

Williams, Patricia J. *The Alchemy of Race and Rights: Diary ofa Law Professor.* Cambridge: Harvard University Press, 1991.

Winter, Cécile "The Master-Signifier of the New Aryans." In *Polemics.* Trans. Steve Corcoran. New York: Verso, 2006. 217–29.

Wolfe, Cary. *Animal Rites: American Culture, the Discourse of Species, and Posthumanist Theory.* Chicago: Chicago University Press, 2003.

Wolfe, Cary. "Echographies from My Life in the Bush of Ghosts." *Angelaki* 13, no. 1 (2008): 85–94.

Wolfe, Cary. *What Is Posthumanism?* Minneapolis: University of Minnesota Press, 2010.

Wood, David. "Comment ne pas manger: Derrida and Humanism." In *Thinking after Heidegger*. Cambridge: Polity Press, 2002. 135–52.

Wood, David. *The Step Back: Ethics and Politics after Deconstruction*. Albany: State University of New York Press, 2005.

Yosef, Raz. "War Fantasies: Memory, Trauma and Ethics in Ari Folman's *Waltz with Bashir*." *Journal of Modern Jewish Studies* 9, no. 3 (2010): 311–26.

Young, Simon. *Designer Evolution: A Transhumanist Manifesto*. New York: Prometheus Books, 2006.

Žižek, Slavoj. *Absolute Recoil: Towards a New Foundation of Dialectical Materialism*. New York: Verso, 2014.

Žižek, Slavoj. "Afterword: Objects, Objects Everywhere." In *Slavoj Žižek and Dialectical Materialism*. Ed. Agon Hamza and Frank Ruda. New York: Palgrave Macmillan, 2016. 177–92.

Žižek, Slavoj. *Against the Double Blackmail: Refugees, Terror and Other Troubles with the Neighbors*. London: Penguin Random House, 2016.

Žižek, Slavoj. "Against the Grain: 'What if violence is needed to keep things as they are?'" *The Independent* (January 24, 2008). https://www.independent.co.uk/news/education/higher/against-the-grain-what-if-violence-is-needed-to-keep-things-as-they-are-772960.html.

Žižek, Slavoj. "Class Struggle or Postmodernism? Yes, Please!" In *Contingency, Hegemony, Universality: Contemporary Dialogues on the Left*. Ed. Judith Butler, Ernesto Laclau, and Slavoj Žižek. New York: Verso, 2000. 90–135.

Žižek, Slavoj. *The Courage of Hopelessness: Chronicles of a Year of Acting Dangerously*. New York: Allen Lane, 2017.

Žižek, Slavoj. *Demanding the Impossible*. Ed. Yong-June Park. Cambridge: Polity Press, 2013.

Žižek, Slavoj. *Disparities*. New York: Bloomsbury, 2016.

Žižek, Slavoj. *First As Tragedy, Then As Farce*. New York: Verso, 2009.

Žižek, Slavoj. *For They Know Not What They Do: Enjoyment as a Political Factor*. New York: Verso, 1991.

Žižek, Slavoj. *The Fright of Real Tears: Krzystof Kieslowski between Theory and Post-Theory*. London: British Film Institute, 2001.

Žižek, Slavoj. *Hegel in A Wired Brain*. New York: Bloomsbury, 2020.

Žižek, Slavoj. "Holding the Place." In *Contingency, Hegemony, Universality: Contemporary Dialogues on the Left*. Ed. Judith Butler, Ernesto Laclau, and Slavoj Žižek. New York: Verso, 2000. 308–29.

Žižek, Slavoj. "How to Begin from the Beginning." *New Left Review* 57 (2009): 43–55.

Žižek, Slavoj. *How to Read Lacan*. New York: Norton, 2006.

Žižek, Slavoj. *The Incontinence of the Void: Economico-Philosophical Spandrels*. Cambridge: MIT Press, 2017.

Žižek, Slavoj. *In Defense of Lost Causes*. New York: Verso, 2008.

Žižek, Slavoj. *Interrogating the Real*. Ed. Rex Butler and Scott Stephens. London: Continuum, 2005.

Žižek, Slavoj. "A Leftist Plea for 'Eurocentrism.'" *Critical Inquiry* 24, no. 4 (1998): 988–1009.

Žižek, Slavoj. *Less than Nothing: Hegel and the Shadow of Dialectical Materialism*. New York: Verso, 2012.

Žižek, Slavoj. *Like a Thief in Broad Daylight*. New York: Allen Lane, 2018.

Žižek, Slavoj. *Living in the End Times*. New York: Verso, 2010.

Žižek, Slavoj. *Looking Awry: An Introduction to Jacques Lacan through Popular Culture*. Cambridge: MIT Press, 1992.

Žižek, Slavoj. "Marx Reads Object-Oriented Ontology." In *Reading Marx*. Ed. Slavoj Žižek, Frank Ruda, and Agon Hamza. Cambridge: Polity Press, 2018. 17–61.

Žižek, Slavoj. *The Metastases of Enjoyment: Six Essays on Women and Causality*. New York: Verso, 1994.

Žižek, Slavoj. "Neighbors and Other Monsters: A Plea for Ethical Violence." In *The Neighbor: Three Inquiries in Political Theology*. Ed. Slavoj Žižek, Eric L. Santner, and Kenneth Reinhard. Chicago: University of Chicago, 2006. 134–90.

Žižek, Slavoj. *Organs without Bodies: On Deleuze and Consequences*. New York: Routledge, 2004.

Žižek, Slavoj. *The Parallax View*. Cambridge: MIT Press, 2006.

Žižek, Slavoj. *The Plague of Fantasies*. New York: Verso, 1997.

Žižek, Slavoj. *Sex and the Failed Absolute*. New York: Bloomsbury, 2020.

Žižek, Slavoj. *The Sublime Object of Ideology*. New York: Verso, 1991.

Žižek, Slavoj. *Tarrying with the Negative: Kant, Hegel, and the Critique of Ideology*. Durham: Duke University Press, 1993.

Žižek, Slavoj. *Trouble in Paradise: From the End of History to the End of Capitalism*. Brooklyn: Melville House, 2014.

Žižek, Slavoj. *Violence: Six Sideways Reflections*. New York: Picador, 2008.

Žižek, Slavoj. "Woman Is One of the Names-of-the-Father, or How Not to Misread Lacan's Formulas of Sexuation." *Lacanian Ink* 10 (1995). http://www.lacan.com/zizwoman.htm.

Žižek, Slavoj. *Welcome to the Desert of the Real! Five Essays on September 11 and Related Dates*. New York: Verso, 2002.

Žižek, Slavoj and Glyn Daly. *Conversations with Žižek*. Cambridge: Polity Press, 2004.

Žižek, Slavoj, Eric L. Santner, and Kenneth Reinhard, "Introduction." In *The Neighbor: Three Inquiries in Political Theology*. Ed. Slavoj Žižek, Eric L. Santner, and Kenneth Reinhard. Chicago: University of Chicago Press, 2006. 1–10.

Zupančič, Alenka. *What Is Sex?* Cambridge: MIT Press, 2017.

Index